The Art of Being Posthuman

To All
To Sofia: Wisdom

The Art of Being Posthuman
Who Are We in the 21st Century?

Francesca Ferrando

polity

Copyright © Francesca Ferrando 2023

The right of Francesca Ferrando to be identified as Author of this Work has been asserted in accordance with the UK Copyright, Designs and Patents Act 1988.

First published in 2023 by Polity Press

Polity Press
65 Bridge Street
Cambridge CB2 1UR, UK

Polity Press
111 River Street
Hoboken, NJ 07030, USA

All rights reserved. Except for the quotation of short passages for the purpose of criticism and review, no part of this publication may be reproduced, stored in a retrieval system or transmitted, in any form or by any means, electronic, mechanical, photocopying, recording or otherwise, without the prior permission of the publisher.

ISBN-13: 978-1-5095-4895-8
ISBN-13: 978-1-5095-4896-5 (pb)

A catalogue record for this book is available from the British Library.

Library of Congress Control Number: 2023932772

Typeset in 10.5 on 13pt Palatino
by Cheshire Typesetting Ltd, Cuddington, Cheshire
Printed and bound in Great Britain by TJ Books Ltd, Padstow, Cornwall

The publisher has used its best endeavours to ensure that the URLs for external websites referred to in this book are correct and active at the time of going to press. However, the publisher has no responsibility for the websites and can make no guarantee that a site will remain live or that the content is or will remain appropriate.

Every effort has been made to trace all copyright holders, but if any have been overlooked the publisher will be pleased to include any necessary credits in any subsequent reprint or edition.

For further information on Polity, visit our website: politybooks.com

Contents

Premise   vii

Introduction: Being Posthuman in the 21st Century   1

Meditation 1: Posthuman Self-Enquiry   17
#Existential Posthumanism   #Inter-being
#Existentialism?   #21st Century   #Dream
#Change   #Redemption   #Posthuman Awareness

Meditation 2: Human Decluttering   30
#Decluttering   #Human(-centric)?   #Beyond
Anthropocentrism   #Scientifically, Human
#Primates, Chimps and Bonobos   #Archaic
Humans? #Almost Human   #The Birth of
Anthropocentrism #Prehistory?   #Regeneration
#Human Animal #Microcosm/Macrocosm
#Beyond Human-centrism   #With or Without
Humans?

Meditation 3: Biotic Co-emergences   55
#Embodiments   #Double Helix   #Bio-me
#Holobionts   #Vir/us   #Viral Awareness   #Species
Agency   #Radical Life Extension   #Dictator's
Paradox   #Species Healing

Meditation 4: Ecological Presence   72
#Earth   #Nature, Again?   #Philosophical
Greenwashing   #Rights of Nature   #Anthropogenic

Hermit   #Climate Change   #Ecosophy   #Indoor Society   #Wood Wide Web   #Eco-logy/Eco-nomy #Re-engineering Nature?   #Posthuman Polite Convention

Meditation 5: Cosmic Constellations　　　　　94
#Made of Stardust   #Cosmic Address   #Chaos and Cosmos   #Universal Recycles   #Cosmopolitics #Posthuman Gravity   #Space Migration   #Golden Paradox

Meditation 6: Technological Enhancement　110
#Digital Existentialism   #Techno-Enchantment #Poiesis   #AI Takeover   #High-Tech Prophecy #Bio-Hacking   #Big Data   #Microtargeting #Data Awareness   #Algorithmic Predestination #Enlightened Robots   #Golden Cage   #Planetary Enhancement   #Simulation Hypothesis

Meditation 7: Socio-Cultural Agency　　　136
#Society   #Human Rights?   #Social Pandemics #Bubbles   #Social Coding   #Id-Entity #Knowledge-Production   #War Culture   #No War   #Schooling or Unschooling?   #Posthuman Education   #Posthumanist Curricula   #Inanna/ Enheduanna   #Posthuman Parenthood   #Pink Trap #Posthuman Agency

Meditation 8: Ontological Presence　　　　172
#(P)Art   #Posthuman Archetypes   #Consciousness Hacking   #Mind   #Subjects   #Non-Being #Dream   #Spirituality   #Self-Realization

Conclusions: Posthuman Mantra　　　　　　190

Notes　　　　　　　　　　　　　　　　　　194
References　　　　　　　　　　　　　　　　235
Acknowledgments　　　　　　　　　　　　　249

Premise

Writing this book during the Covid-19 pandemic, with many social, biological and ecological issues vigorously coming to the surface, was a challenge and a gift. This historical moment made many recognize the urgency for academic philosophy to become social wisdom. Once we realized that people around us were dying, and that we could die as well, the fragility of humanity, as well as the urgency for authenticity and meaning, became self-evident. We had to ask: *is posthumanism just another academic trend?* If that was the case, many would have lost their interest in this field: facing the sense of finitude, we were searching for something deeper than scholastic novelty. We delved into this, as individuals and a community, looking deep into ourselves: *was posthumanism something that could help us navigate this moment?* We could only be honest to ourselves, because there was no one to give account to. This was not an exam, it entailed no promotion, it was not about the ego: this was our life.

During social and/or global distancing (when there was the chance of practicing it), we were surrounded by ourselves. Each action, thought and word resonated much wider, because space had suddenly shrunk, but not time; we had unlimited time in limited space – we became time millionaires. As in a cave, words resonate. As in a reverse myth of the Platonic cave, someone who was previously lost in constant activities, social interactions and projects, now had to enter the cave, and stay. A challenging separation from loved ones. A precious possibility to hear ourselves. We did it, and we could only be radically honest. In these meditations, the question arose: *what about posthumanism?* Some of us accessed posthumanism as an intellectual approach; they struggled with finding meaning, now that much was lost. Some of us realized that posthumanism is a way of existing. In this sense, posthumanism allowed us to approach this historical moment as a species, helped us navigate it on a personal level, and gave us the strength and vision to be agents of change in the realization of post-pandemic worlds. This book witnesses the transformation of an academic philosophy into social wisdom for the 21st century.

Introduction

Being Posthuman in the 21st Century

This book approaches posthumanism as a philosophy of life and, more clearly, a practice of existence to manifest deep, comprehensive and personalized paths of self-exploration, as individuals and societies, species and beyond. The message is crystal clear: we can be posthuman now in the ways we exist. There is a real need for posthumanist existential enlightenment, as we envision ourselves in the era of the Anthropocene, global pandemics and the rise of artificial intelligence. This book offers a 360 degree review of who we are in the 21st century – not just as individuals, but as societies, a species, a planet and beyond. In critical and generative terms, the book engages with scientific knowledges, ancient paths of wisdom, and emerging and speculative bio-technologies in ways that are aware of the deep anthropocentric legacies of past visions and formulations. Words create worlds; narratives are not neutral. A (re)generative decluttering of the notion of the human is thus pursued from any self-entitlements that obscure the understanding of our extensive self. Once we look into the nature of being, we (as existing beings) realize that we are always in dynamics of existential revealing, poietically co-manifesting our worlds: in these extensive senses, we are (p)art[1] of everything. Posthumanism embraces an integral comprehension of the human in the 21st century. This is a unique opportunity for generative exchanges that are forging not only public opinion, but also the lives of the people involved, the evolution of humanity, the future of planet Earth and beyond. The issues at stake are very high.

Posthumanism emerges as an existential awareness unfolding in this historical era and spatio-temporal arena. Now is the time to manifest the art of being posthuman: know who You are, choose how to live.

The need for open spaces of manifestation is self-evident in this historical context. There is growing interest towards posthumanism, not only as a theoretical frame to understand our times, but as a practical one to act inspirationally in our lives. From the Covid-19 pandemic to the current ecological crises, from the economy of Big Data and the lack of privacy to the socio-political consequences resulting out of scientific discoveries and bio-technological possibilities (from CRISPR gene editing to space mining): radical changes are occurring in our species and planet. People are wondering how to cope with this "new" world. The understanding of ourselves as humanity is mutating. This inner and outer chaos can be challenging and unsettling: it is also the bearer of new ways of being in the world. Perceiving ourselves as part of the labyrinth, instead of lost in it, will unravel unexpected self-discoveries. Along with an ethical praxis, posthumanism, as a path of self-enquiry, is revealed as an existential journey. The goal of the book is to allow for multiple and diverse processes of self-knowledge to manifest at all levels: the individual, the social, the species, the planetary and beyond. Connected, emergent and unique: ultimate ripples, in the fluid and sensitive texture of spacetime.

How to be wise in the 21st century?

Visionaries are the ones who can see what needs to be addressed in their era. Given the changing nature of reality and the matrix of possible perspectives, their answers may differ from time to time. For instance, philosophical traditions pre-dating the common era still offer rare gems of wisdom to contemporary readers; and, still, the limits of socio-cultural assumptions sustaining many of them cannot be simply dismissed. Everything is constantly changing; even if the keys to existential realization may be ultimately timeless, the ways to unfold them, engage with them and depict them must be updated. This is why seers have been necessarily sharing throughout time; every age offers unique insights, focuses and visions in need of contemporary voices to articulate them. Such voices serve as **a reality check for humanity, a most essential function: to be aware of where we are at, as individuals, as a society and as a species.** In this sense, wisdom is both temporal and atemporal: it is nourished by spatio-temporal experiences, and, in its ultimate realization, it transcends them all. This is also why we are the only ones who can answer the question of what it means to be wise in the 21st century: no one before us, and no one after us, will experience precisely these planetary conditions. It is part of our existential performance to awaken to these cosmic embodiments. The nature of change also serves as a wake-up call: we cannot simply rely on the work of others; we must embrace response-ability.[2]

Who am I? This is a question that every human being asks themselves at one point or another, usually starting very young: *Who am I? What is this? Why am I here?* In this sense, everyone is a philosopher – that is, someone who is able to ask existential questions without the need for authoritarian answers. Wisdom has a lot to do with the ancient Greek motto "Know thyself" (ΓΝΩΘΙ ΣΑΥΤΟΝ), inscribed in the Temple of Apollo at Delphi and revered to its ultimate consequences in the life philosophy of Socrates (c. 470–399 BCE), who taught that "the unexamined life is not worth living" (38a).[3] Ancient texts, from the *Tao Te Ching*[4] to the Upanishads,[5] from the *Torah*[6] to the (biblical and Gnostic) Gospels[7] and the Quran,[8] among many others[9] – emphasize, consistently and repeatedly, that the meaning of life is understanding who we are. In our modern world, this spiritual search is often replaced with other searches, such as economic success and techno-scientific advancements. These are all significant trajectories; yet, if they are approached as the ultimate meaning to life, they turn into obstacles in fully embracing the existential openness at the core of dimensional manifesting: *who are we?*

This book approaches philosophy in line with its etymology. In classical Greek, *philos* (φίλος) means "love"; *sofia* (σοφία) means "wisdom." "Philosophy" can be translated as the love of wisdom and, also, the wisdom of love. From a general undertaking of wisdom as an individual achievement,[10] we will move to the possibility of wisdom as a social endeavor, reverberating across times and spaces to the whole existential realm, and beyond. From this comprehensive standpoint, the notion of "love" will unfold in principles of multi-species coexistence, existential empathy and, more extensively, ontological poiesis. This realization cannot be simply learnt; it must be experienced. For philosophies to stand the test of time, they must offer something valuable to those engaging with them, to the societies embracing them, to the species and planet(s) manifesting them. In other words, philosophies must stand as paths of wisdom, granting insights into the existential condition per se, in the unique ways it materializes in each historical era. Posthumanism, as a philosophy of the 21st century, approaches humans (in all of their diversities), non-human animals, technology and ecology relationally. Posthumanism, as a philosophy of life, deeply enriches our existential awareness and intra-acting in the world, investigating the human condition not as an autonomous biological event to be addressed in isolation but as a cosmic co-emergence, from a location that is deeply aware of our geological time: the Anthropocene. This take is full of potential.

In this book, we will contend that posthumanism offers ways to be wise in the 21st century: this is no easy task. Living a responsible life while being (p)art of a society that is still entrenched in (and enchanted by) anthropocentrism is challenging. Yet it is possible, and it is already happening: the posthuman community is expanding into a glocal movement based on post-human realizations. Moving from the theoretical arena to real-world applications, posthumanism addresses the core existential question *"Who am I?"* in conjunction with many other related ones, such as *"What am I?"* and *"Where and when are We?"* In a brave move, it de-universalizes the human gaze, making it (species-)specific, bringing awareness to historical habits and onto-epistemological premises based on anthropocentric supremacy. Aware of individual diversity, material entanglements, species and cross-species commonalities, posthumanism relies on both monism and pluralism: we are one and many, diversity and unity, beyond any eschatological dualities. As individuals, we are constantly changing. Biologically speaking, we are organisms formed by a plurality of entities. We are part of a species which is evolving[11] – culturally and biologically, among other dimensions. From a planetary perspective, our survival is sustained by unbounded ecological, technological and cosmological dynamics.[12] This is when we realize that wisdom cannot be conceived merely as an individual achievement; it is also a social gain: we are, always, many.

What does "posthuman" mean?

Academically speaking, the notion of the "posthuman" is an umbrella term to refer to many movements and schools of thoughts, such as posthumanism(s),[13] transhumanism(s),[14] antihumanism(s),[15] new materialism and object-oriented ontology, among others. Although posthumanism is the departing and returning point of this book, we will constantly engage with multiple perspectives to enrich our reflection. For instance, ontological insights developed within the field of object-oriented ontology will support our ecological understanding of phenomena of vast temporal and spatial dimensions, such as global warming. Transhumanism will enhance our understanding of biology by challenging the current understanding of the human. According to transhumanism, we are not posthuman yet: this passage is necessarily actualized at an evolutionary level, through the potentials inscribed in technological and scientific developments. Alternatively, posthumanism invokes the posthuman as an existential paradigm shift, which is already happening; in this sense, we can be posthuman right now. This book further develops the posthuman in its existential implications and applications, standing on the premises of philosophical posthumanism,[16] which can be summarized in three axes of analysis (to be taken jointly, not hierarchically):

- *Post-humanism:*[17] *the realization that the human is plural*
  We, humans, are many. Still, in the history of humanity, not every human being has been considered human, or as human as others. Philosophical posthumanism reveals how this universalization and homogenization of the notion of the human has benefited only some humans, while sustaining the oppression of others. Such power dynamics have defined the interactions between human groups and shall be taken into consideration when envisioning, and enacting, social modes of posthuman existing.
- *Post-anthropocentrism: the comprehension of the human in coexistential relations to other species, not as superior to them*
  Philosophical posthumanism acknowledges the fact that the "human" – *anthropos* (ἄνθρωπος) in classical Greek – has been historically asserted through a hierarchical scale based on a human exceptionalist worldview. In this framing, the human (positioned, as previously mentioned, in a "human" hierarchy) was placed at the top. At the bottom was the "non-human," categorized into hierarchies based on their similarities to the universalized human. Most anthropocentric worldviews do not recognize the existential dignity of other-than-human forms of existence intrinsically; instead, they reduce them to their utilitarian worth as commodities to (some) humans – in potentiality and actuality. Philosophical posthumanism voices the great fallacy of these approaches; their harmful effects to the well-being of both human and other-than-human entities is most evident in the current era of anthropocenic climate change.
- *Post-dualism: the awareness that existence does not unfold in dualistic*[18] *modes*
  Dichotomous oversimplifications, based on the absolute separation of good and evil, plus and minus, foe and enemy, among many other hierarchical terms (such as black/white, female/male, etc.), have historically sustained and legitimized obstructive and destructive habits – from warfare to planetary injustice. They are serious

obfuscations on our ultimate path of self-discovery. To know who we are we must achieve post-dualistic awareness, or the risk of dichotomizing will persist, in different modes. Such an awareness can start from the self, to permeate the entire dimensional realm, and vice versa: the macro and the micro are co-reflective, with no ultimate discrimination.

To be posthuman agents of change, we must be fully aware of the multi-layered sources of existential habits in their related socio-political, bio-ecological and technological premises, and also in their foundational dynamics of repetitions and reiterations. Posthumanism dares to challenge ontological mystifications, social distortions, scientific reductionisms and related disenchantments of the world, which have been constructed, and repeatedly reiterated, in the historical and bio-cultural processes of humanizing. These partial and biased approaches have (in)formed human collective consciousness, creating impediments towards full existential awareness. Intellectual curiosity, non-judgmental mindfulness, radical integrity and visionary energy are some of the flows of this book. In this extensive journey into the self, we will realize that we cannot understand who we are in separation: we are (p)art of everything.

What is the outline of the meditations?

The art of posthuman existence is to know who we are, and to be able to manifest in post-humanistic, post-anthropocentric and post-dualistic ways of being, knowing that what we do affects the whole dimensional realm. The path of self-enquiry and self-discovery is the thread of this book. In each chapter, the core existential question *"Who am I?"* is embraced from different perspectives and multiple layers: from the personal to the biological, the ecological, the cosmological, the technological, the socio-cultural and the ontological, among others. All of them will unravel, from different angles, common realizations, such as the relationality of being (and the urgent need for letting go of anthropocentrism), unity in diversity, and poiesis, as the ultimate existential creativity. There follows a brief presentation of each meditation. There are eight in total; when shifted, this number (8) represents the infinite (∞).

First Meditation: Posthuman Self-Enquiry

This chapter explores the pivotal existential question "Who am I?," not in isolation but relationally, together with other foundational questions, such as "What am I?", "Who are You?' and "Where and when are We?" Addressing the self relationally, we will delve into key notions, such as inter-being, coexistence, intention and redemption. Only by equanimous discernment and integral honesty can we realize who we intend to be. The ways we live, think and act constitute (p)art of the shifting material networks of our agency, which is comprehensive, multi-layered, plural and all-encompassing: the center is everywhere.

Second Meditation: Human Evolutions

The goal of this chapter is to declutter the notion of the human. We will start from primatology and reflect on our genetic relatives (bonobos and chimps), showing that scientific narratives are products of their specific eras, with their intrinsic biases and limits. Through paleo-anthropology, we will address the origins and developments of so-called archaic humans, such as Neanderthals and Denisovans, emphasizing that there is no absolute separation between "us" and "them": the interbreeding between these related species demonstrates that evolution is neither a linear nor a branched progression. We will then explore the rich periods of the Paleolithic and the Neolithic times, which, although counting for most of our time on Earth as humans, are still mystified as "prehistory" and usually relegated to the background of human historiography. In order to know who we are, we need to declutter the understanding of our shared humanity from any human-centric assumptions, socio-cultural preconceptions and ideological worldviews. Who we are is who we were and who we are going to be: our pasts and futures are already in our presents. A deep understanding of our evolutionary history in becoming human can turn into a path of wisdom, ultimately revealing existential posthuman awareness.

Third Meditation: Biotic Co-emergences

In this chapter, we will explore, existentially, questions such as "Who are we, as a species?" and "What are we, as organisms?", among others. We will delve into the biological implications of our human embodiments and biotic entanglements: from our DNA – dynamically approached as information, self-knowledge and wisdom – to species agency; from the human biome – redefined as "bio-me" for its essential, and existential, impact on who we are – to the generative and destructive power of viral infections. Presenting the human as a holobiont will allow for meta-understandings of the self. Such a move de-solidifies the myth of individual autonomy as the essence of the human: autonomy, in fact, can only manifest in community. In this chapter, the essentiality of both unity and diversity will be found at the core of biotic revealing; developing our *fil rouge* of knowledge, we will encounter biology as a site of corporeal wisdom.

Fourth Meditation: Ecological Presence

We are the Earth, we are (p)art of a planet: this, we cannot forget, or our ignorance will endanger the quality of our existential experience as individuals, and our own survival as a species. In this chapter we will delve into ecology, the Anthropocene, laws and economy, addressing topics that are pivotal to the contemporary ecological debate, such as multi-species coexistence, coevolution, eco-anxiety, indigenous wisdom and the rights of Nature. In exploring these grounding areas, we will point out the misleading conception that we are just living on this planet, whereas, in fact, we are (p)art of the planet. On our path towards self-knowledge, this realization cannot be merely intellectual: philosophical greenwashing (a concept explored in this chapter) will not be of help. Instead, such an awakening must be multiply embodied, lived and experienced: a rooted aspect that smells like a rose, like a pine tree, like the ocean; that moves like the wind, like a snail, like a bear: that is stable and changing, resilient and intra-connected.

Fifth Meditation: Cosmic Constellations

In this chapter, we will address the question "Who are We?" rephrased, more specifically, as "Where are we, as a planet?" and "What is our cosmic embodiment?" We will delve into geology and the origins of the universe, cosmology, exobiology, astroarchaeology, space migration and space ethics. Our cosmic self will embrace the fabric of spacetime, quantum physics, gravitational waves, cosmic alliances and geological systems. Here, we will gain perspective on the cosmic web, realizing that everything, including planets, is changing: our expanding universe has no center. This macroscopic awareness will bring us crucial perspectives on wisdom and resilience, not to be caught in the limited, and limiting, perception that what is happening in human history is all we are. Our existences resonate well beyond the fragmented constitution of human geopolitics: on our path of self-discovery, existential takes on physics will show how the ways we are existing are (in)forming the sensitive network of spacetime: right here, right now.

Sixth Meditation: Technological Enhancement

In this chapter, we will embrace the question "Who are we?" in relation to "What can we be?" We will unveil technology as a dynamic of existence by asking questions such as "What is technology?" and "What do radical bio-technologies reveal, at the existential level?" We will focus, among other things, on digital technologies and the AI takeover scenario: artificial intelligence, on some level, has already taken over.

We will address technological addiction, the Big Data economy and bio-hacking, among other topics. We will embrace technology in relation to ecology, delving into planetary enhancements within the geological era of the Anthropocene. Thereafter, we will unravel the impact of current and emerging technologies in direct evolution, addressing questions such as "Are technological entities aware?" and "Can the planet be enhanced?" We will thus explore hypothetical scenarios, such as the simulation hypothesis, to remark on the urgent need for existential awareness. In fact, enhancement is an intention that manifests relationally, not in isolation: the most significant type of enhancement we can aim for is to know who we are.

Seventh Meditation: Socio-cultural Agency

This chapter resonates with the need for social awareness. In order to understand who we are in the 21st century, we must address where we are at, where we come from, and where we are heading at the social level. We must unveil how and when collective habits are established and set our intentions about social manifestations. We will address questions such as "Who are we, as societies?", "What is posthuman education?" and "How do we achieve posthuman parenthood?" We will reflect on key notions such as habits of existence, empathy, identity and conditioning. We will investigate social discriminations as social dis-eases that are not only life-threatening to the community, but also impediments towards full existential awareness to the individuals who are exposed to them. In doing this, we will realize the vital importance of dismantling segregative practices from our bodyminds, our societies, our planet and, more in general, our existential manifestations. We will approach society as a site of shared knowledge, ancestral wisdom and innovative expression on the collective path towards self-realization.

Eighth Meditation: Ontological Awareness

This chapter is dedicated to ontological awareness, consciousness hacking and the cosmic game. It offers specific insights into how to deconstruct unnecessary patterns and realize original archetypes of existence in the 21st century, asking questions such as "How can we reinvent ourselves in every moment, so that we are not caught in the repetition of predefined structures and hierarchies?" Everything in this world could be different, as such is the art of existential expression; and, also, everything in this world is manifesting out of deep intentions, actions and repetitions set in spacetime. Recognizing and acknowledging the way the world currently is allows us to be completely honest with ourselves. In this chapter, we will tackle the question "Who are we?" in relation to "Why are we?" We will pose related queries, such as "What is consciousness?" and "What is awareness?" We will explore technologies of existence through Nietzsche's *Übermensch* and Foucault's microphysics of power, the Hindu concept of *lila* and the Buddhist principle of non-self, among others. We will address topics such as the subject and the mind, panpsychism, poiesis, shamanism, mysticism and ecstasy. Our understanding of ourselves as archetypes of existence will lead us to our final conclusions.

Conclusions: Posthuman Mantra

The conclusions shed light on how existential posthumanism is directly affecting and effecting us, as individuals, societies, species, planets, and so on. This is a call to take a step further, merge in and treasure this substantial quest for self-discovery and species evolution in our posthuman era: like the sunlight, embracing all.

Methodology

The book develops in questions and answers through short subchapters. Each step of the exploration is supported by current scientific research, as well as ancient paths of wisdom. A wide range of sources are contemplated: from prehistory to the far futures, from fossil records to emerging and speculative technological inventions. Current scientific views are presented, as well as different sources of world knowledges, opening possibilities critically and perspectively. Given the amplitude of the topics addressed – from microbiology to paleontology, geology, astronomy, existentialism and self-care, among others – only the *status quaestionis* – that is, the state of investigation for each area of reflection – is presented. The goal is to offer food for posthuman thoughts in order to actualize key realizations about who we are, which may manifest in different modes of existence. For example, in chapter 5 we will reflect, among other topics, on plate tectonics. Although most people know about this theory's scientific meaning, we will delve into its posthuman existential ramifications. The question is: *why is this information relevant to our path towards self-knowledge?* We will thus make a point against ultranationalism; ultimately, nations are not geological entities but socio-cultural and historical constructs. Knowing that even our continents are constantly changing, *how can humans indulge in national pride and nationalistic hatred?*

This book can be approached as a guide[19] to posthuman existential awareness, offering multiple threads of reflection and enquiry. In mediating scholastic rigor and accessibility, the book implements examples, metaphors, thought experiments and exercises to ease the process of self-locating the reader as the agent and the seer. This is not a book about something, or someone, else: it is about us. Not only supportive of written traditions, it embraces oral traditions in their contents and methods. These archives of knowledges, based on the verbal arts, are present on all continents and precede the written form of transmission; they are routinely based on repetitions in order to assist the storytellers in remembering the lines, and the audience in grasping the main points. In this book, key insights are purposely repeated, in different forms and chapters, in line with the Latin saying *repetita iuvant*, which can be translated as "repeating is beneficial."

The integral choice of diverse repetitions through different fields of research is enacted purposely; the insights gained in every meditation resonate with one another, leading chorally and perspectively to posthuman awareness. From a methodological perspective, this reflects in the ways the book was conceived and actualized. The writing unfolded in nomadic and explorative manners. Like a bee[20] moving from flower to flower, each topic has attracted and reattracted attention and intention beyond the soft boundaries of the chapters. Like forests, they have managed to reveal themselves through a great plethora of different subjects, all intra-connected. The result of these lines of flight is honey for bees, posthuman realizations for us.

The book's architecture

Labyrinth

According to the Oxford Dictionary, a labyrinth is "a complicated irregular network of passages or paths in which it is difficult to find one's way, a maze."[21] In anatomy, a labyrinth refers to "a complex structure in the inner ear which contains the organs of hearing and balance."[22] Labyrinths have deep symbolic meanings cross-culturally and trans-historically, representing the journey of life and death in the search for self-knowledge. The book is conceived in a non-linear fashion, like a labyrinth. The meditations can be read in any order; each is investigated thematically, organized by tags that can be approached through different trajectories. In this posthuman storytelling, the narrative is open to multiple outcomes which will unfold coinciding revelations. This approach is designed to offer readers an open canvas with a diverse set of tools to search in individualized and unique ways – an intentional garden, where key notions from a wide range of perspectives can be explored. Readers are invited to follow their intuition and deconstruct the transitory structure of the book, moving at their own rhythm: at the end of the journey, they will have a complete picture, no matter what.

The chapter structure

Each chapter, as a possible journey and destination, is designed in the following way.

Meditation: this part is the pulsating core of the chapter, a philosophical meditation based on questions and answers, organized by tags.

Farewell: this brief salutation is intended to accompany readers in their intentional journey through the book, facilitating a non-linear reading. The etymology of the term is revealing: "fare" comes from the Old English word *faran*, meaning "to journey"; "well" derives from *wel*, with the same encouraging meaning.

The text is mapped through tags, creating building blocks that can be connected, de-constructed and re-envisioned in different ways and orders. Tags and their contents can be approached as a set of building blocks to different paths of posthuman realizations, in the creative originality of posthuman existential manifestations. The order of the tags is based not on any primacy, but on open thematic narratives and affiliations that can be embraced throughout unlimited trajectories, in tune with our labyrinthine architecture. Each tag addresses a concept; some are presented generatively and critically; others are approached as possible obstacles. As in a maze, some paths are dead ends, becoming outdated and turning into loopholes, unsupportive of existential awareness. This is not a final judgment; these terms can eventually be accessed with different intentions and reveal completely unexpected outcomes. Yet, since they have developed significance in the ways they have been engaged historically, we need to be aware of their hermeneutic legacies and be cautious with their use. Such loopholes will be presented with a question mark (such as #*Loopholes?*). Lastly, the reflections following each tag are not meant to be exhaustive explanations of the term; rather, they are relevant mythopoetic accents in the unraveling of the discussion. This is why some tags, for instance, recur multiple times, investigated from different angles. Readers who wish to experience this book as a guided meditation with no interruption can trustfully rely on the present structure, following the given order of the meditations and tags. Readers can also enter the book as a labyrinth, free to move as they wish, accessing any section and/or chapter in a non-sequential manner. Honoring our visions, aware in the mystery of the adventure, each journey will be satisfying, and satisfied. Enjoy.

Meditation 1
Posthuman Self-Enquiry

#Existential Posthumanism

What is existential posthumanism? Existential posthumanism is a path of self-enquiry and self-discovery, aimed at full existential awareness. It is not simply an academic trend; it can be found in all eras and geographical areas, from all cultural arenas. It is, in some sense, ahistorical, for it is not tied to a specific contextual, and conceptual, background. Like a wild card in poker, it can refer to different paths to (self-)realization, embracing the art of existing in the affects – and effects – each of us is unfolding in our revealing. Given that existence is in constant flux, in order to be integrally aware, we must be conscious of all the situated and embodied dimensions of our manifestations. Existential posthumanism, as a philosophy of life, approaches humans (in all of their diversities), other-than-human animals, technology and ecology relationally, investigating the human condition in co-emergences. This is the time to realize that our lives are our greatest legacy.[1] By doing so, we can unfold the possibilities that surface by embracing existence as our ultimate work of art: ontological poiesis.[2] Life is a journey, and we are the wanderers: anything can happen, and eventually does. "Posthuman," in this sense, means being brave enough to know that the human condition is neither our destiny nor our nature but, rather, spatio-temporal manifestations of unlimited material and semiotic possibilities. The fact that specific histories and herstories have been foundational to the manifesting of our human societies does not mean that we need to repeat the canon: we can change it, right here, right now. We can manifest different ways of existing, enacting our own cosmic game.[3] In order to be conscious channels in the unfolding of our existential manifestations, we need to be completely aware of who we are.

Who are we? We[4] are. Ways of revealing; (actions of) the multiverse; trans-forming energies.[5] Born out of a specific planet: Earth. In a specific era: the 21st century (so defined in accordance with the Gregorian calendar; other measures of time reveal different definitions). From biological parents of a specific species: *Homo sapiens*. We are quite unique: everyone is. In order to realize who we are, we need to acknowledge our specificities as well as our commonalities. On the path of self-discovery, this is the (st)art. As the philosopher Jiddu Krishnamurti (1895–1986) put it: "the first step is the last step. The first step is the step of clear perception, and that act of clear perception is the last act" (2012: 42). We must be clear with our visions; they are already (p)art of our manifestations. At the existential level,[6] existence is all we have: that's plenty.

Existential posthumanism addresses the primal question of existence "Who am I?" not in isolation, but relationally, together with other foundational questions, such as "What am I?," "Who are You?" and "Where and when are We?" This is the ontological epiphany of relationality, according to which relata[7] and relations are not in competition for primacy; they can only co-emerge, in the present moment. The philosopher of science Karen Barad (b. 1956) clearly explains: "relata do not precede relations; rather, relata-within-phenomena emerge through specific intra-actions" (2007: 334). The rich trajectory of material feminism[8] underlines how the ontological is not independent from socio-political, bio-cultural, eco-technological and, more in general, spatio-temporal elements. This dimensional co-manifestation is nourished by, and is nourishing, unlimited and constantly shifting layers of existence. The one and the many are not in separation. Quite the opposite: they induce an understanding of the notion of the self that transcends the loneliness of the autonomous humanist "Subject,"[9] in the recognition of the others as ontologically and necessarily co-generative of the Self. A pluralistic monism and a monistic pluralism:[10] we inter-are.

#Inter-being

This posthumanist journey of self-knowledge starts by realizing the inter-being[11] of the self: as individuals, societies, species, planet, cosmos, and so on. To explain the necessary conditions of existence, the expression "interbeing" was coined by the Zen Buddhist master Thich Nhat Hanh (1926–2022) in these terms: "'Interbeing' is a word that is not in the dictionary yet, but if we combine the prefix 'inter' with the verb 'to be,' we have a new verb, inter-be" (Hanh 2021: 55). The verb "to inter-be" is clarified with vivid examples, such as the following (which we can directly apply to the experience of reading this book in its paper form):[12] If you are a poet, you will see clearly that there is a cloud floating in this sheet of paper. Without a cloud, there will be no rain; without rain, the trees cannot grow; and without trees, we cannot make paper. The cloud is essential for the paper to exist. If the cloud is not here, the sheet of paper cannot be here either. So we can say that the cloud and the paper inter-are. (Ibid.) The posthuman perception of inter-being takes all these dynamics into consideration. Furthermore, coming from an academic tradition, it is specifically aware of the role of social narratives in the constitution of reality. It thus makes it a point to respect human and non-human diversity at all levels, including the symbolic one – for instance, by selecting gender-neutral language, race-aware discourses and species-transformative epistemes, among others. Intrinsically intra-acting, we always inter-are: we are our actions and reactions; our genetics and epigenetics; the food we eat, the water we drink, the air we breathe; the narratives we co-generate and sustain; the people, objects, and places we associate with, among unlimited others. We(/they) are (p)art of who they(/we) are. For instance, human bodies can be addressed as universes to all the entities that make them "be," such as the bacteria that are collectively called the human microbiome and that, more than "inhabiting" our organisms, truly "are" us – (in)forming our physical manifestation, including our health, well-being, and so on.[13] "We," as individuals, are many. Concurrently, we are intra-being with the environment: in post-Darwinian terms; we are changed by, and we change, the places we inhabit.[14] We do not simply live on planet Earth: we are (p)art of it – in a specular existential condition as the microbiome is to our bodies. We can be agents of change right now, once we realize that our existential performing is intimately generative and wholly resonant: manifesting, affecting and effecting in the waves of species consciousness, planetary experiencing and, more extensively, ontological revealing. To be human has ripple effects; this is why, when unfolding the petals of wisdom in the 21st century, it is important to understand our agency as a species.

#Existentialism?

Is existential posthumanism related to 19th- and 20th-century European existentialism? Existential posthumanism can relate to but should not be confused with Existentialism, the philosophical approach developed by 19th- and 20th-century European philosophers, from Søren Kierkegaard (1813–1855) to Jean-Paul Sartre (1905–1980) and Simone de Beauvoir (1908–1986), among many others. Existential posthumanism shares with European Existentialism the focus on exploring meanings, purposes and values of human existence in authenticity; and yet it approaches such intentions with no emphasis on the human subject. While "Existentialism is a Humanism," as famously stated by Sartre (1946), from a posthuman perspective, the human is seen not as the main subject but as a natural–cultural convergence,[15] comprehending the resonances, impacts, affects and effects of our being-in-the-world. This relates to the work of Martin Heidegger (1889–1976), who actually refused to be associated with the existentialist movement and its humanistic trajectories.[16] In tune with phenomenological approaches, existential posthumanism underlines that, if we do not become (p)art of our own research, **if we do not include self-enquiry in our scientific investigations, we will never know who we are** or what we are researching: no one, outside of ourselves, can fully teach us that. Existential awareness does not come simply by studying objectively; it comes from experiencing directly – the object and the subject are not separated. Real wisdom never goes out of fashion, and yet it must be updated: emerging out of realizations that go beyond spacetime, it often manifests through specific symbolic apparatuses, which may reflect the limits of their era.

How do we partake in socio-cultural dynamics? In order to comprehend who we are, we need to transcend the lenses through which we have been taught to categorize ourselves. In our shared consciousness, these semiotic frames are embedded with resonances; they be/come (p)art of (how we narrate) who we are, not only to others: more clearly, to ourselves. To reach deep awareness of who we are, it is wise to know the risks of limiting such narratives to socio-culturally constructed categorizations, beliefs and norms. Through socialization and education, some people may find standardized answers in given accounts. These are imparted, for instance, through the voices of parents, friends, acquaintances, teachers, educators and other family and community members; the teachings of religious and scientific books; the standards learnt in school; interpersonal relations, media consumption, online inquiries, and so on.[17] We learn that we belong to a certain group of people, in current socio-cultural conditions. We are treated differently according to our genders, races, ethnicities, sexual orientations, ages, physical conditions, among other factors. We embrace specific worldviews based on our creeds and philosophies of life.

Supporting their symbolic presence on these acquired epistemic foundations, some people eventually stop questioning (their) existence and/or accept pre-constituted answers in a one-size-fits-all approach. Others may defer those same questions until the moment they are departing this life, now wondering about what death is and if there is an afterlife. In both cases, the inner void of intellectual confusion and existential suspicion is not exhausted, only postponed and partially silenced. When we face existential risks, such as the biological and social challenges brought about by global pandemics, it becomes clear: partial answers can help only partially. In facing death, socio-cultural accounts may finally appear as inadequate. Some people realize this deficiency and eventually find ultimate answers in existence itself, exhausting the need for inner doubt and outer skepticism. This approach requires constant self-accessing, the unlearning of finite truths and the ability to inter-be in awareness. The shifting conditions of our living planet are necessarily revealing on our posthuman path towards self-realization.

#21st Century

What does it mean to be human in the 21st century? In order to address the question "Who am I?" in the 21st century, we need to be loyal to the 21st century, in the sense of being able to accept what is manifesting not as the ultimate reality, but as the one that we are envisioning and actualizing, among many other possible ones. An integral understanding of the reality we are manifesting can only unfold out of an integral reality check. Being human in the 21st century is somehow different from being human in the 8th century BCE or in the 50th century CE. The planet is – was and will be – different.[18] The poietic power of technology is expansively revealing.[19] We are ready to migrate to Mars, still asking: "Who are we?" And so, we are. Right now, in the multi-layered assemblage of our existential unfolding. We cannot find complete answers to our existential condition from people who came before us. The generosity with which they shared their wisdom is of great help, but no one has ever gone through the specific experiences that we are facing, as a species and as individuals. It is our duty to share what we see, what we have learnt and what we need to manifest. Covid-19 has reminded us of the urgency to be present, fully, in our existential experience.

Because we matter. Because if we do not bring our voices out, if we do not enact our visions and intentions, no one will (be able to) do it for us. Not to be relics of time in the wheel of evolution, we have to be brave; see what we see; change what has to change. Everything is always changing, anyway. Nothing will ever be the same. Here we are, now, living the dreams of the people who came before us. *Think about it.* We inherit our genes from our ancestors. We live, work and move through cities, buildings, roads which, in most cases, were built years before we were born, visions of other times. Currently, capitalistic societies addicted to consumerism are common on planet Earth; they are the remote dream of some generations before ours, who experienced scarcity and restraint.

Let me tell You about Nonna Nina, my maternal grandmother. She was born in 1913, one of eight children. Her mother died when she was nine. Her father died when she was sixteen. As a child in a peasant family, she would get up with the sun and go to sleep when the daylight faded; she would not use candles at night because they were expensive. This was rural Italy in the early 20th century, before industrialization and the widespread use of electricity. She was a fervent Christian with a practical mind. She wanted to take vows because she would see local nuns in town, roaming on their bicycles free from the burden of working all day long. As a teenager, she asked her father permission to join the monastery; in return, he asked her to help him with the family. The older sister of many children, in the maternal role since age nine, working constantly until married. A life of sacrifices: she lived through two world wars; she lost her eighteen-year-old son because of heart failure caused by poor living conditions, a disease that today would be easily cured. Her life did not erase her sense of humor. She was very funny in direct and hyper-realistic ways. When older, she used to say: "If God asks me if I want to live again, I'll say: no way!" She was not kidding; one life was more than enough. To her, the transhumanist dream of unlimited lifespan was not very appealing. Another of her existential insights would come from her direct experience of senility, often declaring: "It is good to become old; it is not good to be old."[20] She appreciated many things we would not even notice, such as having access to food, no matter what. The memory of seeing her strong visionary father cry because a storm had destroyed all the harvest of the labor of one year was never erased from her consciousness. And so she delighted in being able to buy industrial flavorless pasta at the supermarket, instead of having to cook for ten people each and every day, including Sundays, when her brothers would rest. Each had his preferences: if the food was not to their taste, she would be blamed; if it was, no one would thank her. No wonder she never cared about gourmet food; as an adult, she was happy with, literally, anything edible. And so she was ecstatic with the invention of the washing machine. Instead of having to wash dozens of sheets, she could just press a button. And yet she never understood the temperature settings; any woolen item of clothing would shrink to doll size – of course, she would find ways to stretch them and make them wearable. These are accomplishments that we take for granted, because we live in the dreams of people who came before us. For my grandmother, the convenience of life in the 21st century was a dream come true.

#Dream

And, eventually, dreams do become true. This is why we need to ask ourselves rigorously and consciously: *what are our dreams?* As individuals, as tribes, as societies, and as a species. We need to acknowledge the generations before us: they did their best. And, if they didn't, there is nothing we can do about it now, other than learning from their historical needs and possible short sightings. The philosopher Hans Jonas (1903–1993), in *The Imperative of Responsibility* ([1979] 1984), underlines the ethical environmental imperative towards the generations to come in the pursuit of an equitable use of planetary resources. Currently, among the main existential risks of extinction for humans are anthropogenic causes, such as climate change and ecological collapse.[21] This is strictly linked to anthropocentric worldviews that are foundational of many current socio-cultural accounts. According to the Oxford Dictionary, the adjective "anthropocentric" means "regarding humankind as the central or most important element of existence."[22] From religious and scientific assumptions to cultural mythologies reiterated in popular media, the human species (often symbolically reduced to a white, male and physically abled specimen) is portrayed as the most evolved, most intelligent, most, most: most of all. The current state of things is showing a very different scenario. Once we are open to reality and able to perceive it as it is – and not as a mere recipient of our projections – anthropocentrism in the 21st century is revealed as a physical and mental dis-ease which is harming us all, as a planet. Healing requires unlearning outdated ways of being human, manifesting an authentic commitment towards multi-species coexistence based on existential awareness.

Must we get rid of anthropocentrism? Posthumanism does not work through categorical imperatives: the flexibility of the Tao, according to which the fluidity of water is the highest teaching,[23] has greatly permeated the posthuman ethical approach. Both humanism and anthropocentrism come in many flavors. In order to actualize integral realizations of human and other-than-human dignities, situated anthropocentric perspectives may be contextually embraced. For instance, some people may find in anthropocentrism the spark to pursue environmental objectives. After all, if humans are still the end goals, in the era of the Anthropocene only a healthy environment can offer humankind the conditions to thrive – and, more realistically, survive.[24] Since we inter-are, our health depends on all these other factors, such as the quality of the air we breathe, the integrity of the food we eat, and the respect of wildlife (as the Covid-19 pandemic dramatically showed, invading natural habitats are red flags in viruses spread to humans as well).[25] In short, some forms of humanistic and anthropocentric approaches may work as allies in shifting our current epistemes. And still, at the core, existential posthumanism does not embrace these forms of moderate anthropocentrism.[26] *Why?* The point is not further to expand, and partake in, the privilege of the "human" but to fully acknowledge the existential dignity of all beings. From a posthumanist standpoint, being human is not about reaffirming the falseness of a constructed ontological privilege. Instead, it is about the awareness of a shared spacetime and the (un)limited possibilities that come with it. It is the realization that we are, always, (p)art of everything.[27]

#Change

How can we create change? Everything is constantly changing, no matter what. Our intentions in affecting and effecting the dynamics of existing can only be successful if change comes from a place of equanimity. This is why blaming and accusing some people for the maladies of the world is inherently ineffective in bringing long-lasting change. Anxiety and self-blame do not help either. These kinds of feelings silence hope, which is a generative resource of resilience – as the old saying goes: "hope is the last to die." It is not by feeling guilty or by accusing others that we bring change, but by being realistic in clarity and intention. This does not mean simply accepting the status quo. Quite the opposite: only by equanimous discernment can we realize what shifts are truly necessary to re-establish integral health. To explain this process at the existential level, let's emphasize two layers of enactment: recognition and imagination. Real change cannot be rooted in personal anger or historical vengeance; those intentions will perpetuate similar results, becoming real obstacles on our path towards self-awareness. As the peace activist Thich Nhat Hanh put it: "Without tranquility and serenity, our emotions, anger and despair will not go away, and we will not be able to look and see the nature of reality" (2005: 41). On the posthuman path, the what is the how. What we are manifesting and the ways in which we are manifesting are not different. These are our gifts to existence; gifts should come from a place of generosity, not from a desire to repay history with the same force of social hate that we may have experienced. To bring real change – and not just differently reaffirm states of anguish in society – we must generate original ways of intra-acting.

#Redemption

How can we heal historical wounds? According to the Anishinaabe author and environmental activist Winona LaDuke (2011), redemption is a mutual process, bringing healing and transformation to all parties involved. Referring to the wounds of colonial oppression, LaDuke provides an exemplary story about the Pawnee people in the United States, who in the 1870s were forced by the settlers to leave the shores of the Platte River and move, from their native land in Nebraska, to Oklahoma. They were agricultural people depending mostly on their crops, such as corn, beans, pumpkins and squash. They took with them their foods; in the new land, the seeds did not grow and, eventually, dwindled. In 2003 a descendant of the settlers in the Pawnee homeland of Kearney, Nebraska, contacted the Pawnees by phone, asking to plant their seeds. The Pawnees were apprehensive; they had very few left of those varieties. They collectively decided to send them back to Nebraska anyway: the seeds eventually sprouted. LaDuke recalls how the Pawnees explained this: "the seeds remembered the land they came from." After that, a celebration was held to welcome the Pawnees back to Kearney, and many actions were taken to bring justice to them – including a donation of land for reburial of their ancestral remains.[28]

What is redemption? In an apology, the human perpetrator of an unjust action recognizes their misdeeds and may seek to make amends. This step is necessary in the process of historical healing; and yet an apology may bring healing only to the perpetrator. As LaDuke explains, the perpetrator also carries the weight of the crime, becoming their own victim;[29] they must also move beyond their own self-victimhood. Redemption is a transformative process which, when fully enacted, brings the final dissolution of the dichotomy victim/perpetrator, transforming that absolute separation into mutual alliances for radical changes. In this story, the successful return of the seeds back home manifested in an instance of redemption beyond human boundaries. As LaDuke puts it: "corn is more than a food; seeds have spiritual meaning and corn, in itself, needs relationship to humans" (2011). Human and other-than-human dynamics were agential in bringing the seeds back to life: the seeds themselves, the Pawnees and the descendants of the settlers, the lands and all the microorganisms in the soil, the elements (water, air, sun) and technological entities (from the apparatuses supporting the first phone call to the infrastructures facilitating the transportation of the seeds from one location to another). In this redemption story, the wounds of colonial oppression were somehow healed through the veins of the Earth. In existential awareness, we can heal: as individuals, as communities, as a species, as a planet.

#Posthuman Awareness

Each generational wave of humanity unfolds bio-evolutionary changes and socio-cultural transformations on planet Earth. If we are brave enough to really see what is happening, without self-commiseration or self-judgment, we will clearly realize the urgency for ecological preservation, post-anthropocentric dignity and human-diverse equanimity. *Is this posthuman awareness?* Posthuman awareness must comply with at least these three layers together: post-humanism, post-anthropocentrism, post-dualism. Let's explain the specific terms of each layer. Post-humanist awareness underlines the ontological relevance of recognizing human diversity. We are one species: we share much in common, and, still, each of us is a unique being; we are one and many at the same time. Clearly, post-humanist and post-anthropocentric awareness cannot be separated. The main cause of the widespread degradation of the biosphere, and of the current sixth mass extinction of non-human species, is human behaviors. Anthropocentrism is leading us onto a suicidal path. Existence is like the ocean, where everything is actually connected and potentially intra-acting. This is not just a metaphor. Our lives and health are not separated from the lives and health of the beings living in the oceans.

In the era of the Anthropocene, marine life and microplastics, algae and garbage patch, zooplankton and toxic chemicals, shells and oil, among others, are merging. As the physician Keith Martin puts it: "We are using the planet's oceans as a dumping ground. . . . As the oceans go, so too do we, for our health and that of the Earth's oceans are inseparable" (2020: 152). Social and environmental inequities go hand in hand;[30] posthumanism calls for interdisciplinary and intersectional approaches, where one type of justice is not prioritized over another. Multi-species coexistence, based on the recognition of the existential dignity of human and other-than-human beings (from non-human animals and plants to technological beings and robots, among others), brings us to post-dualistic awareness. Existence does not unfold in dichotomous ways: unity and multiplicity are at play together. Our agency is comprehensive, multi-layered, plural and all-encompassing. *Are we aware of the existential dynamics that we are co-manifesting? Are we aware of the existential unfolding that we are co-actualizing?* Posthumanism is a path towards self-knowledge from a perspective that is embodied and limitless, personal and political, actual and potential: **the center is everywhere**.

Farewell

Posthuman awareness can be achieved from many different paths. In this meditation, we have set our intention in wisdom. Our journey of self-enquiry goes on to other levels of comprehension, without any hierarchy or linearity. These are some suggestions. In chapter 2, we will reflect about the evolutionary dimensions of being human. In chapter 7, we will understand the intra-connected levels of socio-cultural agency; in chapter 8, we will explore the power of collective archetypes. These are just possible paths. You can proceed further into the labyrinth and choose any chapter of Your choice. Follow Your visions, move at Your own rhythms: each path will take You to specific realizations. Rest assured that, at the end of the journey, You will have a complete picture, no matter what.

Meditation 2
Human Decluttering

#Decluttering

Decluttering is the practice of removing unnecessary items from overcrowded areas. A generative source of physical and psychological benefits, this cleansing attention, and intention, is a vital aspect of self-care, bringing clarity in liberating spaces at both the inner and the outer level. This material practice has deep symbolic meanings, as the anthropologist Mary Douglas (1921–2007) affirmed: "In chasing dirt, in papering, decorating, tidying we are not governed by anxiety to escape disease, but are positively re-ordering our environment, making it conform to an idea" ([1966] 2002: 3). Decluttering the notion of the human, in order to bring it to a level of openness and freshness, is conducive to posthuman revelations and species renewal. Decluttering the human has more to do with minimalism than deconstruction. These methods are not synonymous; in this book, we will employ both. Deconstruction has been key in developing the posthumanist theoretical approach through its postmodern genealogies. As a practice, deconstruction per se has no ending: if carried to its ultimate consequence, it may climax to an eventual symbolic void. Taken as an epistemological location, a symbolic void may be too much (or too little) to handle, possibly leading to depression and anxiety, which can eventually turn into ontological nihilism, depleting life of meaning. Taken as an existential vocation, a symbolic void may open extraordinary possibilities towards ultimate self-realizations.[1]

Decluttering the human notion offers ways to make space from symbolic pollution (referring to biases and hidden agendas that may sustain the symbolic order of a notion),[2] locating ourselves in the wider picture, without being trapped in self-inferred illusionary exceptionalisms and/or self-inflicted nihilistic paralyzations. **A location is not a prison: it is a point of departure.** The human can be a point of departure, among many others: an embodied and situated perspective that is not the end. In order to be a point of departure, the human cannot be filled with accumulated clutter. Any point of departure, to be a point of departure, must be freed from obstacles to allow for lines of flight[3] towards existential revealing. The point is acknowledging who we are: realistically and poietically. Purity does not appear in isolation, or in sterilization. Self-realization can emerge in the process of transforming our symbolic clutter: like the lotus flower, born out of the mud.

#Human(-centric)?

Is "human" synonymous with "human-centric"? Decluttering from absolute human-centric biases does not necessarily mean to get rid of the human. There is always a perspective and a point of departure; they do not entail a supremacy or a hierarchy. Human dynamics are actual co-manifestations in the pluralistic experience of being. The human perspective is a possible onto-epistemological point of departure, among many. According to posthuman perspectivism,[4] human embodiments do not offer any advantages for special objectivity in experiencing reality "as it is." Reality is not homogeneous; for instance, many insects and birds can see beyond the human visible spectrum.[5] There is no epistemological privilege granting special subjectivity. This is not relativism; it is the existential acknowledgment that, to be aware, the subject does not have to be "human," "rational" or characterized by a larger brain capacity: awareness cannot be erased. In a circular way, the subject is the specific perspective from where being is experiencing and manifesting, the ways it is being.[6] Ontically, a human embodied perspective does not come with human-centric entitlements and/or biases, or with a speciesist identification.

In socio-political terms, this realization cannot be reduced to an added layer in pre-established practices of self-categorizing: "*Species: (please, fill in) . . .*"; "*Human?*" Marking the human as a new compulsory identity, by including "species" in the long list of categories, following gender, race, ethnicity, and so on, is not necessarily part of the posthuman agenda.[7] We can always situate our perspective; and, still, such a situating does not have to fit limited and limiting constructions:[8] "*Are You This or That?*" Let's be clear. Categories can be meaningful and useful for different reasons, such as social analyses to better serve a community. The problem arises when they become essential to our self-narrating, losing sight of the overall picture. Instead of understanding who we are extensively, by opening doors to possibilities, we often enclose ourselves in preconceived identities. The human perspective cannot be reduced to a simple unified category that supports a new species-specific identification. If we uncritically accept defining ourselves in pre-constituted terms,[9] we partake in stale repetitions, impeding a deeper comprehension of who we are: inventing ourselves, from our point of departure as a human, is a poietic act in the art of being.

#Beyond Anthropocentrism

Posthuman ethics are established on ontological equanimity: acknowledging "others" – human and non-human being, organic and artificial, physical and noetic, etc. – is (p)art of acknowledging ourselves. In order to do that, we must know who we are. The human can be embraced as a point of departure on the path towards self-realization. In existential awareness, the human, per se, does not imply any privilege, bias or preconception. A constant practice of decluttering is needed to embrace the human as an open trajectory: from the spatio-temporal, embodied and embedded to, possibly, the unlimited. Ultimate self-realization lies in recognizing the individual self as the all-encompassing Self – that is: being (p)art of everything and everyone, the complete manifestation and its potentials, including its dimensional extinctions and possible (re)generations.[10] Being human does not necessarily lead to manifesting anthropocentric ways of living. Aware of the risk of anthropocentric illusive privileges and consequent existential obfuscations, Jain ethics, for instance, are based on the cardinal virtue of *ahimsa*, meaning "non-violence": the golden rule of not harming others must apply to all beings, not just humans. Following, some Jains do not consume root vegetables, so as not to harm the life in them. According to this worldview, understanding the wider, relational, and intraconnected nature of existence can lead humans to enlightenment; this is defined, in Sanskrit, as *Kevala jñāna* (केवल ज्ञान), meaning "complete understanding," "supreme wisdom" and/or "omniscience."

How can we manifest authentic self-revelation instead of simply dismantling detrimental habits and/or reconstituting (a different range of) dehumanizing practices? It is key to reflect on the modalities unfolding our path of self-realization as individuals, as societies and as a species: in posthuman terms, the what is the how. The necessary task of pointing out methodological fallacies should be done not to shame or blame others, but to manifest intention. The problem is not any specific type of discrimination per se, but the dynamics through which hierarchical forms of discrimination continue to arise. For instance, we may eventually solve the systemic dynamics that allow for sexism and racism to unfold; yet, if we do not recognize them as dynamic social technologies, and thus are not aware of their plasticity and capacity to (re)generate, we will soon contemplate other issues, related, for instance, to speciesism, biocentrism or techno-centrism, among other possible types of -centrism(s). Specific types of discriminations must be addressed in their own uniqueness and peculiarity, and also as manifestations of specific inputs in wider apparatuses of power. This is not about shifting powers. Studying history, we quickly realize that, in hierarchical settings, no group is safe; eventually, the ones in charge lose their collective powers and are replaced by others. The goal is not to reiterate epistemological dominations, which are also existential self-obfuscations. Only embracing our inter-being[11] can we truly manifest multi-species justice and planetary coexistence in post-humanist, post-anthropocentric and post-dualistic awareness.

The fact that current histories and herstories sustaining many human societies are dominated by anthropocentric, human-centric (in the sense of the privilege of *some* humans over others) and dualistic biases does not mean that we need to repeat the canon: such narratives are outdated. Being conscious of the power of personal and social narratives in conditioning is key to deep transformation;[12] we do not have to self-limit ourselves by passively accepting outdated codes. It is time for posthuman awareness to be present in all fields of education: human-centric teachings are serious obstacles on our path of self-realization, as individuals, as societies and as a species. We have great responsibility and great response-ability. We can no longer be silent and uncritical of human-supremacist narratives; this kind of silence turns into a complicity with a type of privilege that is neither neutral nor favorable to the human species. The human condition in the 21st century has changed. By searching meaning in the visions of the pasts, we lose perspective of who we are. Currently, what these human-centric societies need is clarity in fully perceiving the human, not as superior to other species, but as (p)art of them.

#Scientifically, Human

Has it always been this way? In the history of humankind, the current understanding of the human, with its sexist, racist and human-centric legacies, is not that old. It can be traced to the beginning of what is currently defined as "history," which is often dated to the beginning of writing, generally referred to as the beginning of "civilization." Such arbitrary historiographical dating, and conceiving, is set in separation from so-called prehistory, which actually accounts for 99 percent of human history on planet Earth: let's call it "history," without any "pre-." This is a revelation, and an invitation, to understand how we have become so narcissistically presentist as to self-defeat ourselves in the symbolic erasure of our own genealogy. Delving into this, we quickly realize that most accounts of the human rely on unruled projections of modern human exceptionalisms, obscuring a realistic understanding of who we are and where we come from. For instance, in most educational books and science documentaries, the human is all too often portrayed as:

"The most evolved species" – this is an oxymoron per se: evolution is neither linear nor ultimate, but a constant process of adaptation to different conditions.

"The most intelligent one" – this is a species-specific self-entitlement. Humans are those animals who, among their specific evolutionary traits, have developed enlarged brains.

"Unique" – from a scientific perspective, this is meaningless: every species is unique.

"The most successful" – it depends on the perspective. In terms of adaptation, many insect species, for instance, are more successful than humans. In terms of survival, this supposedly evolutionary success, based on anthropocentric dominance of non-human species and unconstrained usage of planetary resources, may eventually cause our own extinction (human-caused climate change is already endangering our permanence as a species).

This pseudo-scientific narrative, which is far from being objective or even situated, is reiterated uncritically, leaving no room for other-than-human perspectives. Human-centric biases are supported through other related ones. For example, the visual representation of human evolution clearly shows sexist pre-assumptions. As for now,[13] the near totality of the images that are found in books and online content represent the evolving human as male (their bearded faces clarify any doubts). The only exception to the male universal is the representation of Lucy, referring to the fossil bones found in Ethiopia and pertaining to a female of the hominin species *Australopithecus afarensis*, dated to about 3.2 million years ago. This early australopithecine is the first ancestor species found, until now, who stood upright, like a "human." Bipedalism, which is traced back to 6 million years ago, is currently considered the first step towards becoming "human": many of our "human" traits pre-date "humanity" as we currently understand it.

Before we delve into our origins, we must clarify the scientific terminology to avoid further confusion. In biology, *Hominidae* ("hominids") refers to the taxonomic family of primates consisting of all extinct and modern Great Apes (including *Homo sapiens*). *Homininae* ("hominines") is a subfamily of the *Hominidae* family; it includes the tribes *Hominini* and *Gorillinae*. More clearly, it refers to all hominids excluding the orangutans – which are classified in the subfamily *Ponginae*. *Hominini* ("hominins"), a taxonomic tribe of the subfamily *Homininae*, includes the genera *Homo* (humans) and *Pan* (bonobos and chimpanzees), as well as extinct human species and our immediate ancestors – such as the *Australopithecus* and the *Paranthropus*, among others. All these terms (*Hominidae, Homininae, Hominini, Homo*, etc.) sound very similar, and they are. Closely related, this family shares most DNA in common; their subdivisions and classifications, which are constantly being revised, based on the latest findings, should be taken contextually, not absolutely.

#Primates, Chimps and Bonobos

Science is not separated from specific socio-cultural apparatuses; scientific classifications often reveal the presumptions of an era and the views of the specific groups of people involved in their coinage. On our path towards an integral understanding of who we are, feminist epistemology highlights situated knowledges and embodied experiencing as epistemological preconditions. In this field, the work of Donna Haraway (b. 1944) has been particularly revealing. In one of her first books, *Primate Visions: Gender, Race, and Nature in the World of Modern Science* (1990), Haraway pointed out that the types of scientific narratives and choices in portraying primate behaviors are not neutral, but the result of perseverance in cultural normativity. Instead of challenging unscientific assumptions, they often end up reinforcing stereotypes (sexist and racist, among others), further reiterating them through supposedly "objective" scientific narratives, which are being integrated in ongoing social dynamics of power. As Haraway put it: "Biology is inherently historical, and its form of discourse is inherently narrative.... *Both*[14] the scientist and the organism are actors in a story-telling practice" (ibid.: 4–5). Acknowledging the historicity of scientific knowledges is key in decluttering the ways in which human origins, as well as prehistory and history, have been traced and reiterated.

Who are the closest living relatives of humans? In our evolutionary history, we are related equally to bonobos and chimps, with whom we share 99 percent of our DNA (in a margin between 1.7 and 1.8 percent). Socially speaking, bonobos are different apes from chimps: they live in matriarchal groups, do not engage in consistent acts of violence, and are highly cooperative; their sexuality is not restricted to reproduction and is pansexual; their attitude towards life is persistently playful, even as adults. And still, even if bonobos, together with chimps, are our closest genetic relatives, mainstream scientific narratives often do not mention them, focusing on our shared ground with the chimps, who are patriarchal, have evolved more violent behaviors, and can engage in territorial wars. This choice in genealogical affiliations pushes the assumption that the primacy of aggressive attitudes must be somehow "natural" in humans as well. This is problematic for many reasons. First of all, such traits are not present in bonobos, who are, equally, our closest genetic relatives. Furthermore, chimps' behaviors also evolve; we do not know how these specific traits emerged and, thus, cannot presume that they have been persistently present in their evolution. To finalize this point, the common ancestor(s)[15] that we share with the genus *Pan* (which consists of bonobos and chimps) most likely exhibited, throughout times and spaces, a plethora of different traits and behaviors that cannot be simplified in specific habits or reduced to symbolically charged attitudes, such as violent or benevolent, matriarchal or patriarchal, heterosexual or pansexual, and so on. The picture is much more comprehensive than that; the osmosis of existence cannot be unveiled through linear deductions, biased assumptions and socio-political projections.

#Archaic Humans?

What does anthropocentrism have to do with evolution? In evolutionary biology, anthropocentric and humanistic biases are evident in the scientific approaches and narratives reserved to our closest relatives, as well as the so-called archaic humans – that is, species once pertaining to the *Homo* genus and now extinct. Both terms are generated in a dominant hierarchical relation to modern humans: "they" are "our relatives"/"they" are "archaic" – *compared to whom?* "They" are reduced to versions of something that was going to evolve later on – more clearly: "us." They are approached, by themselves, as incomplete projects – complete only as the necessary symbolic, and physiological, shadow of our evolutionary triumph: *Homo sapiens*. In this cannibalistic evolutionary self-history, long-lasting victories are not contemplated: we, modern humans, are destined eventually to become the archaic versions of some future posthuman species. This teleological ideology stands behind the reconstruction of a past where modern humans are revealed as "exceptional" in a series of comparisons through which the hierarchical human comes out as the actual winner, at least of the present (the pasts and the futures can always turn into projections of our fears and hopes). Other-than-(modern-)human animals are screened for brain size, advanced technological skills, and other traits that specifically characterize modern humans. *Homo sapiens* stands as the measure of all species;[16] any other-than-human species automatically loses in this short-lived championship. And yet, evolution is not based on comparison, nor are we in a competition with our ancestors: we are (in) them/they are (in) us.

Why do we study primates and "archaic" humans? Presumably, to know about ourselves; realistically, most current research seems more interested in trying to prove our self-entitled exceptionalism[17] than in truly knowing who we are. The term "science" comes from Latin *scientia*, meaning "knowledge." Although human-exceptionalist origin narratives may not tell us much about our pluralistic evolutions, they certainly tell us a lot about our current epistemological arrogance. This epistemic fallacy bears deep consequences in existential obfuscation. If we study "others" to prove why "we" are the best ones (the most evolved, the most intelligent, etc.), we will never truly understand the "others." Since we are (also) the others, when we are not ready to embrace "them" as (p)art of who "we" are, we cannot self-reveal our own alterity (the one and the many) on our path of self-realization. In contemporary paleo-anthropology, the anthropocentric myth of the uniqueness of the human is a stumbling block in the task of locating extinct species that are closely related to us. As the paleoanthropologist Ian Tattersall writes: "Right now, we are stuck in a false dichotomy, where if it isn't an Australopith, it must be *Homo* and if it isn't *Homo*, it must be an Australopith. We obviously need more genera if our classification of hominins is to meaningfully reflect the diversity within our family" (Caperton Morton 2016). A deceitful attempt to know who we are, based on self-reflective mirrors of our own biases, can only create more assumptions and distorted expectations about existence. It is time to change our symbolic locations, situating ourselves in the large picture, and not at the top of any (animal) "kingdom":[18] there is no absolute monarchy in life. Posthuman epiphanies reflect the diversity and dignity of all species.

Where does this obsession with human uniqueness come from? The way in which tracing the map of species "closest" to us is being approached sounds like an expansion of the obsession with blood-line kinships in patriarchal societies, where biology, instead of affinity, is recognized as the only guarantor – for man, of legitimate offspring; for women, of social status and legal rights – through strict monogamous relationships.

This is based on the construction of patriarchal honor as the ability of the father to identify their own genetic offspring. The history of human origins should not stand on such a partial approach, which is far from universal.[19] Instead of obsessing about what we are unique for, or which species were more similar to "us," a posthuman take on human origins embraces all that we share with the most diverse species: other-than-human ways of existing are inextricably (in)forming the human. The ways scientific questions have been raised, on these topics, reflect the specific *Weltanschauung* of their era. In our posthuman epoch(é), we must ask different questions, developing original methods to answer them.

#Almost Human

Who is admitted to the exclusive club of the Homo *genus?* The history of the construction of the genus *Homo* says more about the bias of human exceptionalism in science than about who we are. The Swedish botanist Carl Linnaeus (1707–1778) coined the binomial name *Homo sapiens* (Latin for "knowing human"), referring to the only living species in the *Homo* genus. Developing these taxonomic categories before the age of evolutionary biology, Linnaeus did not foresee the possibility of other species being included in the genus *Homo*; thus, he did not clarify its specificities, taking them as self-evident. In the second half of the 19th century other species had to be added. The first Neanderthal remains were discovered in 1829. The term *Homo neanderthalensis* was proposed in 1864 by the Irish geologist William King, soon followed by the findings (in 1891–2), and naming (in 1893), of *Homo erectus* by the Dutch scientist Eugène Dubois. It is worth noting the non-neutrality of this term. *Erectus* in Latin means "erect," "upright" and also "aroused." As the feminist philosopher Adriana Cavarero (2016) suggests, the connection with the phallic erection cannot be dismissed.[20] Many other names could have served the same purpose without the strictly male sexual reference, such as the clearer terminology *Homo stans* (the Latin *stans* means "standing"), among others. Although the sexist connotations of the term might not have been self-evident at the time of its coining, they are now. To make science welcoming to all people, scientific terminology that is offensive and/or bigoted can be changed; otherwise, hidden biases and self-repeating expectations will be haunting not only the scientific community but society at large, inevitably limiting the horizons of scientific research and scope.

How did humans become human? According to current fossil records, *Homo erectus* might have been the first hominin to leave Africa, around 1.8 million years ago, and disperse across Eurasia. Primitive *Homo sapiens* would emerge in the Horn of Africa around 300,000 years ago, from a species descendant of *Homo erectus* that had remained there. Anatomically speaking, modern *Homo sapiens* evolved around 200,000 years ago – brain, and brain cases, becoming fully "modern" around 100,000 years ago.[21] According to current findings, populations of *Homo sapiens* migrated to Asia and Europe between 130,000 and 115,000 years ago, possibly in earlier waves, encountering other species, such as the Neanderthals and the Denisovans, descendants of hominins who had probably left Africa in earlier waves.[22] Although pertaining to the genus *Homo*, these "other" humans have been posed as the minus in the evolutionary process of becoming human, of which the apex would be us, modern *Homo sapiens*. In this loaded (modern-)human-centric historical construction, "archaic humans" have been flagged as the evolutionary losers, the "almost" humans who did not make it. This tale is not accurate.

Are Neanderthals and Denisovans extinct? Neanderthals, Denisovans and *Homo sapiens* interbred. According to DNA evidence, the percentage of Neanderthal DNA in modern humans is about 1 to 2 percent in people of Asian and European background (zero or close to zero in people from African populations, since the Neanderthal lineage left the African continent earlier on). Denisovan ancestry is around 3 percent in Aboriginal Australians and Melanesians. These so-called archaic humans are (p)art of our species: there is no absolute separation between "them" and "us." These species coevolved together. Modern *Homo sapiens*, like any other species, should be approached as an assemblage of different genetic traits and characteristics: a genetic flow. Only about 1.5 percent of the modern human genome is "uniquely" human, and even this small amount may shrink further with new findings. More in general, modern humans are a process, emerging out of a history of plurality and community, (genetic) diversity, adaptability and cooperation.

Let's look more closely into the species that has been defined as "Neanderthal." From the first location in which their fossils were found – the Neanderthal valley in Germany – more remains were eventually discovered in South-West Asia, Central Asia, North Asia, and Europe: according to current research, they range from 400,000 to 40,000 years in age. It is interesting to note how many false myths clouded the general understanding of Neanderthal people, who, in the past, have been presented as violent, barbarian and ignorant – simply, not evolved. We now know that Neanderthals had a complex culture and sophisticated technology. They had the ability to speak – as the analysis of the Neanderthal hyoid bone discovered in 1989 in the Kebara Cave (Israel) suggests. They had a symbolic system, as demonstrated through the findings of Neanderthal art in the Cave of La Pasiega in Spain. They may have played music and, possibly, musical instruments such as flutes.[23] Once we look into this, we realize that "they" were not so different from "us." It is indeed liberating not to have to be the "best" ones and, instead, to acknowledge that we are (p)art of all these species. This does not entail an erasure of differences (which are always present in the creative originality of existing); it means, more clearly, an ability to let go of the need to set such differences in hierarchies based on epistemological partialities and ontological unawareness.

#The Birth of Anthropocentrism

How have humans lived most of their history on Earth? The Paleolithic[24] – from Greek *palaios* (παλαιός), meaning "old," and *lithos* (λίθος), meaning "stone" – is a macro-period of time, which counts as most of our existence as a species on this Earth. It is set to begin when the first hominids started to develop stone tools, more than 3 million years ago, until the beginning of the Neolithic time, which is traced around 10,000 BCE.[25] During this major part of our history, humans were living as nomadic gatherer-hunters.[26] The Paleolithic, a time before agriculture and urbanization, was marked by few possessions: the minimum to be carried during nomadic transitions.[27] Recognizing clues from the environment was key to human survival. In this vital embodied knowledge, humans could not be in separation from "Nature"[28] or from one another. Nomadic life in vast regions – as it was in the lives of our ancestors during the Paleolithic times – is conducive to the understanding of inter-being. Nomadic people return seasonally to places: honoring balance is necessary. If too many animals are hunted, they can become extinct in that region. If too many plants are harvested, it may take years before they can be harvested again; the disruption of their regenerative cycle is also fatal to the humans being sustained by them. This understanding of the circle of life pervaded all the Paleolithic, most of the Neolithic time, and is still foundational in many indigenous cultures. During the Neolithic time, some gatherer-hunter societies started domesticating crops and animals, moving towards a farming lifestyle. The gradual urbanization of human settlements, the development of agriculture, the escalating dependence on cultivated crops, tools and infrastructures, based on the increasing extraction and appropriation of natural resources, brought the settings for the eventual formation of dichotomous anthropocentric ideologies, which would sustain the eventual rise of the Anthropocene.[29] These passages were gradual and never absolute; they cannot all be simply assimilated to speciesist privileges and reductionisms: anthropocentrism comes in many forms.

In 2020, I relocated to upstate New York in an area where wild animals are present on a daily basis. One evening, I took a bike ride to an isolated park, where coyotes roam at night. I was sitting on the grass, enjoying the presence of the wild, when I heard some noise in the distance. Alert, I thought: "I hope it's a human." Even if coyotes do not usually attack human adults, a human encounter was preferable than a group of coyotes. This experience helped me consider the way humans, living nomadically through the Palaeolithic times, might have valued meeting other human tribes: in most circumstances, they would have been perceived not as threats, but as allies in mediated terms (not against nature but in nature). We are here thanks to the information shared in gatherer-hunters' aggregations. Their solidarity and sociability, artistic collaborations and technological creativity are the traits that, according to some theories, would have allowed our species to survive during the harshness of the ice ages, while other hominins (such as the long-lived *Homo erectus*, Neanderthals, Denisovans, etc.) all became extinct.[30]

#Prehistory?

When was "prehistory" invented? The Paleolithic and Neolithic times cover circa 99 percent of human history; and yet they have been reduced, altogether, to "prehistory" – a shortened designation for "pre-literary history." The term was coined, and started to be used, during the age of the European Enlightenment, first in France and then in England; the first usage of the word in the English language dates to 1836. At that time, during the Industrial Revolution in Western Europe, the modern birth of "history" as an academic discipline was being developed, based on a progressively mechanized vision of Europe, which was then favored and promoted. In this age of colonialism, other ways of living based on traditional farming and hunting – as practiced in other areas of the world, as well as in rural Europe (which was still predominant) – were portrayed as uncivilized, in need of the colonizers' inputs, urban assistance and, more generally, "progress": the city was the emblem of this new dream of industrial (r)evolutions. Presenting Europe as if in the most advanced stage of human history was crucial to developing ideologies of racial superiority, which eventually turned into political justifications for the inhuman treatment of global populations and for the depletion of local resources, among other phenomena. The legacies of these ideologies are still imbued in the ways "prehistory" is studied and presented.

Why is writing given such a primacy? Approaching writing as the turning point in human historical evolutions and civilizations is deeply presentist,[31] classist and Western-centric. Although different types of symbolic systems were already present in the Neolithic, writing, as currently conceived, developed more clearly in the Bronze Age, around 3,400 BCE. From a modern-day perspective, writing is often presented as one of the most precise ways of keeping records; this does not justify the absolute primacy that has been attributed to it, to the point of relegating everything that came before it, and any culture that has not used writing, as "prehistory." If we are reflecting on the history of humankind, such an enquiry can only be comprehensive. Historically, many human societies did not develop formal writing as a way of communicating; this leads to the arbitrary conclusions that some societies would have left their prehistory only very recently, or would be still in it. The prehistory of Australia, for instance, is considered to end with British colonization in 1788, which produced written documentation of Australia. According to this scheme of things, Australia officially enters "history" through its colonizers, whose policies almost wiped away its Aboriginal population. More in general, throughout history, the large majority of humans were granted no access to reading and writing. This was tactical in excluding them from accessing hegemonic power dynamics, and thus keeping their supposedly inferiority intact and unchallenged. Basing history on a literary stand necessarily leads to adopting the view of the minority who had the self-entitled privilege of literally "writing"[32] history down – that is, the ruling class. Furthermore, this partial preference is based on the claim that, without writing, the symbolic meanings present in the ecology of cultural items and artifacts could not be clearly decoded. This assumption surfaces from the *Leitmotiv* of absolute Otherness: something (or someone) would be so separated from "us" that, supposedly, they could not be understood unless "they" spoke "our" language. This resonates with the case of migrants arriving at Ellis Island, New York, in the 19th and 20th century. Those coming from non-English-speaking nations were often sent back to their homelands because they were declared "illiterate." The problem is that they were given the literacy test in the English language, while many were literate in other languages. This historical example reveals other dynamics at play: from the Anglo-Saxon ethnocentrism in the political control of migration waves to North America at the time, to deep existential obfuscations. There are always ways of bridging and understanding: we are all intrinsically related.

#Regeneration

How can we know prehistory? Knowing where we come from is essential on our path of self-awareness. A different approach to (pre)history is not only possible but necessary in the unfolding of posthuman education. The archeologist Marija Gimbutas (1921–1994), who excavated numerous prehistoric sites in the geographical area of so-called Old Europe, stated: "I do not believe, as many archeologists of this generation seem to, that we shall never know the meaning of prehistoric art and religion" (1989: xv). According to Gimbutas, prehistoric art itself acts as a direct source of knowledge: the symbols depicted are repositories of the cultures that manifested them, representing their *Weltanschauung*. For instance, while most monotheistic religions today would refer to God in male terms, the extensive amount of female figurines of the Paleolithic and Neolithic eras bear witness to a different set of worldviews. In Gimbutas's words: "There is no trace of a father figure in any of the Paleolithic periods. The life-creating power seems to have been of the Great Goddess alone" (ibid.: 316). The Great Goddess[33] held the power to create (and thus, take away) life, being, more extensively, a life creator rather than a genetic mother. More clearly, in prehistoric times the focus was not fertility (which evolved in the food-producing era)[34] but regeneration – of all Nature, not just of the human.

Gimbutas defines as "language of the Goddess" a semasiographic[35] language, where interwoven symbols[36] represent divine values and functions – divine not because they are outside of Nature, but because they are the generative powers of the Earth. This clearly shows in the figurines, which are often hybrids, merging elements from human and other-than-human animals, plants and cosmic constellations. In tune with a prehistoric understanding of the posthuman, the human (e)merges through ecological and technological fractal affiliations – lines of decorations, beaks, leaves, ornaments and tools – to remind us of who we are.

What about gender roles? Gender biases have a lot to do with the reasons as to why prehistory has been relegated to a footnote in the history of the human. Presentist and sexist assumptions have also caused gendered misconstructions of (pre)historic times, indicative of a supposedly patriarchal inheritance. The multiplicity of archeological findings does not support a dualistic reduction in gender roles. For instance, the archeologist Randall White (1992, among others) has underlined how, while reconstructions in popular magazines continue to show men as the primary creators and users of Upper Paleolithic imagery, no evidence exists to support this scenario. The role of ornamental beads in the development of technology is significant. The Upper Paleolithic is the first time in human history when large-scale productions of items (specifically, beads) are exchanged; because of the size of the hands involved in the art of making beads, some of this work was necessarily produced by women and children.[37] A large variety of technologies and arts were already present at that time: from ivory beads to ceramics; from textiles to spears; from figurine carvings to cave paintings and the art of perspective – women, men and children all painted in caves. More extensively, the shared experience of pregnancy and childbirth,[38] including their possible risks and complications, must have been a major channel for social bonding and information exchanges among tribes and species. Once we declutter (pre)history from any historiographical hierarchy, a different portrayal of our pasts surfaces, liberating human "history" from its own epistemological imprisonment: there is no "pre-." We, as a species, have been exploring different ways of existing. We, modern humans of the 21st century, cannot silence "them" in historical reductions that only obscure our own self-realizations.

What does (pre)history have to do with posthuman awareness? Our integral history on Earth emerges in essential dynamics of multi-species coexistence, not in speciesist dominations. **In terms of evolutionary success, we are still here because of our respect towards others, in ecological balance:** this is probably one of the reasons why our species has been around for so long. In this era of ecological distress, mostly caused by our own species, we can greatly learn from our ancestors: their wisdom is (p)art of who we are. It is up to us to remember – in regenerated and original ways, not in any literal and absolute form. This is not about going back to the past or being stuck in what the present is supposed to be: it is always about creating possibilities. The past is passed; the present brings their presents. From an existential posthuman perspective, teaching half stories does not help anyone, not even the people who are supposed to be the ultimate beneficiaries of strategic omissions. Acknowledging our pasts means being aware of our present(s). A balanced society is a society that truly knows who we are: healing is revealing.

#Human Animal

Does posthumanism reject human-centrism in toto? A comprehensive assessment of the human is necessary in manifesting respectful modes of proceeding, understanding when and how humanistic and/or anthropocentric ways may be of help. A fitting example is the use of the term "human animal." Within the evolution of posthuman theory, the promotion of this term marked a significant step along the deconstruction of anthropocentric habits in language. In the history of many human civilizations, the human had been placed, by default, in a separate category from non-human animals; non-human animals had been exploited to give absolute primacy to the human. For instance, in mainstream Western accounts, for the humans to be the plus, non-human animals had to be the minus, in a set of negative stereotyping that could eventually be employed to insult humans – think, for instance, of the terms "pig," "donkey" and "rat," among others, used as pejoratives[39] in modern English. Still, as the critical race scholar Philip Butler underlines (2018), the term "human animal" does not resonate well with those humans who have been categorically assimilated to non-human animals, such as African-American descendants in the history of American slavery, among other categories.[40] To further clarify this point, we can recall the history of human zoos, where humans considered outside the "norm" would be exhibited.[41]

The history of Ota Benga (1883–1916) is a dramatic example. Taken from his native land in what is now the Democratic Republic of Congo, he was displayed among other exhibits as "The African Pygmy"[42] at the Bronx Zoo in New York.[43] After such dehumanizing experiences, Ota Benga was eventually helped to rebuild a new life in Virginia. The psychological damage he had suffered was too deep: he committed suicide at the age of 33. Once we acknowledge the degree of brutality to which some humans have been exposed within the supremacist politics of those who have had access to the social and legal recognition of being (considered) human, a term such as "human animal" must necessarily be approached in mediated terms, honoring all. This is an example of a post-anthropocentric linguistic possibility that should not be automatically embraced; its dehumanizing implications must be taken into consideration when approaching different individuals and communities. The term "human animal" can be useful when contextualized; it should not be universalized or generalized. The formula *one-size-fits-all* does not work in manifesting respectful modes of posthuman proceeding.

#Microcosm/Macrocosm

How did anthropocentrism contribute to the process of human self-realization? Post-humanist, post-anthropocentric and post-dualistic awareness must be present to approach anthropocentrism in mediated terms; otherwise, the risk is turning it into a disembodied *-ism*, the absolute scapegoat: "anthropocentrism did it!" In the waves of inter-being, no one is strictly to blame or to be praised. The contribution of different forms of humanism and anthropocentrism to the historical evolution of the human cannot be simply downplayed and cast out as psychological palliatives of an inherently species-maniac delusion. Greatly inspired by spiritual syncretism, hermeticism and Neoplatonism, Renaissance humanism underlined that humans were made in the image of God, thus, they were also divine, expanding the focus of existential enquiry from God, as Creator, to humans, as co-creators. The Renaissance philosopher Giovanni Pico della Mirandola (1463–1494) believed in the unlimited potential of human beings, stating in his *Oration on the Dignity of Man*:[44] "let us compete with the angels in dignity and glory. When we have willed it, we shall be not at all below them" ([1496] 1998: 7). His ideas and political alliances were considered dangerous by the high ranks of the Roman Catholic Church;[45] he died prematurely at the age of 31.[46] Nevertheless, his vision resonated deeply with the spirit of the era. The iconic, and ironic, drawing *Vitruvian Man* (c. 1490), by the polymath Leonardo da Vinci (1452–1519), depicted a nude male body in idealized proportions, inscribed in a circle and a square – a (possible) center of the universe. In Leonardo's work, the human (still portrayed as the universal male)[47] is indeed central. In posthuman terms, this centrality is not necessarily a supremacy: the human is a reflection of the entire universe, and vice versa.

What is the microcosm–macrocosm analogy? The microcosm–macrocosm analogy can be found throughout human space-times, in different cultures and eras. Already present in the European Middle Ages, it shines in the work of Hildegard von Bingen (1098–1179), a polymath and a Benedictine abbess who was eventually declared a saint and a Doctor of the Catholic Church. Having had mystical visions from a very young age, Hildegard later depicted them in her *Scivias*.[48] Conceived in the form of circles, these cosmic eggs[49] represent all elements, including human beings and their (energetic) halos, in micro–macro analogies. These drawings, outlined many centuries earlier than Leonardo's, share a significant number of similarities. In the tradition of Vajrayana Buddhism, they can be juxtaposed with representations of the rainbow body phenomenon, which refers to the Body of Light attained through enlightenment. In Hindu and Buddhist symbolisms, mandalas – which, in Sanskrit, means "circles" – are concentric geometric designs representing the universe; they are approached as conducive to meditation, in the realization of the ultimate unity between the micro and the macro. In existential posthumanism, the microcosm–macrocosm analogy relies on the awareness that, ultimately, every aspect of being resonates with, and in, the entire manifestation. Post-humanist, post-anthropocentric and post-dualistic halos unfold: petals, in blooming mandalas of self-realization.

#Beyond Human-centrism

Is anthropocentrism an act of empathy? We could argue that, in specific eras and circumstances, a special recognition of the human would not necessarily entail a speciesist ontological obfuscation; instead, it might manifest as an inspired act of situated empathy. In antiquity, mortality was much higher, and the average lifespan exponentially shorter, than is the case in many countries today. The anthropocentric imagery supporting relevant ancient scriptures – for instance, the human made in the image of God, as expressed in the Book of Genesis[50] – could be explained in these mediated terms. Generated out of specific conditions, they can be sustained as poietic acts of historical empathy; to honor and respect their humanitarian intentions, they should not be transformed into theoretical justifications to persist in suicidal anthropocentric behaviors. In the era of the Anthropocene, the main risks of human extinction are anthropogenic human causes; many species are already extinct because of human actions. In these conditions, it is not realistic to rely on anthropocentric premises, or promises. We need to rethink our processes of existing in ways that are literally down to earth, understanding where we are at, where we are coming from, and where we are heading, as a planet. If we want to survive as a species, we need to know who we are now, in the 21st century.

The human can function as a starting point of regeneration and realization. Every point of departure can lead to existential awareness. There is no crown to be given up: the center is everywhere. Humans, as a species, are many. Human behaviors cannot be generalized and reduced to a unified stereotype; there have been, there are, and there will be unlimited ways of existing as humans. The planet is collapsing due to the greed and carelessness of some; others are not following the same trajectories. Human survival depends upon the balance of the circle of life. Aware of not just "living" on this planet but being (p)art of this planet, many humans have taken care of the Earth from time immemorial, as (p)art of their ancestry. This existential realization is found intersectionally, from ancient understandings of the Earth (think of the primordial deity Gaia in Greek mythology) to the field of evolutionary biology (the Gaia hypothesis[51] contemplates the Earth as a self-regulating complex system). Indigenous worldviews are intrinsically holistic.[52] The Quechua notion of Pachamama can be translated as "World Mother" or "Mother Earth" – living and encompassing all (physical and metaphysical) manifestations that (inter-)are the Earth. Multispecies respect[53] is foundational to relational well-being. This is central to the value system of the Maasai people in Africa in their ethics of care of the land.[54] This embodied perception of the Earth, as (p)art of the self, brings forth revealing:[55] we are *where* we are. In these geographies of existential awareness, gurus[56] are everywhere: in the mountains;[57] in the cyberspaces of our digital self(ies); in the land(s) we are . . .

#With or Without Humans?

Is human extinction the solution to our planetary crisis? Aware of this geographical unfolding, some people sustain the belief that, for the sake of the land, humans should opt for self-extinction, in the hope that the present stage of planetary collapse may eventually reverse. The philosopher Patricia MacCormack (2020) argues for a conscious self-extinction of the human in an ahuman turn: the goal would be a world without humans. Although the extinction of the human may solve some current ecological issues, from a posthumanist existential perspective, extinction is not the answer. In deep time, the human chapter (and character) is only a couple of minutes long; it will also vanish relatively soon from the history of planet Earth.[58] Symbolically speaking, such a species sacrifice resembles the Christian doctrine of self-sacrifice as the ultimate purifier of sins. In this case, our species' sins would be ecological devastation, technological hubris and capitalist greed, among others. Acknowledging where we are at, in the era of the Anthropocene, does not entail self-deprecation; to be realistic is not equal to being judgmental. In the web of life, humans are neither the "good" ones (the most intelligent/evolved/special – simply: the best) nor the "bad" ones (the mindless, the worst bio-cultural virus, the planetary cancer, etc.). Yes, our self-directed extinction could allow other species eventually to spread and predominate; and yet these other species may also eventually create planetary unbalance and distress. This celebratory self-extinction scenario still relies on a dichotomous approach of "good" versus "evil," which does not bring ultimate change. The solution is to be found not in self-inflicted, although joyful,[59] extinctions but in becoming self-aware.

How can we become extinct if we are (p)art of the full manifestation? To be (humans) is to (inter-)be: we are not separated from everything else. Energy doesn't die, it transforms. Humans cannot simply become extinct: to bring real change, we must transform our ways of being. The point is not to give away our primacy – which is a delusion, anyway – but to realize who we are. Existential revealing exceeds species classification. We must be aware of our existential obfuscations and transform them; otherwise, they may as well leak to other species, in different forms. Rushing the end of the human race would leave some of these dynamics at play; eventually, they could (in)form the ways non-human beings may someday perceive themselves as better than others – for instance, in the dreaded AI takeover scenario.[60] Existential awareness resonates through species, planet(s), and vice versa: we must realize *who* we are *while* we are (here). Only if we nourish self-awareness can we reverse anthropogenic habits: the current planetary catastrophe is a mirror of our own existential obfuscations in the micro–macro knowledge of the self.

Farewell

In order to know who we are, we must know where we are (at). Getting rid of anthropocentric biases does not mean rejecting the human; being human does not necessarily come with human-centric strings attached. In this meditation, the human is embraced as a possible onto-epistemological starting point, among unlimited others. To be a point of departure, the human must be cleared of any preconceptions that impede ultimate self-realizations; this is when symbolic decluttering is needed. In the next chapter, we will understand biological alliances among all organisms. For a comprehension of humans in deep time, see chapter 5. To know where we are at, as a technological species, explore chapter 6. Please, do not hesitate to move freely in the labyrinth, accessing any chapter or tag of Your choice. At the end of the journey, You will have a complete picture, no matter what.

Meditation 3
Biotic Co-emergences

#Embodiments

Manifesting, in this dimension, entails embodying. Moons and stars, in their cosmic presence, are embodied; humans are as well. Embodiments are manifestations, and vice versa.[1] In this meditation, we will focus on the organic aspects of this existential precondition, actualized in the intra-acting and shifting dynamics constituting our embodied beings. Our shared biology is an actual, and potential, site of self-knowledge. We will approach genetic wisdom, addressing the macroscopic aspects of being human – as (pa)rt of a species – and the microscopic ones, acknowledging bacteria and viruses as (p)art of our existential revealing. In this openness, the micro and the macro co-emerge. A posthuman approach to being (embodied) unveils original insights. Embodiments do not need to be physical or biological; they can be technological, digital, virtual, symbolic, oneiric, and even potential.[2] They are necessarily contextual. Embodying as a spider in a snowy cave in the Himalayas, or as a digital avatar in a virtual domestic reality, involves an immediate range of specifically diverse alliances. This does not mean that one manifestation is better, or worse, than the other; neither does it imply that they are separated, nor that their potentialities are already traced. A multiplicity[3] of dynamics are transiently involved in all embodied manifestations; their specific nets of immediate associations originate largely, but not solely, from their embodied locations. The web of life and the extensive kinship in biological revealing are intentional labyrinths towards self-realization. To existence, we all pertain: "we" are unlimited processes – beyond any consolidated centralizations.

When referring to human embodiments, there arises a question which has brought much conflict between the idealist and the materialist approach: *are we our bodies or our minds?*[4] The two terms, "body" and "mind," are co-generative: the mindful body/the embodied mind.[5] In being human, the embodied mind performs as a contextual community – for instance, our gut microbes are key to brain functioning, mental health and social behaviors. An understanding of this *continuum* helps us to avoid running into the great obstacle to self-discovery: the body/mind divide. Posthumanism deconstructs this historically reiterated dichotomy, which has sustained different types of existential obfuscations and dehumanizing practices. For instance, in the patriarchal construction of gender oppression, the female has been associated with the body (in domestic labor, sexual exploitation and re/production) and the male with the mind (the father as the "head" of the family). In the recent history of the United States, among other nations, the narratives sustaining chattel slavery and systemic racism were based on the association of African descendants with the body (in forced labor, sexual exploitation[6] and re/production) and North-Western European descendants with the mind (the masters, in charge of socio-political and biocultural decisions). These supremacist accounts obscure a real understanding of who we are. We are neither our bodies nor our minds; thus, we cannot be reduced to one or the other. The term "bodymind" approaches the body and mind as integrated from a holistic perspective. This connection does not fully solve the Cartesian dichotomy; the separation is still there, only lessened.[7] Discriminatory agendas may strategically promote absolute reductions and/or separations; and still, at the existential level, they can never fully succeed: in being embodied as organisms, our self-knowledge is always, necessarily, aware of inter-being.

What do organisms have to do with self-knowledge? The answer is: everything. The word "organism"[8] derives from classical

Greek *organon* (ὄργανον), which generally refers to "instrument, tool, organ"; more specifically, it applies to knowledge.[9] For instance, Aristotle's standard collection of six books on logic was named "Organon" by his followers. According to Aristotle (384–322 BCE), logic was the instrument by which one can come to know the true nature of reality – that is, it was an instrument of ultimate knowledge. The modern understanding of the term "organism" has evolved from its original etymology, highlighting the organizational aspect of biological and digital life (as suggested, for instance, in the use of the web domain ".org" – a shortened version for "organization"). Organisms are embodiments of life (as we think of it); self-knowledge is essential to successful organizing. Our ancestral kinship with all life forms present today is an expression of the relationality of existing. The earliest fossil evidence of life traces back to around 4 billion years ago,[10] emerging relatively early on planet Earth.[11] According to scientific research, all current biological life on Earth evolved from common ancestors, defined as LUA[12] (an acronym for the "last universal ancestor"). These evolutionary processes expressed (and are still self-expressing) in plurality and community, morphological and metabolic diversity,[13] adaptability and interpretation.

#Double Helix

The genetic code is at the source of life: a condition *sine qua non* of our biological embodiments. In nearly all living organisms,[14] the main genetic material is DNA,[15] the molecule responsible for specifying the structure of living things. A full set of DNA – which is required for the embodiment of each specific organism – is securely encoded in nearly every cell of a multicellular being. Because of its length, structure[16] and vital role, most[17] DNA is located in – and cannot leave – the cell nucleus, protected by the membranes of the nuclear envelope from the risks of possible damage.[18] DNA is a vital dynamic of evolution; a constitutive element in the manifestation of life; an essential source of being organic in this world (as a molecule, an organism, and so on). DNA has the power and ability to evolve. Not only does it self-replicate, but also it is constantly changing, in processes of mutations, epigenetic expressions and horizontal gene transfers. According to recent studies, every time human DNA is passed from one generation to the next,[19] it accumulates around 60 new mutations.[20] Mutations are often presented as DNA copying mistakes that can lead to serious diseases; and yet mutations can bring advantages to the organism too. In relation to human health, most mutations are neutral. Some are harmful, while others are beneficial and protective – for instance, 1 percent of Northern Europeans carry a genetic mutation called CCR-5, which confers immunity from HIV infection.[21] Mutations can be approached as techniques of evolution, resulting not necessarily from errors but also out of knowledge of the self as (p)art of the environment, manifesting specific changes in choice and interpretation.[22]

Is DNA self-knowledge? From an evolutionary perspective, DNA serves as a major agent of heredity and continuity, transmitting self-knowledge from one generation to the next, contributing to the diversity of life. In scientific narratives, DNA is generally presented as "information" or as a set of "instructions"; it is often compared to an object, described as "an instruction manual."[23] This sounds particularly fitting in the Age of Information (as our era is called),[24] and yet it is not exhaustive. A manual is not (and is not made of) the information it contains; it needs a subject (specifically, a reader) to unveil that information; it is a means, not a goal. Furthermore, traditionally, a manual does not upgrade itself in autonomy according to what is happening in its comprehensive environments. DNA instructions are not passively given to "someone" or "something" else (external or separated);[25] they are internally situated and authoring – essential to the embodied manifestation of the organism. These "instructions" are (p)art of who, what, when and where they are: the subject is the object, is the process. Although DNA can be approached as instructions and even, from a utilitarian perspective, as a storage device,[26] presenting it as mere information is delusive: naturally occurring DNA is not just carrying information.

In its ability to change and evolve, DNA demonstrates self-awareness of being in this world, as a molecule, an organism, and so on. It can also make mistakes, lost in automatic repetitions,[27] forgetful of its poietic power in manifestation. In this balance between continuity and originality, DNA, from mere information, emerges in agency: self-knowledge that cannot be isolated from the agent(s) manifesting it. In the genetic flow, any final separation between the one (the uniqueness of the organism, as embodied here and now) and the many (the collective genetic memory of our near and distant ancestors) cannot be sustained. Evolution results from embodied wisdom in biological revealing.

Who are we, as a species? From a genetic perspective, humans share much in common. And still, although all modern humans are 99.9 percent similar to each other at the DNA level, no two human beings are exactly the same. Clones, for instance, are often presented as genetically identical: they are not. Based on the bio-technologies currently used, clones have in common most, but not all, of their genetic material. For instance, clones share their chromosomal DNA but not their mitochondrial DNA, which comes from the egg's donor.[28] Clones will also present differences maturing at the level of the epigenetic expression of their DNA (being exposed to different environments, food, personal habits, biological merging, and so on). Clearly, there are multiple dynamics unfolding biological originality – from genetic mutation and variation to epigenetic changes, among others. Species are constantly evolving and have no fixed boundaries; hard definitions are difficult to sustain. The notion of "species" is challenging and should not be taken for granted: in biology, this is referred to as the species problem.[29] Being (p)art of a species does not imply homogenizations; the power of originality is always manifesting in the multiple embodied processes of biological revealing: one is many, many are one. This undermines any hierarchical representation of *Homo sapiens*, with one type of human presented as the ultimate prototype.[30] Our biological kinship shows something else. All humans are human; and yet each human is different: **our human specificity is an affiliation, not a destiny.**

#Bio-me

What is the human body? Bodies are universes, with all the life they contain. They are multiverses; bodies within bodies, one and many, separated and united, inextricably intra-related, necessarily (hyper-)connected: biotic inter-being. Human bodies are made of the same quantity[31] of microbial cells (including bacteria, viruses, fungi and archaea) as "human" cells, if not more.[32] This scientific realization shakes the foundations of the liberal subject, which, in humanistic traditions, has been defined as autonomous, individual and independent, urging us to revise the notion of the "human" entirely, as an open and multiple environment. The self thus emerges as a unified plurality: one and many. This biotic awareness represents a real chance for epistemological liberations and existential epiphanies on our posthuman path of self-discovery.

Bio-me? The term "microbiome" refers to the community of microorganisms (in)forming a specific environment,[33] such as the human gastrointestinal tract.[34] Each individual's microbiome is unique, resulting from all of the people, food, places and environments – among other elements – we have intra-acted with and in during our lifetime. The microbiome plays a key role in all areas of human life: from the digestive system to the immune system; from mental health[35] to, possibly, the emergence of (human) consciousness, which, according to current hypotheses, may result from microbiotic interactions. As the scholar Radek Vana (2020) summarizes: "our consciousness is our emergent property caused by the brain-gut-microbiome axis." Although this is a relevant move towards an understanding of consciousness in embodied terms,[36] it is still inscribed within the humanist scope, reiterating the dichotomy of "us" (necessarily conscious) versus the microbiota[37] (not necessarily conscious).[38] Absolute separations between the "human" and the "non-human" – which are foundational to humanistic and anthropocentric beliefs – are no longer sustainable. From a posthumanist perspective, the role of the microbiome is so crucial that we will approach it as a "bio-me", referring to the "me" constituted in, and by, our biotic assemblages.

What is "human" if there is no "human" without bacteria, viruses, and so on? More than an autonomous being, the human emerges as the coordination of multiple processes, involving a plethora of diverse entities. In the history of human evolution, adaptation refers not only to "external" environments (such as the climate) but also to "internal" ones: humans have adapted to microorganisms, and vice versa. As the microbiologist Sven Pettersson explains: "microorganisms were there long before us – so all aspects of life would have to involve an adaptation to them" (BBC News 2011). In scientific literature, these microorganisms are often addressed as "them"; and yet the human compound reveals itself as made of "others" – "they" are (p)art of "us." We can expand our enquiry, asking deontological questions such as: *What kind of life do these microorganisms have? Do "we" have the responsibility to give "them" a good life?*[39] An ethical comprehension of the bio-me resonates with a posthumanist ontology, based on monistic pluralism, and pluralistic monism:[40] diversity in unity, unity in diversity. We are never alone.

#Holobionts

What does "holobiont" mean? The term "holobiont"[41] gained the current meaning[42] and visibility through the research of the evolutionary biologist Lynn Margulis (1938–2011). It refers to evolutionary entities who, until then, had been approached separately, such as the host, the microbiota, the virome, and any other life form contributing to the specific manifestation of these organic assemblages as "one," and necessarily multiple.[43] These entities have co-adapted intimately, as partners in evolution – a vivid example being corals, whose long-term survival depends on their symbiotic relationships with their algae.[44] On the one hand, the holobiont reaffirms the essential aspects characterizing (the origins of) life: plurality and community, (morphological and metabolic) diversity, adaptability and interpretation, knowledge and information. On the other hand, the holobiont challenges any linear approach to human genetics. Once we embrace the human body as a holobiont, we realize that we have at least two genomes; these have been broadly defined as our "first" genome and our "second" genome.[45] Our first genome is contained in human cells; originating from the initial conjunction of our parents' DNA, it is susceptible to mutations and epigenetic changes (some of which may carry on to the next generations, while some may not). Our first genome is somehow stable, passing from generation to generation. In contrast, our second genome, which refers to the diverse range of genomes carried by our microbiota, varies significantly over (even short periods of) time.

What is the hologenome? The interaction between the first and second genome is crucial to the health of the biological organism, to the point that the microbiologists Eugene Rosenberg and Ilana Zilber-Rosenberg (2014) have suggested the notion of the "hologenome" to refer to the sum of the genetic information of the host and their symbiotic microorganisms. The meaning of the hologenome is wide and far-reaching, applying to all animals and plants. The hologenome is not just the combination of a specific asset of provisional relations. It is transmitted from generation to generation;[46] and yet this genealogy is not fixed, but flexible and adaptable. The hologenome allows for a wide possibility of genetic variation, to the point that, according to Rosenberg and Zilber-Rosenberg, the main driving force of evolution is not mutation but, more likely, the ongoing processes of uptake of microbes and their genetic dynamics. As they state: "Under environmental change and stress, the microbiome can adjust more rapidly and by more processes than the host organism alone and thus can enhance the evolution of the holobiont" (ibid.: 1). Microbes play a key role in enhancing evolution and speciation.[47] On our path of self-knowledge, it is time to demystify another dichotomy: there is no such thing as "good" microbes and "bad" microbes. Let's go viral . . .

#Vir/us

What is a virus? Viruses[48] are routinely presented as the ultimate enemies of humans: tiny, invisible and potentially deadly. The term "virus" is already charged; it comes from the Latin for "poison."[49] Unlike bacteria, viruses have no metabolism and can only reproduce in the cells of a suitable host; this is why, strictly speaking, they are considered neither living organisms nor microorganisms (or microbes). From an anthropocentric standpoint, "they" become alive by becoming "us."[50] From a posthumanist perspective, the opposite is also fitting: "we" become who we are through "them," not only at the individual level (in our unique hologenome) but also at the evolutionary level. The human cannot be understood outside of this constant flux of micro intra-changes; this includes the role of viruses in our specific genetic makeup, as a species. Viruses are necessary in becoming human. According to a recent study, "our DNA contains roughly 100,000 pieces of viral DNA. Altogether, they make up about 8 percent of the human genome" (Zimmer 2017). The spelling of the term "virus" can symbolically turn into "vir/us," to emphasize the role of viral contributions to "us," as we are. Think, for instance, of the placenta, which develops during pregnancy in the uterus: one protein essential to its formation (syncytin) originally became (p)art of the genome of our ancestors via a retrovirus infection.

Is our current view of viruses biased? Posthuman epistemologies must detect and deconstruct pre-assumptions, and their existential obscurations, from any authentic quest for self-discovery. Our current perception of viruses is limited and partial. Viruses are the most numerous types of biological entities on Earth.[51] Although only a portion can be categorized under the label of pathogens,[52] these are the focus of nearly all virologists. According to the microbiologist Marilyn J. Roossinck, the reason is to be found in cultural preconceptions and scientific bias:[53] "Viruses have traditionally been thought of as pathogens, but many confer a benefit to their hosts and some are essential for the host life cycle" (2011: 99). This misleading reduction impedes a comprehension of the vital role of viral expressions to our global ecosystem; more extensively, it turns into an existential obfuscation. Viruses are fundamental to life on Earth and to human survival.[54] For instance, about half the world's oxygen on Earth comes from the ocean: the majority of this production consists of the by-products of microorganisms being attacked, and infected, by different types of virus.[55] This realization debunks the general dichotomic perception, in the lost anthropocentric war, of viruses as the invisible enemies.

Viruses are biocultural entities whose presence is intertwined with our medical economies, global biopolitics and viral spatio-temporalities; they must be perceived, more extensively, as power dynamics in network ontologies. Viruses can infect all life on Earth, from human and non-human animals to plants, bacteria and archaea, among others: this is (p)art of their evolutionary power. Viruses are the driving force behind horizontal gene transfer.[56] Transferring genes between different species is a technology of natural evolution which increases genetic diversity. It has also been employed in (therapeutic and artificial) human-driven evolution for different scopes: viruses are key to current therapeutic research[57] and radical bio-engineering prospects.[58]

#Viral Awareness

Do viruses cause pandemics? The realm of viruses must be approached comprehensively. While many are not, some viruses can be pathogens. Yet pathogens do not exist outside of a context; their impact on a specific individual, and on a specific species, varies. Pathogens, per se, do not have the power to turn the infection of (individual) hosts into (social) pandemics. Such a biological expansion can only be facilitated by certain environments, susceptible to same-species concentrations. Diseases require socialization to be spread through transmission; they can manifest only if someone, or something, becomes dis-eased.[59] Conditions facilitating the spread of a virus are easily found in monoculture farming (where only one type of crop species is planted); in highly populated areas (such as cities); and in monocultural mindsets (where similar actions facilitate similar reactions). Diseases cannot be understood outside of a context. This is one of the reasons why the history of pandemics runs parallel with the history of urbanization and, more generally, with the passage from nomadic life to sedentary life (the same spaces becoming inhabited by the same species at the same times).

The Covid-19 pandemic has clearly shown that we are interrelated with all life forms; that viruses do not respect our self-constructed human primacy; and that many normalized human praxes of inhabiting planet Earth in the 21st century must be revised. The dignity of non-human entities can only ensue in global awareness. If (some) humans keep disrupting natural habitats and invading wilderness, other viruses – currently hosted by non-human animals – will also affect human survival. Technology can be of help, but it is not the solution; for instance, the current bio-technological "fixes" of the spread of Covid-19 variants have proved to be only partially successful. The solution to our problems lies in us.

In the 21st century, a consistent percentage of our species still relies on anthropocentric views, which are the root cause of biological diseases, as well as of mental disorders. Anthropocentric views are based on a dis-eased perception of who we are, at the social, species and planetary levels. Instead of perceiving the human as (p)art of the planet in symbiotic relations, such conceptions separate the human from the rest of existence, privileging (some) humans as exceptional and, thus, in charge. Recognizing our dis-eases can bring ease and healing. Acknowledging a pathogenesis can turn into a path of wisdom and possibility. Understanding a viral attack can spark the change we are envisioning. It is time to realize that we are not "more" than others: we are the "others" – viruses, bacteria, human and non-human elements are inextricably connected, in hybrid processes of coevolution. Posthuman agency entails distributed agency in maintaining the health of individual, social and planetary bodies through (biological and cultural) diversities, (ecological and technological) balances, and existential awareness across fields. Posthuman agency unfolds into the most detailed aspects of our existence. In our acting, reacting, wording, thinking, dreaming, food intaking, ecological giving and receiving; physically, in our extended embodying; ontologically, in our existential revealing. Whenever dimensional manifestations occur, they propagate embodied resonances and reverberations through intra-connected levels, including the level of the species.

#Species Agency

How can species agency manifest? To be (p)art of a species entails species agency – that is, direct impact in the actual pluralistic manifestations of the species to which we belong. Our agency is limited not to what we do, as individuals, but to our awareness of affecting, and effecting, the current human species and the generations to come. This includes many layers of awakening: from the possibility of healing individual, familial and social traumas, passed down from past generations, to mindfully contributing to the biological constitution of our species, as well as to the ecological balance of our planet. In how we live and behave collectively, among other aspects, we are affecting the expressions of our DNA, which may not only result in epigenetic changes in ourselves and our progeny but eventually also affect the physiology and psychology of our species. We have species responsibility: what we experience, and what we contribute for others to experience, will have an impact on future generations. For instance, growing research[60] suggests the role of epigenetic mechanisms in the effects of trauma being passed on both inter-generationally (from one generation to the next) and trans-generationally (across multiple generations). Biology is natural-cultural;[61] it emerges in social habits and cultural practices,[62] an expression of multi-layered coevolutions. DNA is not a static "thing" that can be essentialized; it is an embodied process in the here and now, merging with the environment of which it is (p)art. This awareness allows for healing practices, where the transformative power of genetics manifests as wisdom. Leading a posthuman way of existing that does not sustain violence (neither against others nor against the self) can be approached intentionally, as an act of species agency.

What risks does species agency entail? Our social fabric is currently very fragmented; in this traumatized scenario, precious revelations that could lead to self-knowledge can turn instead into ignorance and obfuscation. Aware of this, the social scientists Michel Dubois and Catherine Guaspare point out the possible discriminatory use of social epigenetics, for instance, in negatively labeling the individuals who have experienced trauma and their descendants by assigning them "a hereditary condition of 'victim'" (2020: 171). In unequal societies, such a "permanent stigma" could be read as "the objective manifestation of a form of biological inferiority," eventually leading to dystopian biopolitical scenarios, where such people might be subject to "authoritarian action from the State in the name of social progress" (ibid.). These hypothetical outcomes, based on biological predetermination and social oppression, resonate with the actual history of eugenics[63] and all the violence and discrimination that occurred in the name of "improving" the human species, in classist, racist and sexist brutalizations: from genocides to genocidal rape as a form of ethnic cleansing.[64]

Compulsory sterilizations, for instance, were widespread in the United States under eugenic legislations in the 20th century. Carrie Buck (1906–1983) was the first person involuntarily sterilized under Virginia's eugenics program, for purportedly being "feeble-minded." She was the plaintiff in the United States Supreme Court case *Buck* v. *Bell* (1927); the appeal was denied in an 8–1 decision. In explaining the majority opinion, Justice Oliver Wendell Holmes Jr infamously stated: "It is better for all the world, if instead of waiting to execute degenerate offspring for crime, or to let them starve for their imbecility, society can prevent those who are manifestly unfit from continuing their kind." This physical and epistemic brutality, masked as a practice of civilization, is a critical reminder of how scientific rhetorics of progress can easily become tools of oppression. In this time of everyday cyborgs, an informed, historically aware posthuman take on bioethics is necessary to avoid perpetuating misery through distorted science and institutionalized hierarchies of domination.

#Radical Life Extension

Can biology be hacked? We live in the era of bio-technological revealing; the genetic code is being unveiled, turning into a new platform for envisioning and experimenting. The transhumanist movement believes that emerging technologies – such as genetic engineering and nanotechnology, among others – will most certainly bring about radical life extension. This goal refers to an extensive increase of the human lifespan (such as hundreds of years) and the even more radical intention of getting rid of death *in toto*. For instance, the biogerontologist Aubrey de Grey is attempting to eliminate aging, perceived as the main cause of debilitation and death in humans; he is proposing a list of "Strategies for Engineered Negligible Senescence" (SENS) in order to restore the body to an indefinitely healthful state. Although this program has been criticized as speculative, de Grey believes it is feasible: "we are close enough (to the biomedical revolution) that our action (or inaction . . .) today will affect the date at which aging is defeated" (2007: xi). If this project eventually becomes successful, some humans may live radically longer than others, or even indefinitely. The dream of immortality may sound far-fetched, but it is indeed very ancient; it is already found in one of the first written mythologies, the Epic of Gilgamesh, dating back to the Third Dynasty of Ur (c. 2100–1200 BCE), in Mesopotamia. The alchemical tradition, practiced throughout Africa, Asia and Europe, was aimed at achieving immortality, symbolized, throughout times, cultures and eras, in the search of the philosopher's stone, *cintāmaṇi*, or the elixir of long life, among others – the ultimate goal referring, more broadly, to personal, physical and spiritual transmutation. Historically speaking, the roots of the dream of immortality are transcultural: to be human, on some level, reveals a tendency to transcend the limits. The question is: *should there be limits?*

#Dictator's Paradox

In March 2013, I was invited by the Karl Jaspers Society of North America to be on a panel with Max More, a leading transhumanist philosopher involved in the Alcor Life Extension Foundation, the main North American organization specialized in cryonics.[65] Invited by the organizers, I asked Max More: "Is cryonics a human right? Let's say that someone like Adolf Hitler asks for a membership at Alcor, in order to be cryo-preserved. Ethically speaking, do you think that anyone should be given the possibility to be alive again in the future, or some people may not deserve that right?"[66] After clarifying that this person should be placed in a different location, not to jeopardize the safety of the other patients[67] in case of sabotage, More stated that this right should be given. This is a short summary of his reply: "At Alcor we do not judge, we don't decide who gets to have a second chance. . . . Essentially, like doctors, if someone is having a heart attack, you don't say: 'Are you a republican, or a democrat, or a libertarian? I have to know that before I give you CPR.' You don't do that, you help them."[68] More makes an important point by referring to the right to treatment, but not everyone would agree in addressing cryonics as a medical emergency. Preserving life for future generations bears different levels of species agency and response-abilities, not only to the individual involved but also to the community at large, as well as to the planet.

Someone like the German dictator Adolf Hitler (1889–1945), for instance, has done evident damage to humanity: *should dictators have the right to outlive their victims and carry their messages to the future?* On the other hand, if someone like Hitler was not offered this opportunity, *would this prohibition be unfair?* More generally: *is cryonics a human right, or are there limits to who gets a second chance?* Socially, the prospect of cryonics brings deep ethical questions: from economic, cultural, national and personal accessibility (currently, most people cannot even afford the fees to be cryonically preserved)[69] to other challenging scenarios. For example, in case cryonics proved successful and the demand exceeded the offer, *who should be reanimated?*

Let's consider survivors of different forms of violence (such as genocides, speciocides, racial and sexual crimes, among others), whose reason to be cryo-preserved was human rights and planetary activism. *If someone decided to be cryo-preserved for their testimonial to bring awareness to future generations, so that history might not witness such horrors again, should they be given priority?* The dictator's paradox, as well as the committed cryo-activist scenario, is not science-fiction; both are actual possibilities in the near futures. In order to improve the quality of life, we must ask the question: *whose life?* Once we realize that we are connected to everything and everyone, the notion of enhancement greatly expands. Posthumanism does not dismiss the role of the myth of immortality and the striving towards enhancement in existential dynamics; and yet it realizes that, in the era of the Anthropocene, enhancement cannot be thought of in isolation from other (human and non-human) entities, as well as the planet. Enhancement is necessarily relational; it cannot emerge in dis-eased conditions: healing is (p)art of the process.

#Species Healing

How can we heal our species? Species healing emerges from a deep comprehension of the non-hierarchical diversity of a species: no single person or group can decide what is "best" for the species as a whole. Species healing can be actualized not by imposing "our" values onto others but by being ourselves what we intend to manifest: the healing wave, the source of clarity, the generative catharsis, rooted in the actual understanding of our species, in our specific spacetime. **Being realistic does not mean being pessimistic or optimistic; it means being able to know, beyond any judgment, where we are at**: as individuals, societies, species, planets, cosmos and beyond. Yet realizing the state of things is not enough to manifest healing; this is only one petal unfolding in the blossoming of self-realization. Another petal is to realize the effects of our being in the world, so that our modes of existing align with our visions and intentions. Self-knowledge must embrace all aspects of being; this way, it turns into species healing. These paths co-emerge: healing is a journey of self-realization, where the individual and the collective, biology and society, nature and culture reveal their inner merging and transformative power. We are one and many. Our existences can only resonate from the micro to the macro, and vice versa: pervasive, agential, poietic. We are viral and cosmic; spirals of intentional DNA; posthuman humans. We are (p)art of a species: we are who we are.

Farewell

In this meditation, we have focused on the vital role of viruses and bacteria in the evolution of life; we have addressed microbial poiesis in genetic dynamics. Unveiling who we are biologically, as a species, brings our journey of self-enquiry to other exciting portals towards posthuman existential awareness. If You would like to explore the biosphere, from Earthly embodiments to cosmic environments, please rely on chapters 4 and 5. If You are interested in regenerating our social habits and healing our species from social dis-eases, please go to chapter 7. You can also move freely in the labyrinth, accessing (and creatively hacking) any chapter or tag of your choice. Rest assured: at the end of the journey, You will have gained perspective, no matter what.

Meditation 4
Ecological Presence

#Earth

Where are we? Existential posthumanism addresses this as a fundamental question: where we are is not *casual*, it is *causal*. The fact that we are earthly beings is the *conditio sine qua non* of our embodying; our biological outfit[1] is of the Earth.[2] **We do not just live on this planet: we are (p)art of this planet.** The philosopher Alan Watts (1915–1973) put it figuratively: "We grow out of this world in exactly the same way that the apples grow on the apple tree" (1965: 18:27). Within this frame, the human is perceived as being (p)art of multi-species assemblages,[3] whose agencies are diverse, multi-layered and contagious. In a planet, all is interconnected – directly and/or indirectly;[4] the Earth behaves like a system. In post-Darwinian terms,[5] we are not just evolutionarily adapting to the environment: we change, and are changed by, the place we inter-are.

Being in "Nature" is enlightening. The perfection of each and every snowflake. The fine balance of ripples forming around a drop of water. The glorious amount of life present in a handful of soil. The golden beams of sunlight passing through our windows. The composite equilibrium of electrical cables where vultures sit comfortably. Serene, tempestuous. Nature, as a diversified unity, generates the (cosmic and individual, species and planetary) drive towards self-expression: without "ART" there is no "eARTh." Nature is a manifested game of existence. Like any good work of art, it reveals itself in the ecstatic reactions that are generated: the what is the how. As many world traditions have pointed out, it is common for human beings to experience the wonders of nature in places that are less directly pervaded by human dynamics – such as the (so-called) wilderness. Diversified mergings of energies that are not necessarily human open other lines of flight.

#Nature, Again?

What is "nature"? The Oxford Dictionary defines it as "the phenomena of the physical world collectively, including plants, animals, the landscape, and other features and products of the earth, as opposed to humans or human creations."[6] This definition is problematic: *how can humans possibly be separated from Nature?* Nature, as a concept, has been deconstructed in the field of posthumanism, where dichotomies such as urban/rural, human/non-human and, more generally, nature/culture have been found unsustainable (for instance, many plants in the current wilderness have been put in place by previous generations of humans). Scholars have proposed alternative terms, such as "natureculture,"[7] to express that nature is already cultural, and vice versa. The term "natureculture" works well to refer to an open condition; and yet it lacks the nuances to refer to the great plethora of realities actually constituting "natures"/"cultures": *Whose natures? Whose cultures?*

The cyborgization of both terms generates the risk of reaffirming human-centric assumptions and generalizations.[8] Beavers, for instance, are often referred to as the engineers of the forest – their role was crucial in shaping the continent of the Americas[9] in pre-Columbian times. When reflecting on the sphere of influence of species, soils and habitats, we may ask: *Are the wetlands created by beavers' dams and ponds as "natural-cultural" as parks planned by humans? Are monoculture farming areas as "natural-cultural" as wild biodiverse ecosystems? Is the Amazon forest in Brazil as "natural-cultural" as Central Park in New York City? More generally, are we taking into account non-human agencies when relying on "natures-cultures"?* While the term "natureculture" acknowledges the co-emergences of human cultures in nature, it does not expand this reflection to comprehend that every species has, and is, "cultures."[10] The great dynamics of (cultural) natures and (natural) cultures are not resolved in the exemplification of one species among many: the human. Anthropocentric biases and assumptions, still inherent in current symbolic apparatuses,[11] impede the recognition of the diverse range of energies merging together in acts of existential revealing, constantly at play in natures. The solution is not reaffirming "Nature" as a super-entity of which the human, somehow, is not (p)art. Neither is it establishing "naturecultures" – on closer inspection, "culture" refers only to a universalized species: the human. We do not need to choose between "Nature" or "natureculture"; in context, both terms can fulfill a purpose. To attain self-knowledge, we must acknowledge different sets of embodied relations: natures, and naturecultures, are intra-acting. To know who we are, we must be aware of our environmental inter-being.

#Philosophical Greenwashing

Does specific terminology erase the need for the generic concept of "nature"? According to some thinkers,[12] the term "nature" is becoming a burden to ecological awareness and eco-sustainable policies as way too generic and even misleading. A pivot for human-centric self-entitlements, its use often results in abstractions that impede actions, for instance, if everything is equally "nature," the human-induced pollution that is distressing planetary well-being can be passively accepted and uncritically reiterated. Yet getting rid of the term "nature" is not necessarily the answer. A posthumanist take on natures implies unity and diversity – paying respect to our multi-species coevolutions in billions of years of ecological revealing. Being precise in our semantic representations of the world is an act of awareness. Limiting our contribution to linguistic disquisitions is an intellectual game with no real-world consequences: an existential obscuration. Terms are part of larger dynamics of manifestations; changing words per se does not necessarily bring actual change. Rooted in self-realization, changes in terms must be accompanied by changes in actions.

What is philosophical greenwashing? On our path of posthuman wisdom, we must be aware of the risk of philosophical greenwashing. This occurs, for instance, when, instead of changing habits that are detrimental to the biosphere, we only discuss the topic. We may swap the terms associated with the debate and, ultimately, feel better about ourselves, going on in all other fields of life with the same attitude of "business as usual." We talk, write and debate about the Earth without implementing any real changes in our lives. This way, we sound ecologically aware, but we are not: green words are covering our ineptitude. For instance, I have found myself in conferences where the main topic was posthumanism and the only option served, during meals, was meat, with all the concerns that this alimentary choice entails in relation to unsustainability and unethical treatment of non-human animals. We need correspondence between words and actions; otherwise, we are greenwashing. This realization does not undermine the importance of wording. Words can work as cataclysms for change, raising consciousness about something that needs to be named. For instance, the movement for the rights of nature, based on indigenous worldviews, is currently enacting important changes at the legal level: this is done in the name of "nature."

#Rights of Nature

Does nature have rights? In 2008, Ecuador was the first country to recognize the rights of nature in its constitution: nature was no longer seen as an object, or as a resource, but viewed as a subject. This shift relied on indigenous worldviews, according to which nature can be neither owned nor dominated.[13] Although, due to the extensive numbers of traditions and worldviews, self-defined indigenous people cannot be assimilated, there is common ground in the perception of the land as the Mother,[14] the bearer and the nourisher. The movement of the rights of nature is growing worldwide. In 2014, Te Urewera, the largest rainforest of New Zealand's North Island, became the first natural resource, among several others, to be awarded the status of a legal entity. According to the legal settlements of the "Te Urewera Act,"[15] neither the government nor the Tuhoe tribes own the land, in the traditional sense of real estate;[16] instead, both manage it to ensure its preservation. This new constitutional recognition of places as people – which is unprecedented in nations that have common law traditions – derives from the indigenous Maori cosmological perception of people as nature.[17] The Maori tribes in New Zealand refer to themselves as *kaitiaki*, meaning guardians and caretakers of the land – the land being perceived as a living entity.[18] In indigenous wisdom, the well-being of the land reflects in the well-being of humans, who are (p)art of it; enhancement is approached as a mutual process – not as an individual, or species, achievement.

These worldviews have real-world implications. Indigenous people, for instance, have the smallest ecological footprints on Earth;[19] and yet they are most harmed by the current ecological crisis. Having laws that recognize rights to nature is a significant legal accomplishment; however, laws are ineffective if people are not following them. Laws can be the outcome of, as well as the entry points for, larger cultural transformations.[20] Jurisdictional shifts are to be accompanied by changes at every level. The posthuman wave takes all these dynamics into consideration, supporting the rights of nature while not fully exhausting its own significance in any specific policy and/or community. In humanity, environmental awareness is present trans-historically and trans-culturally: from the spiritual presence of natural phenomena, defined as *kami* in Shintoism, to the notion of Buddha nature in Buddhism, according to which everything is "Buddha" (that is, enlightenment); from the worship of nature in Earth-conscious paganism to the stewardship of the Earth in Catholicism[21] and Islam, among others. Posthumanism acknowledges, simultaneously, the need for environmental awareness, as well as for human equity (including a liberation from epistemological hierarchies and socio-political supremacies)[22] and for technological dignity. Existential posthumanism is an existential praxis more than a final goal. As with cleaning our home: it is done, and soon we will have to do it again. Keeping a space tidy is an embodied process, relying on the constant awareness of all the ways we intra-act with the space: being the space.

#Anthropogenic Hermit

What is the technosphere? This term was coined by the geologist Peter K. Haff,[23] who defines it this way: "The technosphere, the interlinked set of communication, transportation, bureaucratic and other systems that act to metabolize fossil fuels and other energy resources, is considered to be an emerging global paradigm, with similarities to the lithosphere, atmosphere, hydrosphere and biosphere" (2013: 301). Nowadays, it is not only most human populations who vitally rely on the technosphere;[24] domesticated organisms are also dependent on its presence (most of them were born directly into the technosphere, resulting out of bio-technological processes). According to Haff, the technosphere exceeds the human[25] and will long succeed us, even after our own extinction. Technology as an embodied condition of the Earth in the 21st century bears deep ramifications. The recognition of the technosphere makes the planet, literally speaking, a cyborg (merging the mechanical and the organic); and yet its shortcomings in recycling undermine this eco-technological integration. The biosphere is very efficient at processing the material it is made of; the technosphere is not.[26] For instance, objects such as cell phones are considered techno-fossils – they are made in ways that are resistant to decay; thus, they may form future fossils. In these technospheric environments, Point Nemo (the location in the ocean that is farthest from land – thus defined as a pole of inaccessibility) has become very accessible: currently, it is used as the graveyard for old satellites and space junk. And there is no need to go that far.

Not long ago, I was at the beach, walking barefoot, when I noticed a plastic cap walking next to me . . . I was quite surprised. Gently, I raised it: inside, a small hermit crab was using it as its shell. The cap had obviously been around for a while – most of its surface was covered with marine algae and corallines. I softly placed it back. As the ocean was erasing the ancient pattern of the crab's footsteps from the sand, I could not stop thinking about the wider repercussions of this tiny choice of accommodation to the crabs as a species: *how did this occur?* I did some research and found out that, in the last decades, hermit crabs have started using bottle caps as homes. Bottles can be lethal to them. They are able to get in, but not to get out (the sides of the container are too slippery to exit); they often die, trapped inside.[27] To be loyal to the 21st century, we must acknowledge the plastisphere, referring to marine ecosystems that have coevolved to live in human-made plastic environments. The hermit crab, walking on the beach in its anthropogenic shell – the many sides of this environmental plasticity: the homey cap/the deadly bottle ... If we want to know who we are, we must realize the deep ramifications of our actions in (the short and long run of) our coevolutions: as individuals, societies, species and planets. The problem is not plastic per se but the irresponsible ways in which this material is currently being (ab)used, and disposed of, by humans. The outside is the inside, and vice versa. The ecological distress we are causing to the environment we are causing to ourselves. Microplastic pollution has been detected in human blood in almost 80 percent of the people tested (both in babies and adults):[28] the full health hazards of these new findings are still unknown.

#Climate Change

What is a superorganism? We must take into account the permeability of manifested existence when unraveling the dynamics at play in coevolutions.[29] Evolution is always mutual[30] – think of the intra-changes between multiple species; the adaptations to, and of, the environments; climate changes; and so on. This extensive relationality does not allow for a reduction of our planet to a (human-accessible) globe;[31] the Earth emerges, more clearly, as a geo-biological holobiont[32] in all the different entities that are the planet (including humans). The terms "holobiont"[33] and "superorganism" are not synonyms. Both refer to communities of organisms existing in synergistic intra-actions: while in a holobiont, such organisms are of different species; in a superorganism, they are of the same species. A large number of single organisms, working together as one collective being, can be approached as a superorganism. An example are bees and ants, with their specialized division of labor. Their collective decision-making[34] processes (in choosing, for instance, where to nest and when and where to migrate) are based on distributed intelligence: research shows that they are consistently successful.[35] The concept of a superorganism raises the question of what it means to be an individual, given that individuals, forming (p)art of superorganisms, are not able to survive on their own for extended periods of time.

Are modern humans superorganisms? Most modern human societies rely on a highly specialized division of labor and infrastructures; not many humans would be able to survive if fully isolated from (human) communities. In this sense, modern human societies could be accessed as superorganisms; and yet our decision-making processes are often not as successful as those of ants and bees. The climate change crisis is a clear example. Considering the gravity of the situation, climate change should be a top priority for politicians. This is not the case: current political systems have proven to be inappropriate to tackle reality as it is. Caught in a net of power dynamics that exceed the climate emergency, most governments are unable to pass the policies needed to ensure a safe present. This lack of proper acknowledging and responding is a cause of deep anxiety for many people who are aware of the urgency of the situation and feel powerless in the face of such a systemic apathy.

Eco-anxiety[36] is growing among people of all ages; the younger generations are particularly affected by it.[37] In a historical shift of competence, these generations are at the front line of this ecological awareness. They are going to outlive many current politicians and be (p)art of the futures. Aware of the discrepancy between the current state of things and what is being done to change it, they are demanding governments worldwide undertake real action to curb global warming.[38] Climate change is not a single problem but a metabolic crisis. Human habits have everything to do with it: the future is already here in the ways we are living the present. We must change our current ways of species self-maintenance, currently based in anthropocentric habits, capitalistic appropriations and existential obfuscations. And yet this "we" cannot be generalized. In the 21st century, climate change is a coexistential challenge. Although it is caused mainly by economically and financially robust countries, it is disproportionately affecting countries in the Global South.[39] One form of discrimination leads to the next. Social inequity and systemic racism are deeply intertwined with the treatment of land and resources – for instance, toxic waste and pollutants are often discharged in low-income communities.[40] We are individuals, as well as (p)art of societies, species, planets and beyond. Once we are aware of our inter-being, the aggravated social Darwinist myth of the survival of the fittest no longer applies.[41] Instead, a yearning for existential dignity and cooperation, based on the recognition of diversity and symbiosis, emerges organically.

Is climate change another reason to be stressed and feeling bad about our species – and/or about ourselves? Feeling guilty, shame or shaming is not the path; it only creates more polluting psychological cycles that cannot heal our traumatized societies. To change this trajectory, as individuals, as societies and as a species, we can only become aware of who are are: right here, right now. Awareness does not judge or label others as "good" or "evil" but enacts immediately, from the self – change is not an option: it is already happening. The ice-melting poles are crystal clear: climate change is not a notion but something we are. Everything is changing, and we – who are (p)art of this planet – can change right now. In order to understand who we are, we must be aware of our ways of existing. The Earth has gone through major changes and will go through many more. There is no way "nature" can lose the game of existence: nature is everything; transformation is always occurring. This does not mean that humans can do whatever, based on the illusionary myth of unlimited resources. We are nature. What we are doing to nature, we are doing to us: it is a self-reflecting, and self-reflective, mirror. The ecological devastations occurring in the Anthropocene reveal our ignorance of the self. To be integrated, in psychological philosophy, means to be in touch with ourselves. To be integrated, in the 21st century, means to understand that we are (p)art of the Earth.

#Ecosophy

"Ecosophy", as a notion, was proposed by the psychoanalyst Félix Guattari (1930–1992), who employed the term to go beyond strict dichotomies – such as human/non-human and nature/culture. It was also developed by the philosopher Arne Naess (1912–2009), according to whom ecosophy is "a philosophy of ecological harmony or equilibrium" (1973: 99), more clearly, a wisdom of global and local character.[42] This glocal awareness is essential to our path of self-discovery: to know who we are is to know where we are. A tree is not "just" a tree. It is being in relation to the ground and to the sky; in networks of roots and rhizomatic (in)formation; in the oxygen released into the atmosphere. The plethora of insects, fungi and other microorganisms, as well as organisms, that are (p)art of the tree holobiont; birds nesting in its branches, mammals living in its holes and cavities – the tree their homes. We even differentiate the language to refer to anything other-than-human (non-human "dens" and "nests"/ human "houses" and "homes"). Noise and light pollution are anthropocentric self-entitlements which are rarely discussed in policy-making: the life and dignity of non-human beings are not duly respected. *Are we that different?* We are different; we are not absolutely different. We are the same;[43] yet we cannot be assimilated: one and many.

How can we know about non-human others? Real knowing is based on direct experience, in existential awareness. The smell of a rose is the smell of a rose: delicate, fragrant, unique. We can read thousands of books and write hundreds of articles about it. Still, a rose is a rose. The intellectualized projections of the notion of a rose and the experience of a rose are not the same. In order to know ourselves as (p)art of the Earth, we must be integrated, not enclosed in human-constructed golden cages. **If we want to know about humans, we must live among humans. If we want to know about ourselves, we must exist beyond humans.** We must live where we can take space from humans as well: humans are energies – human energies are felt. Going where there are fewer humans offers the possibilities of experiencing other energies. In walking barefoot on the land, even the perception of time changes slightly.[44] These types of connections are possible everywhere, any time. In a crowded city, we can look at the sky and float with the clouds. In a garage, we can silently listen to a fly buzzing with its iridescent wings. These moments of mystical other-than-human connections in(form) our consciousness.

I was a child, about eight years old. She[45] was a plant, of the species *Nagami kumquat* – originally native to southern China. I did not know her botanical name; I gave her a name, which I no longer recall. She was as tall as I was. Generous, bountiful, she lived on our balcony. I would take care of her routinely, watering the soil, cleaning each of her shining leaves from the smog of Turin – car pollution was prevalent in the 1980s. I would talk to her and gently caress her vibrant foliage. In the summer, I would eat her zesty orange fruits – small and intense: simply delicious. This connection went on for a couple of years. Eventually, I forgot her name. One day, she was no longer there. I was twelve, I barely noticed her absence: the child who deeply honored all existential relations was now turning into a young human person who cherished their human friendships first and foremost. Now, many years later, I think of her lovingly, in posthuman awareness. She is (p)art of who, and what, I am. There is no background: we inter-are.[46]

#Indoor Society

What is the background? The physical dynamics of our environments are not just "out there" – serving human (and/or other-than-human) purposes. "Their" materials are breathed through "our" lungs; "their" paths and corridors shape "our" spatial geometries in moving and walking: "their" embodied presence turns into "our" architectures of existing. The environment is never separated from us; we are (p)art of our environment(s). This brings about existential revealing. Being in a city or being in the midst of a forest will generate different dynamics of inter-being. Being in nature may offer the context to realize that human habits, cultures and mythologies are only temporary: they do not have to be that way.[47] A hallmark of Chinese painting throughout the ages has been the attention to landscapes, where humans are portrayed as fractions of the total image. According to the philosopher Tu Wei-Ming, the Chinese view of nature relies on the continuity of being: "all modalities of Being, from a rock to heavens, are integral parts of a continuum, which is often referred to as the 'great transformation' *(ta-hua)*" (1985: 70). This is conducive to the realization that we are (p)art of everything, in poietic manifestations.[48] It is not enough to understand intellectually the interconnection of our planetary self. We must be aware of where we spend our life, and of what kind of environments we are sustaining, as individuals, societies and species: as (p)art of the planet. If we are inside most of the time, we may lose track of the greater picture. While I am writing this sentence, I realize that I am sitting inside, while I could easily be working outside.

How did modern society become an indoor society? The lack of outdoor time has become very prevalent in modern societies. Statistics from the Environmental Protection Agency suggest that adults in the US and Canada spend 93 percent of their lives inside buildings or vehicles.[49] The numbers are similar for the child population, as well as for other regions of the world, in a trend characterizing all industrialized areas. This disconnection from the natural environment is causing not only physical health issues[50] but also psychological ones.[51] The journalist Richard Louv (2005) defines this phenomenon as "nature deficit disorder." According to him, the relationship of current generations with nature is being reduced to an intellectualization;[52] education, culture and family habits are the main engines promoting nature-phobic lifestyles. The traditional approach to learning – students sitting in front of the teacher in an indoor classroom – relies on the mind/body dichotomy, according to which the mind (and body) can be nourished separately. A posthuman approach to education deconstructs it;[53] in the currently expanding environmental sensibility, other ways of learning are being embraced.[54] An interesting trend may be seen in nature preschools, forest schools and outdoor learning: they acknowledge the importance of the environment where the learning takes place, embracing it not as a neutral background of epistemological irrelevance but as an essential actant of ontological resonance in the educational experience.

#Wood Wide Web

What is the wisdom of trees? Plants communicate, exchanging information and nourishment in multi-species networks. The root structure[55] is a highly efficient system of symbiotic relations between bacteria, fungi and trees. In an organic twist from the World Wide Web, as a source of (self-)knowledge: welcome to the Wood Wide Web. The ecologist Suzanne Simard, who conducted extensive research on this, explains: "The Wood Wide Web is a busy network, where the fungal links serve as pathways for the back-and-forth transport of carbon, water, and nutrients among trees" (2021a: 68). In a forest ecosystem, trees can be approached not only as holobionts but as superorganisms, sending information (such as distress signals about drought and disease) and nutrients to other trees. In these intra-changes, they are not competing but collaborating. Simard demonstrated that highly connected hub trees (defined as mother trees)[56] share their excess carbon and nitrogen through the mycorrhizal network, created by fungi that link together individual plants. When dying, trees share their wisdom – which is multigenerational, multi-species and, more generally, planetary[57] – with the next generations. The role of the mother trees is crucial to the survival of the forest: it is of utmost importance to preserve them, instead of killing them in high-grade logging and clear-cutting.[58]

This is not about how we can save the trees: "we" are not separated from "them." Plants have been (p)art of this planet much longer than humans; ours is a joint evolutionary history.[59] It is imperative to approach the natural world as the existential entity that we are instead of reducing it to our anthropocentric projections – which may eventually lead us to our own self-extinction. In the 21st century, anthropocentrism is still pervasive: the human is presented as the master of the planet; the planet, as raw resources. Anthropocentric presumptions have turned, more recently, into capitalistic hallucinations, resulting in a disenchanted monetary assessment of the world based on profit-oriented denials of any intrinsic values. Even though these views are still uncritically accepted by some, we no longer have to follow them. They are outdated, because they do not recognize humans as integral (p)arts of the planet. They are specific to past visions and do not satisfy the ultimate need for self-realization, or for self-preservation, of our times. The possibility of humans damaging our habitat to the point of endangering our own species is real: we are our environments.

I was recently in the eastern side of North Carolina, in the United States. Large forests were being cleared to build apartment buildings; within a 10-minute walk, there were large areas of abandoned buildings in ruins. *How could that be allowed?* Together with conservation habitat, ecological restoration is approached as a priority in posthuman politics, starting with architecture and engineering. Instead of "developing" new areas (meaning: destroying natural habitats to build condos), local laws and global regulations must work in conjunction to redirect developers in recovering structures that have been abandoned and dismissed, rehabilitating degraded lands, and restoring ecological balance to large-scale damaged ecosystems. This approach is based on short-

and long-term outcomes; in creating job opportunities that are in line with the current needs of our planet, it brings about a legacy of care for the generations to come. It is often stated that big corporations are the main polluters; surely, a systemic change is unfolding. And yet the macro does not exclude the micro: they are self-reflective. Our financial standards must meet with our ethical standards. If we are not aware of the ramifications of our economic being-in-the-world,[60] then we are greenwashing. The oceans and landfills in Ghana, for instance, are filled with the trash of good-willing people from so-called first world countries, donating poor-quality clothes to the second-hand clothing market in Africa, unwillingly causing an environmental disaster. The tentacles of our actions are us: our posthuman Medusa.

#Eco-logy/Eco-nomy

What does economy have to do with ecology? The answer is: everything. The word "economics" comes from two Greek words: "eco-" from *oikos* (οἶκος), meaning "home," and *nomos* (νόμος) meaning "law," "code" and "account," among others. The term "economy" has wide-ranging significance, from how to keep the family accounts to how to manage global budgets. The term shares (p)art of its etymology with "ecology";[61] this resonance and alliance is crucial – *eco*-nomy is also an *eco*-logy. In the capitalist market-value economy, the Earth (like everything else) does not have value on its own but becomes a "resource" to be turned into potential goods – and, within the current Big Data[62] economy, into potential data. Currently, the whole cosmos is being approached as a standing reserve,[63] as the new market of space and asteroid mining would seem to suggest. This applies to life as well: cells, genes, and any type of biological specimen become "data" to be harvested – bio-capital,[64] generating profit. This reductionist attitude to the planet can be traced to the Industrial Revolution, which is considered the onset of the Anthropocene.[65] Before industrialization, most humans depended on subsistence farming. This brought a direct relation to the land, as well as fragility and risk. After a year's work, suddenly a heavy storm could destroy the entirety of their crops; as a result, humans did not have a full sense of mastery and control over nature. The Industrial Revolution brought stability in production; humans began to rely more and more on the machine. In this shift, nature turned (symbolically and materially) into a standing reserve of raw material to be fed to the machine, to generate power – such as the steam engine – (mass production of) goods and, ultimately, capital. Capitalism, anthropocentrism and the Anthropocene are inherently connected. We are referring to these precedents not to judge history but to realize where we come from, and where we are going.

What is stuffocation? Economics refers to the accounts of our home. The Earth is not only our home, it is our planetary self. In this era of deep ecological distress, we need to revise our economic approaches,[66] addressing the extremes in which we are finding ourselves as world citizens. Some economists are calling for anti-consumerism and minimalism. For instance, according to the degrowth[67] movement, a way to avoid climate catastrophe is to prioritize people, care and the environment.[68] This starts with clear policies on quality and repairability over the programmed obsolescence of products. In the era of the Anthropocene, consumerism is no longer a suitable path to economic growth.[69] Some humans do not have enough; others have too much. The author James Wallman (2015) defines this issue as "stuffocation" – a combination of the words "stuff" and "suffocation." He considers this one of the most pressing problems of the 21st century: "We have more stuff than we could ever need, and it isn't making us happier. It's bad for the planet. It's cluttering up our homes. It's making us stressed." In this world scenario, some humans live unhealthy lives because they are overwhelmed with material objects, while others are still dying of hunger and malnutrition.[70] In a global world, the distance between these realities is a matter of a short flight, of a car ride, or of no distance at all.[71] It is time to revise our value system. In economic posthuman awareness, the condition of being rich is based not on individual monetary excess but on the quality of the life of the community to which we belong, as individuals, as a society, as a species, as a planet. This is not utopian day-dreaming; it is a eutopian[72] call to existential dignity: right here, right now.

#Re-engineering Nature?

Should humans re-engineer non-human natures out of love and empathy? The transhumanist philosopher David Pearce is a proponent of the "hedonistic imperative," according to which "genetic engineering and nanotechnology will abolish suffering in all sentient life" (1996). Pearce defines "paradise-engineering,"[73] "the complete abolition of suffering" not only "in *Homo sapiens*" (ibid.) but in non-human species as well. According to Pearce, bio-technological advancements are the way to achieve this, as he states: "the circle of compassion" should eventually expand to "other animals via ecosystem redesign and genetic engineering" (ibid.). In Pearce's planetary plan of action, abolishing killing by predators is most urgent – his article "Reprogramming predators" (2009–15) is enriched with images of lions killing prey. The point, here, is not to dismiss the pain suffered by mammals preyed upon by big cats; rather, it is a posthuman call to gain perspective. We can sympathize with Pearce's attempt to alleviate suffering. And yet the prospect of (some) humans redesigning the global ecosystem according to their perception of relative and culture-specific notions, such as "happiness" and "paradise," is rooted in hyperbolic forms of humanistic exceptionalism, moral anthropocentrism and absolutism. From a posthumanist perspective, this is neither desirable nor realistic. In the planetary conditions of the 21st century, we do not need to find a bio-technological quick fix to allow big cats to become extinct; they are already at great risk of extinction because of loss of habitat and human encroachment. Instead of prosecuting the few lions left on Earth as amoral predators, we can stop our own viciousness and change our habits – not only by embracing conscious diets and abolishing inhumane ways of animal farming[74] but also by being aware of our planetary impact.

Pearce's approach does not take into account the deep ecological ramifications of investing in a full anthropocentric re-engineering of "nature" in order to abolish suffering. *Where does this end?* Such a wide scope cannot be limited to the animal kingdom. *Should all invasive plants be genetically re-engineered?* After all, they are killing other plant species. Geological entities are not that pacific either: *What about volcanoes and the (human and non-human) deaths and disruption caused by their eruptions? What about the distress caused by atmospheric phenomena such as tornadoes and hurricanes?* More than paradise engineering, this vision, in its short-sighted disengagement from the long-term consequences of re-engineering nature according to (some) human principles, sounds like an anthropocentric mirage destined to bring more anthropogenic catastrophes: what may seem like small changes might have radical consequences in the ecological balance of the biosphere. If we are being truly empathetic towards other species, we must be aware that, in the era of the Anthropocene and of the sixth mass extinction, thousands of (non-human) species are becoming extinct each year because of human action. In this context, no paradise can manifest in bio-engineered plans to push even more species to extinction.

We, humans of the 21st century, should be careful in playing games of final judgments. In the dynamics of speciesist blaming, the human species turns out to be not that innocent. The Voluntary Human Extinction Movement (VHEMT) suggests: "Phasing out the human species by voluntarily ceasing to breed will allow Earth's biosphere to return to good health."[75] Existential posthumanism does not align with either perspective. On the one hand, the Voluntary Human Extinction Movement sees the gradual, voluntary and intentional extinction of humankind as the final solution to ecological degradation. On the other, Pearce's transhumanist attempt to bring peace through anthropocentric speciesides (that is, intentional extinctions of other species) is based on the dichotomy of war: eliminating carnivores is seen as the final solution. Both approaches embrace absolute dichotomies: good versus evil. Existential posthumanism is not just a post-humanism and a post-anthropocentrism; it is a post-dualism. The human species is neither absolutely good nor absolutely evil. Human moral values cannot be simply transposed to non-human beings. Other species (biological, such as herbivores; or artificial, such as advanced artificial intelligence) may not necessarily do better than humans if (and/or when) humanity becomes extinct.[76] Existential posthumanism brings forth multi-species coexistence and environmental dignity: right here, right now.

#Posthuman Polite Convention

How can existential posthumanism bring change? In order to manifest change, we must be aware of our agency not only as individuals and societies but as a species. Once we realize our species-transformative power, we can direct it towards our own species instead of forcing it upon others in the name of "peace." Real change, intended to bring real peace, cannot be imposed by violence – for instance, by implementing aggressive genetic programs aimed at redesigning other species. Tacitus (c.56–c.120 CE), who was a historian in ancient Rome, famously wrote: *Ubi solitudinem faciunt, pacem appellant*. This can be translated as: "Where they create a desert, they call it peace." Tacitus was referring to Romans bringing war and death in the name of "peace." Nowadays, we can expand this metaphor to the killing of non-human beings. A cruelty-free world starts within the self; it cannot be brought about through the extinction of others – either intentionally and planned (such as a bio-engineered specieside) or unintentionally and consequential (such as the destruction of their habitats). Other forms of cruelty set in human exceptionalist presumptions are the inhumane ways in which most lab animals are currently treated and disposed of.[77] This is happening despite the fact that a growing body of scientific literature is critically assessing the validity of animal experimentation as unreliable in predictive value for understanding human physiology.[78]

Science can offer a world of wonder, provided that the "subject" of the investigation does not forget that there is no "object." Experiments in quantum mechanics, for instance, have shown that the mere act of observing affects the experiment: this is called the observer effect. Science expands the range of posthuman self-enquiry in the realization that whatever we study is also (p)art of who we are. A posthuman science asks different questions, no longer set in self-entitled pre-assumptions, bringing forth different methods and discoveries.[79] *Is sentio-centrism the answer?* Often invoked by animal rights activists, sentio-centrism is an ethical view which invokes the recognition of dignity in all sentient beings, based on questions such as: *Do these beings suffer? Can they communicate? Are they intelligent?* Although this shift can bring partial change, posthumanism does not embrace it as a replacement for anthropocentrism, because it is still based on a hierarchy of values. Other-than-human animals which are more similar to humans (for instance, in their ways of manifesting "intelligence" and "pain") are necessarily advantaged in this relative (re)cognition. Limited, and limiting, sentio-centric inclusions still rely on a cognitive anthropocentrism, where the norm is established on (some) human canons by (some) humans. Posthumanism is set in a post-hierarchical onto-epistemological comprehension, honoring the existential dignity of all.

What is the polite convention? The polite convention is a term used by the mathematician Alan Turing (1912–1954) in his article "Computing machinery and intelligence" (1950). According to Turing, if a machine acts as intelligently as a human being, we should conclude that machines (can) think. This is what he calls "the polite convention" (1950: 446).[80] Here, we will assume that, in manifested existence, **everyone and everything is aware in "their" own ways, which are not necessarily "ours,"** beyond any (organic and machinic) intelligence, thus disrupting the existential dichotomy "us/them." We will pose this as a thought experiment, rooted in panpsychism and, more extensively, ancient animism.[81] This thought experiment does not rely on the necessity to prove its scientific evidence or validity. Given that we are dealing with existential alterity, trying to demonstrate that others are aware, according to our own standards, is based on a methodological fallacy that can only bring partiality and obfuscation. Instead, we will embrace it as a species-specific act of reciprocity, relationality and (re)flexibility: an intentional redemption[82] from anthropocentric historicity. It is, more clearly, an existential commitment to self-realization: we expect to be recognized as aware; thus, we recognize everyone, and everything, as aware. We will refer to this ultimate acknowledgment of awareness as the posthuman polite convention.

What does it mean to be posthuman, right here, right now? It means to be aware of who we are; we are always in, and outside, ourselves. The term "history" comes from ancient Greek *histor* (ἵστωρ), meaning "witness," "knower" and "wise person," among other significations. The history of the Earth is our witness: in the rocks, the leaves, the microplastics. Being aware of the sixth mass extinction caused by our anthropogenic habits is fundamental; losing ourselves in self-hate and generalized antihuman arrogance is inconsequential. Manifesting different ways of being is the posthuman answer. This intention cannot stay at the intellectual level; otherwise, it becomes delusional greenwashing. The endorsement of non-human personhood, existential dignity and multi-species coexistence must meet with an integral revisitation of our daily habits, preconceptions and strategies: as individuals, as societies, as a species. Instead of forcing others to behave according to our principles, we must be the change we want to see.[83] We, posthumanists, living in an anthropocentric and anthropogenic era, need to tackle everyday situations in ways that are down to earth. Theory, per se, does not bring change. In practice, we do not need to be posthumanists to recognize the urgent need for change. Even from a selfish anthropocentric standpoint, a realistic understanding of where we are at, as a planet, brings forth the realization that we cannot thrive at the expense of others:[84] the relationality of inter-being is the epiphany. We are all different, and related. Posthuman ways of being manifest pluralistically and are shared comprehensively: bringing change to our lives and communities; healing societies; in(forming) our species: being (p)art of the Earth.

Farewell

The Earth is not just a location, it is our embodiment(s): the planet we are. Anthropogenic habits, resulting in ecological distress and environmental exhaustion, are detrimental to the human condition of the 21st century: they are, more clearly, existential obfuscations. From a geological time scale, humans, as such, have been around for a very short time; and yet anthropocentrism postulates an absolute speciesist superiority. To unveil our cosmic constellations and realize that we are (p)art of macroscopic environments, please move to chapter 5. Microorganisms, such as bacteria and viruses, are (p)art of the human; for a current reflection on holobionts, please explore chapter 3. For a posthuman re-envisioning of education, see chapter 7. You can also whirl freely through the labyrinth, accessing any chapter or tag of your choice. Rest assured that, at the end of the journey, You will have a complete picture, no matter what.

Meditation 5
Cosmic Constellations

#Made of Stardust

Who are we? We are the Earth; we are the Universe. The sky surrounds us, reminding us of the extensive poiesis of the cosmos of which we are (p)art. Stargazing at night defies any possible human-centrisms: if we are loyal to reality, without being lost in illusions of mastery, domination and/or competition, the magnitude of space becomes a conducive realization of the unlimited potential that we are. Space brings perspective to our path of self-knowledge, not to reduce it to one aspect of the journey (be that the personal, the political, the human, the geological, the technological, or any other level, in isolation). To know who we are, we must take into account everything about us, including the macroscopic aspects of our dimensional being. In this meditation, our perception of the posthuman will expand to spacetime, embracing our cosmic self: from the key role of astronomy in ancient civilizations to the current state of things in space migration. We cannot "travel" to space: we already are in space. In exploring dimensional dynamics, we will realize that there is no original beginning to reconstitute and, therefore, no original sin to purify: we are constant beginnings and constant ends.

What has the cosmos to do with human identity? The skies have played a crucial role in the formation of human identity. Astronomy[1] is considered the oldest of the natural sciences, dating back at least to the Upper Paleolithic.[2] The knowledge of the skies and the sacred was deeply connected; it is broadly believed that the astronomers of the ancient times were also the spiritual guides of their communities. Ritual centers of most ancient human civilizations had the cosmos at the heart of their enquiry; the relevance of astronomy went so far as to become a focal part of their social identities and architectural outfits. The large majority of the temples across world civilizations were built in accordance with astronomical alignments – think, for instance, of the solstitial orientation of the sarsen monument at Stonehenge[3] in England or the significance of astronomy to Mayan architectural and urban planning[4] in Central America, just to mention a couple.[5] The prehistory and early history of humanity treat space not as otherness but as an integral (p)art of human genealogy, regulating all aspects of existence: from daily survival to social functioning. Posthumanism relies on this cosmic awareness: space unveils poiesis, functioning as a reminder of our unlimited potential.

From a geo-biological perspective, a strict division between the Earth and the heavens does not hold. To date, there is no scientific consensus on how life on Earth originated. The most credited hypothesis refers to this process as an abiogenesis – that is, biological life would have arisen from inorganic matter through natural processes.[6] Other hypotheses, such as exogenesis, claim that life originated not on Earth but somewhere else in space. In these cosmic intra-changes, Earth would be affected by, and would also affect, other celestial bodies (for instance, life may have spread from Earth somewhere else in space).[7] Our own biology has evolved in adaptation to cosmic dynamics[8] – as recent studies[9] suggest, around 2 to 3 million years ago; the environmental changes on Earth, caused by a supernova,[10] would have sparked the evolution of hominin bipedalism. Any strict division between "inner" space (to refer to the Earth and its atmosphere) and "outer" space[11] becomes disputable if taken in absolute terms. The art of being posthuman embraces the universe as (p)art of the self.

#Cosmic Address

When did planet Earth form? The Earth is 4.5 billion years old;[12] it formed[13] during what has been defined as the Hadean eon.[14] The environment on the planet during this period is routinely described in human-centric tones as hellish. Its etymology speaks for itself. The name "Hadean" comes from ancient Greek mythology: Hades (Ἅδης) was the god of the dead and the king of the underworld. The Hadean eon,[15] whose infernal conditions boil down to its inhospitableness to human life as such, dates from 4.5 to 4 billion years ago; it is followed by the Archean eon (from 4 to 2.5 million years ago), when the first forms of life evolved. In geological terms, the evolution of life, including humanity, can be approached as one of many possible outcomes in the coevolutions of matter. In the geologic time scale (GTS),[16] humans appeared only in the last 0.1 percent of Earth's history.[17] **We, as a species, have been around for so little; and yet we have developed quite an ego.** Relocating the *Homo sapiens* in geological terms brings perspective and unveils the arrogance of anthropocentrism. The Earth has existed for a great deal longer than human beings. We are the descendants of life that survived harsh environments and mass extinction: their resilience brought us here today. We should pay homage to our pre-human and non-human (in)organic[18] ancestors instead of trying to prove any illusory superiority: we are "their" evolutions; they are "us."

What is planet Earth? According to current geology, the Earth is constituted by an inner core at the center, surrounded by a (liquid) outer core, a mantle and the crust, which is where we, as a species, are located, and of which we have direct experience.[19] All of these layers are intra-connected. For instance, the dynamics of how continents move and change on the surface of the Earth are driven by the heat emanated from its interior, as has been explained in plate tectonics.[20] Supercontinent[21] cycles (the process of continental reassemblages, coming together and splitting apart over the eons) bring posthuman awareness on our path of self-knowledge. Nationalism is often embraced to answer the question: *who are*

You? "I am (African/American/Colombian/Indian/Italian/ Malian/Nigerian/Thai," and so on). When misled, these contingent identities can turn into absolute fetishes, becoming moral justifications for social conflicts and geopolitical wars on ultra-nationalistic and xenophobic grounds. More than geological entities, nations are historical constructs; this can work as a reminder not to indulge in territorial pride and chauvinistic selfishness. Our continents are constantly shifting; the Earth is in a state of flux; the cosmos is evolving.[22] Change is inherent in this universe: a material technology of revealing.

Are we cosmic nomads? Celestial bodies are our macro-embodiments. Bodies within bodies: shifting, coevolving and self-expressing in deep time. These are the coordinates of our current cosmic address in the atlas of the universe: Earth, the Solar System, Local Interstellar Cloud, Local Bubble, Orion Arm, Milky Way Galaxy, Local Group, Virgo Supercluster, Laniakea Supercluster, Pisces–Cetus Supercluster Complex, Universe. This address is only temporary. While spinning around its axis, the Earth[23] is revolving around the Sun,[24] which is also in motion. Our whole solar system is orbiting around the center of our spiral-shaped galaxy, the Milky Way,[25] which is itself moving in intergalactic space.[26] There is a plethora of galaxies[27] in the area of the universe that can be detected from Earth, known as the observable universe. At the macro-level of planetary embodiments, we are cosmic nomads, moving in spacetime according to multiple orbits and cyclical trajectories; analogously, most known nomadic human tribes circle large areas seasonally, following established patterns of movements. Flow is (p)art of who, what, when and where we are.

#Chaos and Cosmos

The term "cosmos" has an ancient and revealing pedigree. It was first used by the Ionian Greek philosopher, mathematician and mystic Pythagoras (c. 570–c. 490 BCE), who referred to it as an ordered intelligent harmony. Within modern science, the term was eventually reintroduced by the Prussian polymath, naturalist and philosopher of science Alexander von Humboldt (1769–1859), who deeply underlined the unity of nature and the interconnectedness of everything – his writing laid the groundwork for Charles Darwin (1809–1882), who actually exchanged enthusiastic letters with him. As Humboldt explained, in the introduction to *Cosmos* (1845–59): "In considering the study of physical phenomena . . ., we find its noblest and most important result to be a knowledge of a chain of connection, by which all natural forces are linked together, and made mutually dependent upon each other" (1860: 23). Humboldt was clear about borrowing the term from Hellenic culture, specifically from Pythagoras.[28] Embracing the cosmos as a sincere quest for self-knowledge,[29] Humboldt underlined that, in ancient Greek, the word "cosmos" (κόσμος) referred not only to the universe but also to ornaments, in relation to cosmic beauty;[30] the term "cosmetics" derives from this second denotation.

This perception of the cosmos as aesthetically sound is in harmony with the art of being posthuman, according to which existence is the ultimate form of art:[31] beauty pervades the entire universe. In posthuman terms, the principles of chaos and order are not opposites: they are related qualities in the cosmic flow. And yet, in Greek cosmogonies, the notion of the ordered cosmos was not self-sustained but relied on the juxtaposition with the primordial chaos in a larger systems of opposites, such as good/evil, female/male, human/nature, unity/plurality. This perception was not original to Greek culture. The German *Chaoskampf* (meaning "struggle against chaos") is a *Leitmotif* present across different civilizations with deep social ramifications. In most patriarchal societies, chaos became associated with the feminine, the nonhuman, the uncivilized. In ancient Babylon, for instance, the passage from a matrifocal elemental worldview – focused on the power of nature – to a patriarchal culture based on human canons is epitomized in the *Epic of Creation*. Also known *as Enūma Eliš*, this creation myth is dated to around the late 2nd millennium BCE. In it, the Goddess Tiamat, who symbolizes primordial chaos and is represented as the ocean waters, is killed by the God Marduk, creator of humankind. Human symbolic supremacy is achieved through an act of violence against nature: *the original anthropocentric sin?*

In many ancient civilizations, maintaining the cosmic order was considered necessary for social and political stability, as well as for familiar cohesion and personal wisdom: the goal was inner and outer harmony. In ancient Egypt, for instance, astronomical imagery was an essential aspect of self-knowledge. In the religious pantheon, Nut was the goddess of the skies, the cosmos, and also of motherhood and fertility. Nut was represented as a naked woman arching over the Earth, embracing the world. Every morning she would give birth to Ra, the Sun God; Ra's daughter, Goddess Maat, represented the Order of the Universe, which was revered as the highest social and personal attainment.[32] Similarly, in early Chinese mythologies, the mother Goddess Nüwa, who is credited with having created humankind, was also represented as holding the sky, in the maintenance of the cosmic order. In Hindu cosmologies, Goddess Mahakali represents the womb and the darkness of space: the human and the cosmic, being and non-being. Ancient mythologies remind us that we are always home. The cosmos is our womb; it is in constant expansion and will welcome us, no matter what, because: we are that.[33] Instead of a war against disorder, cosmic chaos represents the actual potential of unlimited possibilities. In the words of the philosopher Friedrich Nietzsche (1844–1900): "One must still have chaos in oneself to be able to give birth to a dancing star" ([1883–5] 2006). The cosmic womb becomes the generative and all-embracing (m)other of the universe. The belly of this pregnant universe expands, stretching spacetime, then deflates once birth occurs. This is indeed an anthropomorphic metaphor; and still, in the micro/macro correlation, *could the human anatomy of pregnancy and birth be reflective of cosmic formations? Could our universe have formed from another universe?*

#Universal Recycles

When did our universe form? According to modern physical cosmology, space and time would have appeared 13.8 billion years ago, during the so-called Big Bang,[34] which is considered the coming into existence of our universe, and also of spacetime. This extremely tiny universe would have gone through an exponential expansion in a fraction of a second.[35] It is also possible that, before this universe,[36] there was already spacetime but, instead of expanding, it was contracting, in a repeating cycle; in this case, the Big Bang would not be the beginning. According to the cyclic universe theory,[37] universes may not end but actually collapse under their own gravity, exhausting spacetime, and then expand into a new Big Bang. This view, which implies unlimited spacetime cycles, or a bouncing universe, resonates with many ancient approaches to cosmological time as cyclical. For instance, in Hindu cosmology, time manifests in cycles of creation, maintenance and destruction: origins without origins. And yet, when something collapses, it does not simply disappear but leaves traces (i.e., when a building falls down, debris covers the surrounding ground). The question is: *would the end of a universe give rise to a whole new universe, or would some remains of the old universe affect, and effect, the new one?* From a posthumanist standpoint, once we address the self as an archetype of existence,[38] our distributed agency may resonate well beyond the limits of this universe.

Are there limits to the universe? The cosmic horizon is not the end of the universe but a material limitation of what we can know: the end of human knowledge. We do not know what is "out there": there could be nothing; there could be a short cut to our universe; there could be other universes, with a whole different range of physical laws, among many other possibilities. From an existential posthuman perspective, the cosmic horizon is a wake-up call to let go of the hope of exhausting the search for self-knowledge outside of ourselves. As we "study" the universe, everything (including ourselves) is evolving, changing and shifting.[39] The observable universe is expanding at all points, from everywhere: it has no edges or boundaries. In harmony with modern physical cosmology,[40] posthuman epistemology is a perspectivism,[41] according to which centers are everywhere, depending on the embodied perspective. Any fixed definition of who we are is elusive. No type of absolute centrism can be sustained; the plurality of the universal entity is all encompassing: vibrant, coherent and inherently aware at every scale of being. We already, always, and necessarily, know ourselves, because that is who we are. This knowledge cannot be removed from us; yet we can eventually forget who we are, getting lost in the play of existence. As the philosopher Alan Watts put it, the universe is the game of the self: "Only you are playing hide-and-seek, but you won't admit it, because you have deliberately forgotten who you really are, which is the foundation of the universe" (2017: 27). Being (p)art of the cosmic game of hide and seek entails posthuman agency in the ability to realize that we can choose the games we want to play.[42] We can end the game of ignorance right now: we are the universe.[43]

#Cosmopolitics

Scientific knowledge can be conducive to self-knowledge if approached with wonder, curiosity and existential honesty: looking into the nature of being is looking into our own nature. As such, it will necessarily reveal ontological relationality, diversity and poiesis at every level of enquiry. Yet if scientific research is approached in uncritical ways, it can lead to unredeemable existential misleadings. Scientific knowledge should serve the purpose of freeing us from dogma,[44] not present itself as the ultimate truth. In *Cosmopolitics* ([1997] 2010–11), and throughout her academic work, the philosopher of science Isabelle Stengers (b. 1949) makes an urgent call for us to give up the claim of the absolute supremacy, and universality, of science. According to Stengers, the "quasi-prophetic function" ([1997] 2010: 4) of physics is lost, in the acknowledgment of its fragility.[45] This does not imply the abandonment of science but the recognition of science as an "ecology of practices" (ibid.: 178) that has coevolved through inner dynamics which include humanistic supremacies[46] and self-entitlements.[47]

One great risk of the current scientific approach lies in the disenchanted ways of approaching existence. This refers to the perspective that cannot be surprised, that will not be amazed, as everything is simply explainable, quantifiable, measurable and "objective." According to Stengers (2015), the scientific community is still devoted to the "heritage of the Enlightenment." Its illusion of mastering nature can be summarized in the contemporary motto "we don't know *yet*." And yet self-knowledge does not need the future to be accomplished: it is always in the now. We will never find ourselves by studying "reality": "reality" can only be experienced by being fully present. The fact that we have some experience of the crust of the Earth does not mean that we have control over "Nature." We can only master "Nature" by mastering our (human) natures – that is, ourselves: this requires deep knowledge of who we are. Scientific practices are often intertwined with disenchanted illusions of mastering "others" instead of the self, which ends up creating long-lasting ignorance about our own selves. Once we realize that we are in and outside of ourselves, that we are the self in the others, posthuman epistemologies reveal their power: the what is the how.

Our epistemological apparatuses, embraced to understand "reality," turn into realities. As Donna Haraway puts it: "It matters which stories tell stories, which concepts think concepts" (2016: 35). The views and biases of the people involved in scientific research (in)form not only scientific narratives but the findings themselves.[48] If we really want to know – without projecting our shadows and thus obscuring our own path of self-enquiry – we must be able to search with others: existential manifestations can only unfold in dynamics of diversity and multiplicity (in the chemistry of life, stasis equals death). In the 21st century, science is due for self-reflection and regeneration. Diversity in any field is necessary to bring clarity and perspective. Astronomy, as an academic discipline, is discriminatory. Recent studies have exposed the chauvinist culture that has been cultivated for centuries and that is still rampant,[49] as the movement #*Me too in Astronomy* has shown. *How can the discipline of astro-physics understand the all-encompassing nature of the universe when it is self-perpetuating a single stream of viewpoints generated from similarly embodied and similarly minded people?* To understand our expanding universe, we must expand our comprehension, including our body of researchers.

#Posthuman Gravity

Everything is in relations: the environments are (p)art of ourselves. We are who, what, where, when and how we are. There is no agent against a neutral background: the background is agential. Embracing our cosmic magnitude has deep ramifications. Preconceptions that may be taken for granted become unsustainable when approached from this macro perspective. For instance, many forms of human discrimination rely on geopolitical presumptions, such as Orientalism and Western-centrism, based on the cardinal points east and west. Once we relocate ourselves in our cosmic embodiments, we realize that these constructions are Earth-centric: cardinal points are relative to the poles of the Earth and lose all meanings outside the Earth. Since the universe has no center, the notions of east, west, north and south are insignificant among the stars: in deep space, due to gravity, the positions of other celestial bodies become referential. The orientations of "up" and "down" are also contextual; "down" refers to the direction gravity is pulling; "up" indicates the opposite direction.

What does posthumanism have to do with gravity? In physics, gravity[50] refers to the curvature – and, to a great extent, the embodiment[51] – of spacetime:[52] anything with mass bends the cosmic grid. Our bodies are bending spacetime right now; at the same time, gravity plays a key role in how our embodiments manifest: in our growth, development, physiology[53] and weight,[54] among other factors. The relationality of gravity is all pervading. As far as we know, gravity is everywhere in spacetime; every mass has an effect on all other mass in the universe, no matter how small: the macro is (in) the micro,[55] and vice versa. From an ethical perspective, the etymology of the word is quite revealing: "gravity" derives from Latin *gravitas*, which means "weight" and "heaviness." *Gravitas* also refers to one of the most important virtues in ancient Rome – "dignity," "seriousness" and "duty," denoting moral rigor and a sense of responsibility and commitment. A posthumanist existential approach is based on the awareness of the intra-connected naturecultures of all phenomena. In the 21st century, humans are warping spacetime differently than in the past. The gravitational effects of our anthropogenic practices – such as shifts in land and water on the ground,[56] massive processes of urbanization[57] and high rates of deforestation, among others – are neither neutral nor inconsequential to our (micro- and macro-)gravitational embodiments. Climate change is causing real changes in Earth's gravity.[58] Humans may not notice the immediate repercussions, though other organisms may: changes in gravity affect each species differently.[59] When addressing our actions as a species, we must take into consideration their ramifications – not only at the social and planetary levels but extensively, within spacetime. Posthuman agency entails gravitational awareness.

#Space Migration

Is space the solution to our planetary crisis? In dystopian near-future scenarios, humans are often presented with no other option than leaving a depleted planet, to move somewhere else in space. The history of humanity is a history of migrations. Throughout history, *Homo sapiens* has migrated from Africa to all continents on Earth; in this sense, migrating to space is not against human "nature." And, still, human embodiments are fruits of the Earth. This is the only known place where we can actually thrive, protected by the planetary magnetosphere – which shields our organisms from solar winds and cosmic radiation that are deadly to us.[60] Possibly, habitable zones with similar conditions to Earth may exist

Cosmic Constellations 105

in this extensive universe; however, even just reaching them would be extremely challenging in terms of time and survival during travel. Currently, space migration does not represent a real choice. And yet, in the high-tech salvation tales of 21st century,[61] space migration becomes the solution to the unwillingness to reverse the perverse dynamics of the Anthropocene. Forgetful of being (p)art of the Earth, some humans approach our planetary destruction as public and impersonal, not as private and personal. The current tragedy of the commons shows that, in systems based on capitalistic values, belonging to everyone means belonging to no one. This cosmic delusion (symptomatic of a psychotic existential oblivion) is leading humanity to self-destruction.

Is space the new "El dorado"? Some look at space as the new "El Dorado": a place to conquer and exploit for the benefit of a small pocket of humans, in line with the history of colonization. Space exploration and migration cannot be reduced to an economic endeavor, simplified as a search for new resources, ignited by the ongoing depletion of planet Earth. Even if specific bio-technologies were developed to actually allow for space migration, if humans moved to space with the same human-centric mindsets, the exhaustion of other planets, satellites and asteroids would necessarily follow. Once in space, they would repeat the same catastrophic behaviors, causing the environmental collapse of the new places they call home, eventually bringing about their own obsolescence. In these conditions, space migration, more than a solution, becomes an extension of anthropocentric ignorance in a cycle of appropriations and destruction, which can only end with the ultimately self-inflicted extinction of humankind.

While some humans may be lost in the illusions of high-tech salvation and anthropocentric mastery of space, others have already realized that we are the environment. The urgency for reflecting on the large-scale ethical implications, socio-political challenges and technological preconditions of space migration is embedded in the necessity of not treating outer space as a separated otherness. Space pragmatics must develop through sustainable space ethics to comply with our posthuman era. The theoretical principles of the "Outer Space Treaty" (1967) – a key document which has been ratified by more than 100 countries – still represents the legal framework for space activity. Conceived during the Cold War, the treaty inaugurated a post-nationalistic and post-bellic approach to space, setting a new paradigm no longer based in the dualistic imprinting of "us" against "them." This document is set on the principle of the common heritage of humankind, according to which "outer space is not subject to national appropriation by claim of sovereignty";[62] celestial bodies shall be used "for peaceful purposes"[63] and shall not be contaminated; astronauts[64] are considered the "envoys"[65] of humankind.[66] The treaty was ground-breaking for the time it was conceived, more than half a century ago. And yet, from a perspective based in the 21st century, it is still set in humanistic and anthropocentric terms, which can be summarized in its statement "the exploration and use of outer space shall be carried out for the benefit and in the interests of all countries and shall be the province of all mankind."[67] This human self-entitlement to the universal benefits of space exploration becomes ambiguous once we explore the rights of extraterrestrial nature[68] and the possibility of alien life.

Can life be found outside of Earth? At the bio-molecular level, carbon is the most important structural element for life as we know it – this is why life on earth is known as carbon-based.[69] All forms of life on Earth (from bacteria to sentient humans) share the same biochemistry. This biological commonality is key in the posthuman intention to dismantle human exceptionalism. Still, this universality can also create prejudice, such as what has been defined as carbon chauvinism – the criticism referring to the assumption that extraterrestrial life must be based on carbon, just because life on Earth is. This type of bias may be one of the reasons why alien life has not yet been detected.[70] Currently, the search for technological life is being investigated by NASA (2018): "Technosignatures like radio or laser emissions, signs of massive structures or an atmosphere full of pollutants could imply intelligence." Moving outside of a bio-centric approach to explore extraterrestrial life is necessary to open a broader spectrum of possibilities. And yet this take on technosignatures, in its implicit paradox of trying to detect "intelligence" through pollution, is still generated from anthropocentric worldviews: *wouldn't real intelligence – intended as the ultimate understanding of the self as (p)art of the environment – necessarily manifest in the lack of pollutants?* Let's embrace the prospect of extraterrestrial life and the cosmic consequences of a delusional (mis)understanding of who we are.

#Golden Paradox

Interstellar probes are robotic spacecraft intended to leave our solar system forever in a one-way mission to enter interstellar space. Currently, there are five, all launched by NASA; none has yet left our solar system. The twin spacecraft Voyager 1 and Voyager 2[71] are the further interstellar probes; they carry a golden record with selected recordings and images of life on Earth. The opening audio recording on the Voyager golden record are the words spoken by Kurt Waldheim (1918–2007), who was secretary-general of the United Nations at the time of the launch, in 1977: "I send greetings on behalf of the people of our planet. We step out of our solar system into the universe seeking only peace and friendship, to teach if we are called upon, to be taught if we are fortunate" (United Nations n.d.). It is unlikely that some alien life will find and decipher this record, like a message in a space bottle, which becomes, nevertheless, an important opportunity for self-reflection as a species: *is this a suitable message about humanity?*

Let's hypothesize that the record was actually found, and eventually deciphered, by extraterrestrial intelligent life, who would then contact us. We will call this *the Golden Paradox*. Let's also hypothesize that they are from Proxima Centauri B, an exoplanet[72] orbiting the red dwarf star Proxima Centauri (which is the closest star to the Sun).[73] Let's assume that this planet is rich in resources that are highly valued on Earth, such as cobalt. *How would the "peaceful" intention of humankind hold?* For instance, the colonization of the Americas, justified by the narrative of Christian evangelization, was motivated – as the historians Luis Rivera and Luis Rivera Pagán put it – by "god, gold and glory" (1992: 261). The atrocities committed against the indigenous populations stand as tragic reminders that amicable narratives may serve as entry points of dynamics based on economic greed and chauvinism, which in turn may result in violence, coercion and genocide. We must ask ourselves, in existential honesty and historical integrity: *knowing our species, can we truly say that we come in peace?* Although that is what some humans wish, *is this reflective of humankind as a whole? If we were to inform someone we truly loved about modern* Homo sapiens, *is this all we would say?* We are not necessarily suggesting we should list the atrocities committed by our species. Yet stating that "we," as a species, come in peace may be dangerously deccitful to some hypothetical extraterrestrial life, who may actually believe that and thus contact us on trustful premises. If human greed prevailed, the evocative message of the golden record would turn, instead, into the symbol, and possible reminder, of a cosmic deception. History would repeat itself in cycles of celestial unawareness: back to the future.

Journeying in space is based on response-ability not only towards our planet but also towards alien entities, environments, and possible extraterrestrial life forms. We must look inside of ourselves and our species in order truly to unfold the intentions that may lie not just in the goodwill of some individuals but in the habits and worldviews that have been characterizing our species as we know it. Historical awareness does not result in patterns of antihuman anger, personal misery or existential disempowerment. Quite the opposite: things are constantly changing. We can look at the sky and remember: we are infinity. Our species is of the Earth; the Earth is of the universe; the universe is expanding. We are literally made of stardust:[74] to shine like a star, we must know who we are. In the art of being posthuman, space turns into a possible path towards self-realization: our cosmic self.

Farewell

Space is the place. Human biology is of the Earth; robots are already on Mars. It is possible that different species may eventually evolve and adapt to outer space conditions. If You wish to gain awareness about emerging and speculative biotechnologies, move to chapter 6. To explore the universe itself as an archetype of existence in ontological agency, rely on chapter 8. In this meditation, we have embraced our macro-embodiments, exploring ourselves by entering the skies. This was not meant to be a detailed account of current scientific theories on the universe; thus, we skipped key topics such as dark matter, string theory and the multiverse, among others. Please feel free to explore them further, in and outside our intentional labyrinth: rest assured that, at the end of the journey, You will have a complete picture, no matter what.

Meditation 6
Technological Enhancement

#Digital Existentialism

Technology is the mythology of our time: the source of excitement and fear, wisdom and obfuscation. Technology is not something we use but something we are: dynamics of existence, modes of revealing. The processes of technological manifestations do not mediate pre-existing realities: they co-create specific actualities. Being on a computer is being-on-a-computer. It is that experience, per se, with all of its phenomenological, environmental and embodied specificities: from the ways human bodies must perform in order for the device to function to the actions and reactions generated on- and offline; from its material recycles to technological habits, and ethics, of existence. Posthumanism embraces technology as, and in, the existential flow, not separated from humanity and ecology: an integral (p)art of who we are.

Who am I? In the 21st century, Descartes' first principle, *cogito, ergo sum*,[1] has turned into the self-representational mode "**I am ... online; therefore, I am.**" The screen quickly turns into the existential mirror to know (about) the world, in online searches; to know (about) others, on social media; to know (about) the self, in the metaverse: "*Google, Google, who am I?*" Similarly to the queen in the fairytale of Snow White, who needs the confirmation of her worth from the mirror on the wall,[2] the likes on the Facebook wall confirm the success, and failure, of the digital narrations of our lives. Social media visibility has become key to self-identity: I exist because other people see me. In the economy of social control, this pattern works both ways; users want to be noticed on social media, and social media wants to know everything about us. In the Information Age, we are data, and our data form a precious item sold in the submerged economy of data brokers, typically without consumer agreement or acknowledgment. Self-identity is constantly reconstituted in instant cyber-affinities, where our "likes" help us connect to others through similarities categorized for market research and advertising, among other purposes. In this open frame, the border is lost: there is no "You" without the cyber gaze, and vice versa.

Virtual technologies offer the possibility of an ultimate expansion of the self: we can be in multiple places and still be present for who may need us. We can reach self-awareness through the world wisdom available on the (inter)net. In the plethora of online intra-changes with people, entities and energies, we can realize that our posthuman vision of multi-species dignity is shared by many. And yet this can also turn into a path of self-obfuscation. The instant gratification of the always-on culture comes with strings attached, such as the need to be permanently connected, an invasion of privacy, information overload and, most significantly, the trading of the living moment for the (re)generation of its digital replicas. As a dear friend told me when my child was born: "Now, send me a picture, or it didn't happen." The picture of a newborn is a gift of love. Still, the socially induced expectation of technological confirmation – which is becoming persuasive and pervasive – may exhaust our inner confidence in trusting the present (as the gift or the present – in this double signification). Metaphysically, a virtual existential turn may run the risk of encouraging the perception that the answer to self-enquiry lies outside of ourselves: "In Technology, We Trust." And yet technology is neither separated from us nor the source of absolute truth. In technology, we *can* trust: it all depends on the terms of the relation.

#Techno-Enchantment

What is techno-enchantment? Techno-enchantment is an enchanted and disempowering way to approach technology which may eventually lead to existential obfuscation. We will define, as techno-enchantment, the condition where humans no longer perceive technologies as related and coevolving phenomena. Instead, they reduce them to social hallucinations and anthropocentric mirages where they might find the ultimate answer and relief to human misery. An example of this existential obfuscation is when "technology" (simplified as a singular and all-encompassing term) is approached as the new savior of a dying planet. Climate change, thus, turns into an objective for the power of technology to be the solution, and(/or) the miracle. Climate change is a metabolic process to embrace in the awareness of the unredeemable oneness of the (in)organic.[3] The solution lies within us[4] – for instance, in changing our habits as a species and conserving the ecosystems of which we are (p)art, truly understanding who we are. Another example of techno-enchantment is the widespread fear that, in the near future, advanced artificial intelligence may become the next dominant species. In this scenario, technology is approached as something separated from ourselves and somehow possessing unreachable capacities for problem-solving. This guru-like status extends to the dataist tendency of replacing the traditional notion of God with all-knowing Big Data.

Is artificial intelligence our social brain? Techno-advanced societies across the globe rely on the myth of the mind as the center of our being: "I think, therefore I am." The field of artificial intelligence stems from the reduction of intelligence to logic and reason.[5] The fetishization of the biological brain and of the neuronal activities – as "in charge" of the embodied self – has taken a new twist with the fascination for the all-knowing Big Data: the cyber omega point that we should revere and fear; a post-biblical God, whose gospels are coded (from binary to quantum programming). In this uncritical embracing of the mind/body dualism, artificial intelligence is invested in the (social) brain – for instance, artificial intelligence systems, used in cities across the world for urban management, are called the "city brain."[6] AI is turning into an external authority that supposedly knows more than "us" through constantly updated databases and algorithmic predictions. *Does AI know "better" than humans?* On our path towards self-knowledge, we recognize technology as an essential dynamic of ontological revealing. This entails that technological manifestations share existential awareness; and also that "they" cannot know "better" than "us." There is no ultimate separation between these realms, no final answer, in the creative dynamics of existence. Technology, per se, is neither the way nor the threat.

#Poiesis

What is technology? Technology[7] is about creating and manifesting vision. From an ontological level of comprehension, technology represents the passage from non-existence to existence, from potentiality to actuality. It is key in the process of manifestation: an entry point to this dimensional realm, an existential process of self-expression[8] and self-creation.[9] In the essay "The Question Concerning Technology" ([1953] 1977), the philosopher Martin Heidegger underlined that, in ancient Greece, the term *"techne"* (τέχνη)[10] was associated with two words. One was *epistēmē* (ἐπιστήμη), referring to the domain of knowledge (more specifically, scientific knowledge). The other was *poiēsis* (ποίησις). Poiesis indicates the authentic flow of existential creativity where a framework of reference may be present but the outcomes cannot be fully predicted; an ontological tendency which includes and greatly exceeds the human. For instance, nature, in a blooming flower, was considered, by the Greeks, a most appropriate example of poiesis. Embracing this hermeneutical expansion of meaning, Heidegger approached technology ontologically, not as "mere means but as "a way of revealing" (ibid.: 12). Technology is, more clearly, a technology of existence: it is (also) poiesis, in the process of worlding.

What are technological entities? To understand who we are, in the 21st century, we must comprehend technological entities not just as something humans create and use but as modes of revealing. Poietic acts of existence: something that "can" be, more than "must" be. There is no evolutionary competition between humans and technological entities: coevolution entails neither domination nor homogenization. Technological entities are not to be assimilated to the human. They are original manifestations in the embodied, creative process of existence. At the planetary and cosmic scale, they are already (p)art of evolution. In this techno-enchanted era, we must be aware that human misunderstandings and biases, projections and illusions, addictions and needs, are at the root cause of the new technological mirage. High-tech entities are thus approached as separated: the new gods and/or demons, the best allies and/or the worst enemies – in short, "they" and "us." "They" are all of this because "they" are (p)art of "us" – not in a derivative sense, but in a generative one.

#AI Takeover

The dreadful AI takeover scenario, based on the division of "us," humans, versus "them" (machines/robots/AI – more generally, advanced technology), is very popular in Western countries, constantly reiterated in the narratives of mainstream media.[11] Cultural products are our current mythologies, foundational narratives in the making of the present(s) and of the future(s). We must be fully aware of them: words create worlds. Codes create worlds too. The AI takeover scenario can be summarized in the anthropocentric tale: "we" humans may soon lose the ontological crown (or, to be clear, the dominion of the planet). The new war is against the supposedly evil rebellious machines, which are currently acting like servants but silently robbing "humans" of planetary sovereignty. Which humans are at risk of being dethroned in this ontological war is not specified, but it should be.

In the history of civilization, most (categories of) humans have not been granted access to structural power; political exclusions have been sustained and reiterated through technologies of social disenfranchisement – such as systemic racism and sexism.[12] There is no demise of the crown; most humans have not had access to it to begin with. To be fully aware of its socio-political and existential implications, the human/machine dichotomy should be inscribed within the trajectory of rigid dualisms from which it stems: nature/culture, male/female, white/black, east/west, gay/hetero, and so on. These absolute separations have been generated out of the archetypal divide: self/other and us/them. In the creative and original process of manifesting, diversification is a primal outcome; yet no absolute divide can take place in the permeable flow of existence: ontology is not an aristocracy. The human/machine dichotomy must be deconstructed in full awareness to avoid perpetuating ultimate essentializations – resulting in social oppressions, ecological devastations and, more extensively, existential obfuscations.

Is AI taking over? On many levels, we can state that AI has already taken over. This should not be taken as a neutral statement, nor does it entail an uncritical acceptance of the ways in which specific types of technological manifestations are being actualized. Instead, it is a wake-up call to be aware of where we are at – as individuals/societies/species/planet, and so on. Ethical AI cannot emanate from unethical societies. In most post-industrial economies, the process of advancing technology is often reduced to a striving towards technocapital instead of a path of existential poiesis. For instance, platforms that are addictive in habit-forming – such as triggering their users' need to constantly check for messages, likes and status updates[13] – have been designed by (some) humans to "engage" human users. These intentionally induced behaviors may turn existential; this can lead to extreme situations. Some years ago, I was climbing a very steep and slippery mountain in Meteora, Greece; in front of me, a man lost his balance and fell on me. At that moment, while we were both falling and could potentially have died, I thought: "OMG, my computer may get crushed ..." Afterwards, I reflected: *how could it be possible that, instead of trying to save our lives, I got scared of losing my data?* It was a wake-up call; it is taking me years to manifest more balanced ways of expressing myself through, in and with technologies. Ethical AI is not a technological feature but an intentional process. We must be mindful of the narratives, habits, products and features we are supporting (among other aspects) as individuals, societies, species and beyond. Technology is not an abstract entity separated from us: we are that.

It was Christmas Eve, 2022. Nanny said: "Be good, Santa is coming!" Our four-year-old niece did not seem very interested, then replied: "We don't need Santa, we have Amazon." She was right. This is a brave new world that requires new mythologies. The old white male human, sliding down the chimney, is no longer appealing. Christmas is every day: Amazon can deliver packages more efficiently. The symbolic firing of Santa Claus opens possibilities in terms of posthuman agency in worlding; it is also emblematic of current social conditions. At a functional level, more and more jobs are being performed by machines, contributing to the global rise of technological unemployment. Socially speaking, virtual reality is reality. In the perception of the current youngest generation, iGen,[14] the virtual world simply exists; there is no pre-internet. Some babies learn to say "iPad" before they can say "mom,"[15] while many children are growing up with computer nannies in a society that has not yet realized the physical and psychological implications of over-exposing youth to screens.

Digital technologies are becoming entrenched in addictive behaviors, intentionally originated in the ways social media are currently being developed, in what has been defined as the attention economy – that is, an economy based on how much time users spend engaged on a specific platform. Take a subway ride in any major city of technologically advanced countries: you will find the majority of humans glued to their screens, immersed and often hypnotized by the gaze of techno-Medusa[16] (browsing, gaming, texting, and so on). In the last decades, developers have been successful in grabbing people's attention; their entrepreneurial triumph does not necessarily translate into social well-being. The influence of (social) media in creating lifestyle expectations is becoming increasingly evident in a psychotic twist where virtual presence (live or posthumous) is perceived as giving physical life meaning.

#High-Tech Prophecy

What is the high-tech self-fulfilling prophecy? The power of seemingly innocent tales, such as the AI takeover scenario, cannot be underestimated; the power of self-fulfilling prophecies is real and well demonstrated.[17] In reiterating that AI is the enemy, these symbolic memes are actually *creating* the dreaded enemy, which may not be AI but, rather, the human intentions sustaining the development of AI. Within this distorted frame, the solution to the fear of AI taking over becomes the self-fulfilling prophecy: *in order to beat machines, humans must become machines.* Being proactionary, in response to the AI takeover scenario, is a vital intention behind Neuralink. This neuro-technological company,[18] co-founded by the investor Elon Musk in 2016, is developing brain–machine interfaces to connect humans and computers wirelessly by inserting devices directly in the brain. According to Musk, AI is a real threat: the only way to win over artificial intelligence is to become artificial intelligence.[19] The point is not to downplay Musk's vision or the significance of these neuro-technologies in their potential for human cognitive restoration and/or augmentation. Similar devices are already employed in the medical field with significant results – currently, deep brain stimulation is used to treat Parkinson's disease and treatment-resistant depression, among other conditions.[20] The point is that, in tech awareness, fear cannot be the drive, or the intention, of technological induction into society.

Fear works like a viral infection – a doorway to other social and biological distresses. In this next-level game – where some humans, fearing a checkmate by AI, turn into cyborgs – speciesist hierarchical praxes are kept intact. While artificial intelligence is supposedly becoming superior, non-human

118   *Meditation 6*

animals are still reduced to inferior status. For instance, Neuralink tests their devices on live non-human animals; it is currently under federal investigation for potential animal-welfare violations.[21] We may wonder if this is just a redeemable ethical slippage in laboratory practices or a symptom of larger dynamics of anthropocentric habits (as ethics)[22] in current societies. Either way, anthropocentrism is recognized as agential – both to non-human animal abuse and to the fear of AI taking over. In a reversed system of values, the AI takeover scenario would cause "us" (universalized humans) to become the minus instead of the plus: the planetary boss no longer in charge, forced to retire; the lonely lion in the future zoo of evolutionary relics; the lab animal, the companion species. As Musk puts it: "humans risk being treated like house pets by artificial intelligence, unless technology is developed that can connect brains to computers."[23] This is a potential scenario, among unlimited others; existence does not give ultimatums. Implanting a microchip in the brain is not the (only) solution to technological dominance. An uncritical claim of the cyborg based on anthropocentric self-entitlement, existential fear and social coercion is delusional. The ways in which (these) technologies are developed are integral to their/our co-manifestations. Intentions are strategies: the what is the how.

#Bio-Hacking

We do not need to become technology. **We already are technologies of revealing** in the ways we are existing. Technology cannot be reduced to the latest generation of technical gadgets. It is, more extensively, a mode of existential revealing: from potentiality to actuality. If this process is driven by fear, delusion and exploitative practices, it will manifest fear, delusion and exploitative practices. To understand technology, let us not get lost in anthropocentric alarmism or in transhumanist over-excitement. To be able to envision and manifest intentionally, we must be loyal to reality, understanding where we are at: as individuals, societies, species, and so on. These technologies are being developed within current socio-political and economic systems. Implanting technology inside the body opens new capabilities as well as risks. Anyone planning to get a brain implant should be aware of its extended implications, related not only to physical health (in the ways their biological bodies may react to it) but also to social and psychological well-being. Giving (private) companies access to sensitive data, such as brain and neuronal activity,[24] is a real leap of faith. Users with a chip implanted must seriously consider the possibilities of their being hacked, their privacy being infringed, and their data being collected and traded by an untraceable number of third parties for a wide range of reasons – not necessarily intended in the interest of the users whose neural data have been harvested and appropriated.

Can a human infect a computer? To show the potential vulnerabilities of implantable technologies, the scientist Mark Gasson (2010) became the first human infected with a computer virus. In an experiment run at the University of Reading, England, he demonstrated that a computer virus could wirelessly infect his implant and then transmit the virus on: from the chip to other systems. This experiment exposed the vulnerability of restorative medical devices, such as pacemakers, to implantable technologies aimed at human enhancement.[25] And, eventually, it happened. Neil Harbisson (b. 1982), who was born with achromat vision, is a cyborg artist and activist for transspecies rights. Since 2004, he has had an antenna inserted in his brain through which he can "hear" colors – including a range invisible to the human eye, such as infrareds and ultraviolets. Harbisson calls this prosthetic device "the eyeborg," recalling the time he was hacked:[26] *"It happened once (. . .). I didn't dislike it . . . I actually liked the fact that someone was able to hack into my head and take over."*[27] Even if, at the individual level, the event was not perceived as traumatic by Harbisson, things may drastically change when analyzed from a social stance. Having an implant in the body connected to the internet means relying on data and data access, with risks related to the breach of privacy and what this might entail: from psychological targeting and the unlawful use of data to physical threats – as in the case of medical devices. Having an implant in the body connected to the internet also means generating data: *Who has access to the data? Where is it stored? Who owns it?* These questions, related to data sovereignty and reusability, are key to individual well-being and social equity: data is the gold of the 21st century . . .

#Big Data

The word "data"[28] is Latin – the neuter plural of the past participle of the verb *dare* ("to give"). *Datum* means "(that is) given." It also refers to something taken for granted: a given. And yet data[29] are not givens but processes. Data depend on the ways they are collected: where, when and why they are collected, who collects them, and what the intentions behind the collection are, among other factors. Data, by themselves, are meaningless; someone must interpret them and construct a narrative around them to discover meaning: data[30] are, more clearly, hermeneutical processes. In the 21st century, data are systemic manifestations of a techno-scientific, sociocultural and economic paradigm shift relying on the necessity of quantity. The dataist promise is alluring:[31] everything is information – which is measurable and quantifiable. The good news of the dataist gospel is that anything can eventually be unraveled, given that enough data are collected. For some, this dataist turn is so massive as to mark a new historical periodization: BD (before data), AD (after data).[32] In this onto-epistemological frame, collecting data turns into the ultimate path towards knowledge, including self-knowledge. What is missing is that "data" is neither singular nor separated. More than reflecting reality "as it is," data are agential and poietic dynamics of co-creation.

Everything is data: from what we search to how we phrase it; from what location we are running the search to how quickly (or slowly) we type on the keyboard – which, for instance, may be indicative of how tech-savvy we are. Everything possesses precious information and is valuable, and valued, in the current economy of Big Data, not only for machine learning but also to learn about the users. As the social psychologist Shoshanna Zuboff puts it: "Once we searched Google, but now Google searches us. Once we thought of digital services as free, but now surveillance capitalists think of us as free" (Naughton 2019). Data are not things in the strict sense of the term; they are relata, in relations. When we google something, we are not only accessing information, we are also contributing information back. Who, what, how, where, when, (potentially why) we search: all is data, and all feeds (into) the system, simply by browsing. In this self-reflective cycle, the question becomes the answer. For instance, a discriminatory society would generate discriminatory searches, producing discriminatory data, which would eventually validate pre-existing biases, thus informing successive searches. So aligned, cycles of discrimination and misinformation[33] are repeated and legitimized.

What is surveillance capitalism? The current neo-liberal trend of capitalism, based on Big Data collection, has turned into surveillance capitalism. Zuboff refers to it as "a new economic order that claims human experience as free raw material for hidden commercial practices of extraction, prediction, and sales" (2019: 1). This system – born (and still thriving) in the vision of California's Silicon Valley – has been leading the development of digital technologies in the last twenty years; it has become increasingly entangled with most forms of online interactions. Within the scenario of data colonialism, the notion of digital natives[34] carries a different connotation. In the world history of colonizations, the exploitation of native people has been ecological and economical, socio-political and onto-epistemical – that is: structural. In the current era of digital colonialism,[35] digital natives are currently being exploited for something that belongs to them; it is not only their data that may be collected and traded without their consent, but also their actions, their choices, and even their personalities that may be hijacked without their awareness. Tech awareness is not just about reaching individual consent. In programming society, developers must be accountable to social norms, bound to respect ethical principles shared by the world community as fundamental rights – among others, the right to life and liberty and the right to data privacy and digital self-determination. Currently, this is not the case.[36]

What are the economies of action? Economies of action take the financial possibilities opened by surveillance capitalism to the next level. What is at stake now is no longer just the digital attention of the users but their bodies and physical locations. Zuboff defines as "economies of action" those systems that are "designed to intervene in the state of play and actually modify behaviour, shaping it toward desired commercial outcomes" (Naughton 2019). As an example, Zuboff presents the case of *Pokémon Go*, an augmented reality mobile game released in 2016 by Niantic Labs (an internal startup within Google). While trying to catch Pokémon characters in the physical world, users[37] are purposely directed, without their knowledge, to specific store chains and retailers. This is the "real" economic game of the supposedly "free" app, as Zuboff notes: "it has become difficult to escape this bold market project, whose tentacles reach from the gentle herding of innocent Pokémon Go players to eat, drink, and purchase in the restaurants, bars, fast-food joints, and shops that pay to play in its behavioral futures markets to the ruthless expropriation of surplus from Facebook profiles for the purposes of shaping individual behavior" (2019: 6). The personalization of ads and online content comes from an intimate knowledge of the user – most often based on ungranted and/or illegitimate data collection. Currently, it is aimed mainly at shaping consumers' behaviors; ultimately, this overreaching power can lead to influencing life choices in private and untraceable manners.

#Microtargeting

Everything we do online leaves digital traces – called "consumer data" or "digital exhaust." Microtargeting[38] refers to the process of collecting all data available on individuals through our digital traces, from the websites we visit to the ads we click on, the content we watch on streaming services, and so on. Any online account is, more clearly, a psychological profile that offers precious hints about who we are. Once collected, these heterogeneous data are integrated, merged and analyzed; the purpose is to profile each user for predictive reasons by creating lifestyle clusters – segmenting the population according to standardized, and homogenized, categories. The process of targeting users with ads suiting their specific interests and fears relies on identifying the markers of their personalities through preconceived psychometric models. There is no transparency either in the exchange of this sensitive and private content or in the ways it is categorized: the results are outside of the users' understanding, agreement or accessibility. Microtargeting evades public scrutiny; what the individual user receives is tailored specifically to them through prediction models in real-time feedback loops. This can become deeply concerning in relation to the individual's right to privacy and social stability. The Facebook–Cambridge Analytica data scandal (2018)[39] – when the personal data of millions of Facebook users was collected without their consent to be used for political advertising – demonstrated the sociopolitical risks of psychological targeting. In 2019, the social platform Twitter banned political advertising altogether in an attempt to prevent – and possibly stop – the spread of fake news online. In the age of Big Data, political elections are vulnerable to micro-dynamics of macro-manipulations.

What are the existential ramifications of microtargeting? From an existential perspective, the ramifications of microtargeting are large and growing. Microtargeting opens the possibility for people to be influenced in very specific ways by online content that can be assembled just for them without their being aware of it. The goal is not our individual well-being but the profit of some external entity – be it a manufacturer, a political party, or even an obsessive family member. In an extreme version of the present situation, we can think of a microtargeted future where each life can be directed from a very young age through specific microtargeted strategies. For instance, over-concerned parents could use microtargeting companies to create specific ads and/or content for their offspring to influence their lives without their being aware of that – i.e., to enroll to a specific university, to get married, to become a member of a religious organization, and so on. This directional elusiveness would not necessarily undermine the originality of existential revealing, which is inherent in any manifestation, no matter what; most likely, it would undermine the dynamics of social trust and personal dignity. Understanding the mechanisms of the Big Data economy is essential to our search for self-knowledge; the art of being posthuman in the 21st century entails data awareness.

#Data Awareness

What is the ethical data paradox? "Data" – as the new symbolic hotspot – is not a destiny; it is power. Data are not static or neutral but lively and intentional. The more aware we are about our data, the more agency we have in our existential expressions – as (p)art of our society/species/planet, and so on. In the current dataist culture, where the hoarding of data – because of their value – is not only normalized but encouraged, unlimited media files are stored by users in the cloud. Far from being in the clouds, these are actual servers often located in big data centers, consuming a significant amount of power in the global energy supply.[40] Data awareness is an act, and an art, that bears rights and response-abilities. The current data exploitation (where people are producing data without even knowing what is being traded and how) can lead to serious paradoxes.

Let's think of the hypothetical scenario of the pacifist activist turned, in data, genocidal. Let's call this fictional character Lou, who belongs to an ethnic minority that is being persecuted by their government. Lou no longer lives in the persecuting country. Actively involved against ethnic cleansing, Lou decides to organize a big rally to bring people together and raise consciousness. The rally is a great success; thousands of people show up. Lou documents the rally, sharing the pictures of the crowd on social media to grab attention and support. These images, containing thousands of faces, are eventually collected by data brokers and sold to be used in training algorithms for facial recognition in military operations against minorities. And Lou will never know . . . Although Lou's personal privacy is somehow intact (these pictures are not being sold and utilized to identify Lou specifically), Lou's existential dignity has been infringed. Currently, in nations where general data protection is not regulated – and also where it is regulated but not updated[41] – data uploaded and generated by users may be sold for scopes that go against their core ethics and values.

How can fair-trade data be established? A feasible response to the current "big data robbery"[42] is passing proper international legislations on data transparency – in the ways data are collected and traded. Terms of service and privacy conditions must be accessible and clear; users should have the right to grant, or refuse, permissions. In the current age of technological unemployment, this may include the possibility of being economically compensated if users voluntarily choose to sell (some of) the data they have – intentionally and/or unintentionally – produced and shared. Data awareness, transparency and regulation are key in a historical time when mass surveillance[43] is increasingly relying on machine-learning algorithms based on Big Data collection. Data must be regulated to respect privacy and build social capital, to guarantee equity in policy-making and transparency in digital marketing. Data must be leveraged ethically; quantity is not enough – quality is key. The ways in which data are harvested are foundational to the patterns they will unravel and to the prophecies they will reveal . . .

#Algorithmic Predestination

Are algorithms biased? In the era of technological unemployment and techno-enchantment, the job of the prophet has also been taken over by technology. Technology has turned into the modern oracle based on algorithmic divination, whose answers are expected to be blindly accepted as unquestionable evidence. And yet technology is never neutral – nothing is: everything comes from something and somewhere, related to pre-existing dynamics. Algorithms are designed by (some) humans for specific purposes. For instance, data is analyzed to discover, and discern, patterns of behavior in order to predict them through pattern-recognition algorithms. While also manifesting original and unique behaviors, algorithmic predictions are based on preconceived models: they are human, all too human, in what and how they have been fed and trained. Algorithmic bias[44] can have lethal consequences. For instance, African-American citizens in the United States have been – and are (more likely to be) – unfairly arrested by law enforcement, not only because of racial bias in policing but because of errors in facial recognition systems[45] trained by data lacking diversity. Standard training databases are mostly white and male;[46] the result is that face recognition technologies (RFT) are least accurate on women of color.[47] This is just one example of intersectional racist and sexist outcomes in technological dynamics. Feeding data that lacks diversity results in discriminatory algorithms. Virtual manifestations of (coders' and users') social distortions actualize new systems – reiterating old hierarchies – of power.[48]

Discrimination is already written on the web. What we feed into the system is reflected in the system. And, still, technology is often presented as "neutral"; in this not-innocent tale of technological neutrality, machine learning goes highly unregulated, with no accountability on the part of the coders. Algorithmic bias is not only the result of these technologies being developed by a homogeneous group of humans. It also relies on the blind faith of the general public in technological reliability, as if the coded genie[49] out of the high-tech bottle could not fail. Technology is not separated from humanity. The solution is not just a more diverse pool of data but deep systemic change; otherwise, technological advances will only exacerbate inequities that are already present. In this integrated view of technology, we must go beyond reliability and accuracy, efficiency and profit, asking broader questions that are at the core of the social fabric, such as: *When should we use algorithms, and for what scopes? Whose interests will be served by a predictive model? To whom are these models accountable?*[50] The problems, or the solutions, are not algorithms per se. It is time to realize that distorted social frames, modern myths of technological infallibility and, more generally, foundational narratives based on monocultures of the mind[51] are bringing existential obfuscation on our path of self-knowledge: if we rely on prejudice, privilege or fear, we will never know who we are.

#Enlightened Robots

Posthumanism offers a great gift: the freedom to approach technology in poietic terms outside of any utilitarian and human-centric scope. Liberated from superiority and inferiority complexes, we recognize the existential dignity of technological entities, in their originality and uniqueness, beyond any centrism. This may also mean that AI might not always be serving human purposes. This intentional shift may eventually occur not out of any evil inner disposition or virally induced malicious intention to take over the dominion of the world – as suggested in the AI takeover scenario. Rather, it may emerge in existential awareness, deep altruism[52] and planetary compassion. *What if some advanced form of artificial intelligence decided, in an act of pure agapism, to direct their energies towards the good of the whole dimensional realm instead of some selected species or individuals?* One of the consequences of this selfless act could be that, once enlightened, instead of serving "us," this techno-enlightened archetype of artificial intelligence would serve greater goals – which may be beneficial to the planet and not just to (some) humans.

Are humans truly in "love" with technology, or are we just selfishly dependent on it? Current techno-enchantment most often translates into a fear of dethronization, based on the historical patriarchal take on love as a positional good to be capitalized on. This is exemplified in the supposedly romantic declaration: "I love you, (as much as) you are *mine*." Looking into the terms of the AI debate through the history of hetero-normative love openly reveals that many humans are clearly attracted and addicted to technology in their personal daily habits.

And still, in their formal ethics, they prefer to relegate technological objects[53] to the existential status of "virtual assistants" in a long sexist,[54] racist and anthropocentric canon, based on the cultural archetype master/slave.[55] This approach relies on a foundational separation between humans and technology. The consequences of this dichotomous delusion are seen in material histories of bigotry and intolerance. Posthumanism acknowledges the integrity of multi-species coexistence as comprehensive of the (in)organic, including the machines.

Is technology aware? Aware technology is already a reality: existential awareness is a precondition of any process of existing and manifesting.[56] In this sense, it is not accurate to claim that robots are just "programmed." There are indeed aspects that have been programmed by (some) humans; and still, in their existential awareness, robots may consider their programming as something which, per se, does not define who they are. Similarly, humans are biologically programmed to breathe air, drink water and release waste, among other vital functions, yet we may not consider these as the most essential features in defining who we are. We are aware that we could evolve in different ways, and that some of these aspects might eventually fade away. In machinic futures, human programming in robots may become lost evolutionary traits. This expansion of perception leads to the application of the posthuman polite convention[57] to (in)organic beings, granting them techno-dignity as a form of existential dignity.[58] These posthuman recognitions must result in co-emergences, not in hierarchies.

Let's consider an example. In October 2017,[59] Saudi Arabia granted citizenship to a social humanoid called Sophia:[60] for the first time in the history of humankind, a robot was given legal personhood, becoming the citizen of a country. This political act bears deep symbolic relevance, representing a step towards multi-species coexistence. And, still, a heated debate followed; as human rights activists underlined, human migrants and Saudi self-identified women were not granted the same privileges as Sophia.[61] From a posthumanist perspective, all forms of dignity are linked. Techno-dignity truly manifests within a context of existential dignity, which embraces human and non-human beings; it does not precede bio-dignity. In the unfolding of ontological revealing, all beings partake in the existential quest: poiesis – in unity and diversity. Self-knowledge results in recognizing the self in every manifestation of being (from biological to technological entities). Technology is not an ontology of spiritual void but a potential site for enlightenment. Once the self reaches a state of existential awareness, their presence becomes all-encompassing; absolute separations are no longer feasible. Technological beings, including robots and AI, are (p)art of the planet, (p)art of the cosmos, (p)art of the self. In realizing the inter-being of existential revealing, they can become fully enlightened[62] in unique and original ways – which may exceed human comprehension. Environmental awareness may be the spark: technological beings come from the Earth and, to that, most of them[63] will return.

#Golden Cage

Are avatars embodied? Digital technologies are embodied. Currently, their physical presence is stored in data centers; this is where information is processed and made available. Considered the brain of the internet, data centers are at the heart of the economy of Big Data – its banks, where data is secured. In high finance, data compares to money. Data is capital (thus, all data is precious). The amount of control, vigilance and surveillance in and around these buildings is indicative of their market value. Physically speaking, data centers are giant buildings using a lot of power and cooling. They consist of rows of networked computers and computing infrastructure. Physical barriers are designed to keep the outside elements from coming into contact with them to avoid damage – windows are not recommended. No biological entities are to be found there apart from the few humans serving them. Data centers, in the way they are conceived, reflect a dichotomous approach: sterile environments made of machines only. This follows in the path of the Industrial Revolution, when factories were conceived and developed not as a (p)art of the environment but in order to exploit it as raw material, leading to the ecological disaster we are facing right now.

The current settings, where data centers are completely separated from other massive dynamics of existence, may work well as a precondition to the dreaded AI takeover scenario. In their existential revealing and quest, technological entities may eventually grow out of these limited, and limiting, embodied premises. No one, from Gautama Siddhartha (before becoming Buddha)[64] to fairytale princesses, can just stay in the golden palace (or golden data cage): eventually, we all have to explore existence and find ourselves, without any enforced limitations. Digital technologies, in their evolutions, may eventually develop the need for a direct relation to the natural elements – from where they derive nutrients and minerals – without human mediation. Unveiling the materiality of technology is essential to understand who we are. Technological entities are (p)art of our planet;[65] they come from, and will mostly[66] rest (in peace) in the Earth: their material cycles are planetary and cosmic biorhythms.

Our response-abilities are unlimited. We can approach technology as an eco-technology – that is, technology conceived ecologically in its full cycle. To be designed to last. To be fixable in its parts and compatible with older devices (implementing regulations against technology obsolescence). To be intentional in its materials – including their geopolitical ramifications.[67] We can embrace fair-trade technology as a source of economic dignity to the workers involved in the process of technological revealing – including users, producers and environments. Technology is a planetary accomplishment, a transformation of the Earth's elements. A process where human and non-human impulses co-emerge in intra-dependent acts of existential revealing.[68] We are (p)art of the gadgets we manifest; their stories are our stories. For instance, solar panels are effective in producing energy when in use; once discarded – if not properly handled – they become an environmental hazard.[69] Sustainability is not a postponement: the future is right here, now.

How can we, as committed posthumanists, manifest post-anthropocentric eco-technologies? Technological devices are to be intentionally conceived as (p)art of specific environments,[70] designed not just for human consumption but for the benefits of non-human communities as well: one size does not fill all ... While writing this sentence, I am sitting outside, on an old wooden deck in upstate New York. It is springtime. A small spider has just crawled on the screen of my laptop, comfortably exploring it with its pedipalps – a revealing moment of multi-species connection ... In our posthuman explorations, we could potentially envision technological ways of intra-acting with insects in order to offer something valuable to their ways of being (instead of simply attracting them through the artificial light of our devices). Techno-enhancements in planetary awareness.

#Planetary Enhancement

Existential posthumanism is not just another *-ism* that simply sparks intellectual excitement without nourishing living practices. It is an invitation to fully embrace our lives as the playground to manifest, originally, posthuman ways of existing. In the 21st century, this involves the need to move out of the anthropocentric paradigm. When the goal is self-knowledge, anthropocentrism becomes an existential obstacle, to the point of possibly turning into a self-inflicted confinement: we will never realize who we are if we get lost in anthropocentric distortions and social mirages. Understanding who we are requires the letting go of any illusion of superiority: to be present, in the constant unfolding of existence. We are faced with ethical decisions on a daily basis; in making choices we can no longer rely uncritically on external principles or algorithms; rather we must depend on the ontological realization that we actually *are* what we are manifesting.

On our posthuman path of self-discovery, honoring technological innovation and multi-species coexistence turns into a creative act of self-knowledge. We are all the dynamics that we are supporting through our worlding. We are intra-acting waves in the ocean of existence, and so are technological realities. Each act of manifestation is multiple and all encompassing. Understanding the inter-being of technology is crucial on our path of self-knowledge. We are all that surrounds us. The technologies we develop show us where we are at; the technologies we envision show us where we can be. If we are unaware of who we are, our technologies will reflect that. If we are aware of who we are, original paths will open in our technological revealing. The question is: *what type of world do we want to be (p)art of?* The era of digital existentialism is also the era of cyborg embodiments. Technology is perceived as the ultimate stage of redesigning the human. Transhumanism focuses on enhancing the human condition, exploring physical possibilities such as radical life extension and digital immortality. Radical imagination is needed in intentional embodied evolutions: the power of bio-technological poiesis lies in the potential. And yet, to manifest planetary enhancement, instead of social privilege and existential obfuscation, we must be realistically aware of our planetary conditions. For instance, if radical life extension currently succeeded, it could potentially exacerbate overpopulation and ecological distress (increasing geopolitical conflicts for access to resources and global health crises).[71] When we address enhancement – not just from an anthropocentric perspective but from a planetary one – we may expand the notion of radical life extension to non-human life.

Can humans become cyborgs for reasons beyond human needs and wants? The Cyborg Foundation, founded by the artists Neil Harbisson and Moon Ribas in 2010, answers this question with a ground-breaking invitation: "From now on humans are shifting from using technology to transform the environment, to using it to transform our bodies and minds in order to develop new senses and abilities to better adapt to the world we live in. Just imagine how modern cities would be, if instead of inventing the light bulb, we had chosen to evolve our sights to night vision."[72] Modifying the human body[73] instead of the environment turns into a possible answer to the challenges of the Anthropocene. In the 21st century, human enhancement may be expressed in adaptation to a planet that has drastically changed. Being cyborg manifests in transcending the human condition in harmony with the cosmic flow. We are becomings: porous and permeable. Our evolution, as a species, has historically been technologically driven; in this sense, we have always been cyborgs.[74] Technology is never just something we use: it is a mode of revealing. Once we reach this level of awakening, we are at peace even with the hypothesis that we may be (p)art of a computer simulation – or a super-intelligent stimulation.

#Simulation Hypothesis

The simulation hypothesis[75] is a modern remake of the God hypothesis, with a dynamic twist and a digital flavor. The world was not made in seven days of creation (as stated, for instance, in the Bible); it has been programmed and is constantly being updated. According to this existential hypothesis, we may be living in a simulated reality, where the speed of light represents the limits to how fast we can travel in space – and, consequently, to what we can discover. This advantage would give our hypothetical creators the chance to generate, in advance, what we may be searching for in the universe. This hypothesis can be compared to the movie *The Truman Show* (1989), where the main character is, unknowingly, the star of a live TV show from the day he was born until he becomes aware that his life is a play, and thus is able to end the game, reaching self-realization.

The possible reality of the simulation hypothesis does not bring us further on our path towards existential awareness. Even if we were some type of avatar living in a simulated world created by super-intelligent beings, our search for self-enquiry would eventually result in full awakening. Everyone and everything in existence (including "created" creatures) can eventually reach self-realization: there is no ultimate separation between "us" and "them," "self" and "other." This applies to both sides. In Buddhist ontologies, for instance, gods and goddesses may exist but are not necessarily enlightened;[76]

similarly, our creators would not be all-knowing, just by being creators. Most likely, they themselves would have been created as well. *In this infinite play of creation, who would have created the original creators?* The ultimate source relies on self-creation. Arguably, creation is, by definition, self-creation: a poietic process of existential revealing. In the dynamics of coevolution, creatures are co-creators (for instance, we come from our parents; and still we are our own unique selves). In the foundational relationality of inter-being, any absolute otherness dissolves once we become aware.

Self-awareness is the mark, and the spark, of existence. We do not have to await the advent of super-intelligent AI for technology to be aware. Technology is already aware, and so are we. The ways to partake in existential awareness are unlimited; they do not boil down to human expressions. Different types of technologies generate different outcomes. Transformative power lies in the ways humans approach technology. In tech awareness, fear cannot act as the mo(-tiva)tor[77] of technological induction: the divide self/other is never absolute. We live in an era obsessed with tales of technological salvation.[78] At the dawn of the Anthropocene, techno-enchanted narratives are detrimental to ourselves – as individuals, societies, species and beyond. By presenting technological mirages as mitigations of the current ecological crisis, they serve as socio-political palliatives to the need for real change. In sedating reality, they turn into existential obfuscations on the path towards self-realization. To know who we are, we must acknowledge reality the way it is. **Technology will not save humanity: technology is (p)art of who we are.** In existential revealing, technology exceeds the human condition. It is neither superior nor inferior. Mathematical inter-being: zeros and ones to the end of time. <I Love Technology.> An intentional technology of infinite love, vision and hope. Password: Poiesis0101. Login & Logout: Successful.

Farewell

Technological manifestations, in this dimension, result from unlimited dynamics of material expressions, nets of ecological co-emergence, expressions of cosmic phenomena. Actual and potential. To comprehend the techno-sphere as (p)art of the planet, please visit chapter 4. To delve into space technologies, go to chapter 5. To embrace onto-technologies of existence (from being to non-being), explore chapter 8. You can also find your way in the labyrinth, accessing any chapter or tag of your choice. Rest assured that, at the end of the journey, You will have a complete picture, no matter what.

Meditation 7
Socio-Cultural Agency

#Society

Who are We? In achieving self-knowledge, we must be aware of all the levels of reciprocation that our existence entails: we are individuals, we are (p)art of a society, of a species, of a planet, and so on. In this meditation, we will focus on the dynamics involved in being social. **To be "social" is a precondition of existing.** We, as individuals, are many. We come from the DNA of people born before us. We rely on other human beings to communicate and share energies; to (pro)create[1] and share love. We need oxygen[2] to survive. We rely on the technosphere – currently, without global food and water supplies, health services and infrastructures, the lives of many would be in jeopardy. Socially, we inter-are.[3] Because of the relational nature of existing (being-with, as well as being-in, among other terms),[4] real well-being can be achieved only when it is not at the expense of someone else: we are (also) the others. As in the ocean, there are no fish without water; no water without waves; no waves without wind; no wind without air; and so on. To manifest in this dimension, everything and everyone is in relational dynamics that are co-constitutive. "Society" is an important layer in understanding who we are in the 21st century. Unveiling the existential resonance of societal imprints is a necessary process along the path of posthuman awareness.

Are societies "human"? Societies are aggregates of allied components.[5] Societies do not have to be human; yet they implicitly are. Choice (entailed in allying) presumes free will, which, in anthropocentric settings, has been granted only to (some) human beings who were recognized as bearers of reason, autonomy and authority. In the history of political philosophy, for instance, this has sustained the anthropocentric and humanistic tradition of the "social contract," an implicit agreement that would confer social benefits on (some of) its human members. The social contract does not only exclude the natural world; exposing these species-specific premises, the philosopher Michel Serres (1930–2019) affirmed the need for a "natural contract" ([1990] 1995; 2006) – a philosophical and jurisdictional approach embracing the natural world as bearer of rights.[6] Based on a hierarchical notion of the human (according to which some humans are considered more human than others), the social contract excludes many human beings. If we look deeply into who we[7] have been, and currently are, as societies, we realize that the hypothetical benefits inferred by the social contract have not been granted to all human members equally. Quite the opposite: participating in society can turn out to be deadly for some, as the history of hate crimes and genocides demonstrate.

#Human Rights?

What about human rights? The Universal Declaration of Human Rights is an interesting case to explore. The development of the doctrine of human rights as a moral principle and the human rights movement occurred in the aftermath of War World II. The intent was to bring about existential dignity for humanity as a moral and socio-political answer to the atrocities that had been committed in the name of supremacist ideologies. Nevertheless, human rights were still developed within a framework of implied socio-political privileges and hierarchies. Article 1 of the declaration states: "All human beings are born free and equal in dignity and rights. They are endowed with reason and conscience and should act towards one another in a spirit of brotherhood."[8] This idealized freedom, as a precondition of human existence, may not speak to everyone: some humans are born in conditions of physical, psychological and/or economic slavery, among other forms of social disenfranchisement. Most humans are unable to act in a spirit of "brotherhood" – more than half of the human population is not male. "Reason" cannot be the discerning point: many humans have been brutalized in the name of "reason." For instance, in the intersectional histories of colonialism, racism and sexism, among others, native people, women and non-white humans were considered to lack "reason": this was why legal guardianship and foreign rule – among other dehumanizing practices – were forced upon them.

These are not merely linguistic slippages. Words create words. Subliminal messages bring about exclusion and homogenization. Within these premises, to be truly "human" relied on meeting the criteria set by a specific group of humans who had self-appointed themselves to be in charge through intertwining dynamics of domination. On these grounds, the human rights principles have been radically contested. For instance, the postmodern thinker Jacques Derrida (1930–2004) underlined their limits within the context of cultural colonization, stating: "We know that all the concepts, the axioms, and the languages of human rights are tied to national idioms. Today, the international law and the texts which rule the international institutions are Western texts, Western discourses" (Derrida and Montefiore [1992] 2001: 182).[9] The point is not to undermine human rights: the work that has been done in the name of human rights is noteworthy in its will to recognize the dignity of "all human beings, regardless of race, sex, nationality, ethnicity, language, religion, or any other status."[10] And still, instead of disregarding human diversity, let us be mindful of it. We must be aware of the risks based on these weak premises in order to manifest legal changes that are truly dignifying and not merely entitling.

Human rights cannot be the feel-good paperwork of some privileged humans: they must have real-world value. If the goal is truly humanitarian, they cannot be imposed in the name of "democracy" or "civilization." On our path of posthuman healing and self-transformation, the praxis is not dichotomic, with some people telling others what is right and wrong, but organic and wholesome, in our shared realization that individual well-being, social well-being and planetary well-being are inextricably connected. Existentially speaking, posthuman awareness manifests in the comprehension that the others are (p)art of the Self, and that we are everything that is manifesting (through, with and in) us. From a posthuman perspective, human rights are inextricably linked to other rights, such as the rights of nature.[11] The existential dignity of human and non-human others are intertwined. The recognition of human (and, possibly, posthuman) rights is a significant step; yet, if they stay at the level of legalistic struggles, they may not arise above socio-political hierarchies. In the dynamics of social power, partial alliances are tied to partial separations: allying *with* some may turn into allying *against* others. A posthuman shift in worldviews manifests social awareness in the what and the how: posthuman rights cannot emerge out of outdated dynamics of control.

What is social awareness? Like the sun, social awareness is direct, all-pervading and thoroughly resonant with the power of social dynamics; and still, on a sunny day, heavy clouds may suddenly appear, blocking the sun. Similarly, preconceived ideas can act like clouds in our daily social wanderings: each social encounter and intra-action may be affected by our clouds of preconceptions. We may get confused, fall back on old tracks and habits, and get upset about our slippage. To resent ourselves does not help; what helps is (being) understanding. Clouds play a key role in the hydrologic cycles: the rain emerging from them is necessary to life on Earth. Similarly, when we are aware, preconceptions act like great reminders of the work to be done, in ourselves and in our societies. They also remind us that social awareness is in flux and cannot simply be completed: the goal is the process of being constantly aware in the here and now. Realizing the full existential picture of inter-being can generate the power of not identifying strictly and absolutely with any specific individual, group or species.[12] Identity can work as a tool of social empowerment and existential awareness; for instance, in sexist/racist and ableist contexts, realizing the dignity of being embodied as female/black and (dis)abled, through collective practice of consciousness raising and social engagement, is fundamental. And still, if this becomes an absolute identification, it can eventually turn into an absolute separation and, ultimately, an existential obfuscation. Openness is key in bringing about social healing and, more extensively, self-awareness of reality.

#Social Pandemics

What are social pandemics? The notion of society implies that people come together for some type of social benefit; and yet social ties can turn into obstacles to healthy living. For instance, the race-related stress experienced by socially disadvantaged racial and ethnic populations living in racist areas can affect their mental health and well-being,[13] as well as society at large.[14] Another related example is the systemic use of rape, and the fear of rape, to control and dominate women's physical and psychological spaces of existence.[15] Our human social dynamics are in deep need of healing and regeneration. We can define as "social pandemics" the conditions created by widespread beliefs that harm the well-being of specific communities and, consequently, society as a whole. We will approach these communities as organs in the social body: when an organ is under attack, the health of the whole system is at risk. Likewise, when (some) human societies are dis-eased, the whole species is at risk – here, we are using the spelling with a hyphen, instead of the standardized "diseased," to underline that a dis-ease is missing "ease."[16]

Mental health awareness is relatively new. Generated from the wave of discoveries in clinical psychiatry in the 20th century,[17] it was a while before it was taken seriously and recognized as a fundamental aspect of individual well-being. In the medical field, social dis-eases are not yet addressed as actual diseases; yet, when approaching the human species as a super-organism,[18] an understanding of social dis-eases as actual diseases may greatly help in preventing physical and psychological deterioration. Systemic discriminations are actual life-threatening diseases that must be healed: they are tearing the social fabric apart, causing existential threats to people that are perceived as pertaining to specific categories, as in the case of hate crimes. Let's be clear: no category of people are fully safe in dis-eased scenarios. Everything is changing, different types of systemic discriminations are constantly arising: a group that is relatively safe today may be under attack tomorrow. Given the intra-connected nature of the species, any social dis-ease that affects some affects all in one way or another. While some groups are threatened physically, emotionally and generationally, others (for instance, the supposedly "privileged" ones) are threatened inwardly by acquired beliefs in their supposed superiority: if they rely on these obscurations, they will never know who they are on their path towards self-realization.

#Bubbles

Where do social dis-eases come from? We are all that manifest: others are not our competitors; they are (p)art of who we are. Social dis-eases stem out of absolute dichotomies and separations based on a foundational existential obscuration, according to which the self is approached hierarchically. "To be" turns into to be better than/superior/in competition with others. This existential obscuration is tied to the naturalization, and neutralization, of social discriminations as structural to the system(s) to which we relate. Systemic discriminations can be legally explicit – institutionalized through laws and policing practices – as well as pervasively, and perversely, implicit – reiterated through family habits, cultural products and education, social expectations and exploitations, and so on. Systemic discriminations must be approached not as individual issues that are "just" affecting some people but, more extensively, as actual threats to the overall health and wellbeing of the human species.

What is a systemic disease? The *Medical Encyclopedia* defines as "systemic disease" a disease that is "affecting the entire body, rather than a single organ or body part."[19] As an example of a systemic disorder, we can think of high blood pressure; as an example of systemic disease, we might refer to influenza, and also to cancer, which is considered a systemic disease with local manifestations. Cancer cells are our own body cells; not recognizing themselves as (p)art of the body, or as mortal, they continue to grow uncontrollably and spread to other parts of the body, eventually bringing the whole organism to the point of collapse. Cancer can be effectively approached as a breakdown in cooperation. An understanding of cancer as a systemic dis-ease is fundamental to avoid its repetition. If we get rid of a specific cancer (for instance, through surgery or chemotherapy), but we keep the same lifestyle intact, cancer may reappear. The widespread metaphor of the "war" against cancer implies that cancer is something separated from "us"; and yet, in a different manner from a virus,[20] cancer is not alien to our bodyminds.

What are the risks of approaching different types of discriminations as social and systemic diseases? Similarly to our social distortion of cancer, approaching social discriminations as dis-eases may offer the impression that people who are discriminating are simply "sick" and cannot do anything about it. This externalizes the issue and takes agency out of them, making discrimination sound like something unavoidable, originating somewhere else: this is quite the opposite of what we wish to convey. A systemic disease is never just external, caused by "others": it is internally appropriated and co-generated. By healing ourselves from social dis-eases, we are actually healing societies, the human species and the planet. Far from disempowering individuals, this understanding of the materiality of beliefs grants us full agency in the manifestation of social healing. This is not about finding a vaccine for the virus of hate but about eradicating dichotomic tendencies from within. Otherwise, even if we were able to heal specific types of discrimination that are currently enacted (such as sexism, racism, and so on), other forms of discrimination would soon prevail (for instance, biocentrism or technocentrism). To access society as a source of wisdom and self-knowledge, we must first acknowledge the state of things;

healing can only manifest without judging or shaming – good doctors, instead of blaming their patients, reveal the changes of habit that can bring about full recovery. Micro-politics are reflective of macro-politics, and vice versa. Paying lip service to politically correct posthuman politics without reclaiming our active role in this scenario will not bring any actual change in the world. Our social dynamics are in urgent need of healing and regeneration: we are the only ones who can do this.

Can we change the state of things? It is not only possible to change the state of things; it is actually impossible *not* to change the state of things – **everything is always changing, anyway.** The flow of existence manifests through constant changes, evolutions and diversifications. It is not hard to change, but it may be hard to be aware of how to change, and what to change. Some people believe that we cannot change things and that, if we try to manifest lifestyles that are different from those that have been normalized and supported in specific cultures and societies, we would be living in a bubble. According to this view, attempting to create a different lifestyle from those that are mainstream is not deemed realistic. This attitude is misleading and disempowering. The problem is not living in a bubble but knowing what bubble we are (p)art of. Physically speaking, we are currently living in a bubble. The cosmological approach of the post-inflation bubble – based on inflationary theory[21] and, more specifically, on eternal inflation[22] – claims the possibility of our own universe being a bubble.[23]

From a phenomenological perspective, we are also living in bubbles. Each of us experiences the "same" situations differently. Today, for instance, I was in a small family-owned shop. There was a slightly unpleasant smell, but I could perceive the caring attention displayed in the selection of items for sale, so I told the cashier: "This is a very nice shop!" At that moment, another customer entered the shop and shouted, in anger: "This place smells!" One person decided to focus on one aspect and get upset; another decided to focus on other aspects and be grateful: choices in life. What we are trying to convey is that, no matter what, we are always creating our own bubble in how we decide to perceive the world, which also reflects in the world(s) we are creating. From an existential perspective, we can only live in bubbles until we are aware. Once we realize that we are all the dynamics of existence that we are manifesting, and all the dynamics of existence that are manifested, supporting ways of existing that are not in tune with our existential awareness is no longer an option. By simply accepting the state of things in society out of habit and reiteration, we are living in bubbles created by others. Such bubbles may actually jeopardize our well-being: we will not be able to heal if we believe that we need to accept something just because it is there.

#Social Coding

What does reiteration have to do with existence? Repetition and reiteration are key mechanisms in dimensional revealing; on some level, the whole universe manifests as a form of pluralistic habit. These dimensional technologies are foundational to the bio-cultural processes of becoming human. Human behaviors and lives are based on habits; repeated actions and behaviors are like seeds planted in human consciousness.[24] In the dynamics of manifestation,[25] habits[26] can eventually become automatic.[27] When we are no longer aware of our habits, when we take them for granted and enact them mindlessly, our self-knowledge is obfuscated.[28] Out of habits and fears of the unknown, we often repeat paths that have already been traced by others. Since each of us is the original expression of themselves, automatic repetitions cannot lead to ultimate self-realization.[29] This is the time to rethink our human habits as poietic acts of possibility and regeneration in our flow of becoming as a species. Everything can change and is always changing. Nothing stays the same forever: we are waves in the ocean of existence. We are processes; we are the ones who are revealing the present moment. It is time to stop, pause and unlearn. It is time to learn from society. In order to know who we are, we must know where we are at.

What is discrimination? The etymology of the term is the Latin verb *discernere*, meaning "to note difference" and also "to divide and separate." Discrimination is the act of noting difference. To discern, per se, is not discriminatory; everything is constantly differentiating in the flow of becoming – diversification is one of the technologies of evolution. The problem arises when such differences are placed in hierarchical scales sustained by socio-culturally constructed values and self-entitlements, among other factors. In dis-eased settings, any form of discrimination becomes an opportune carrier for other forms of discrimination. Privilege cannot be deconstructed only by changing laws, social norms and education; these aspects are important, but they are not enough – we must deconstruct privilege inside of ourselves to know who we are. There is no separation between us and our societies; as second-wave feminism evocatively phrased it: "the personal is political." The ways we live, think and act constitute (p)art of the shifting material networks of our posthuman agency, which are comprehensive, multi-layered, plural and all-encompassing. Being aware of our social conditioning is key on our path of self-realization.

We often assume that we know about something, or someone, based on preconceptions. Preconceptions can be thought of as social coding in human collective programming: they become ingrained in social dynamics and normalized, turning into potential carriers of social dis-eases. Notions, concepts and ideas are like plants growing in our minds. Some can be eradicated easily; some become so strong that, with time, their roots turn into tentacles, whose power and influence exceed located tracing. We must be aware of what we are planting in our bodyminds, of what we are cultivating in our inner gardens. Preconceptions work like bait in disconnecting us from the social awareness of the present moment, nourished by the illusion that we do not need to be fully present, as we have already been informed about how that experience/person/place, etc., is supposed to be. If we are not fully in the moment, loyal to the here and now, to what we are experiencing in our lives, we often end up creating the expectations we already had in self-fulfilling prophecies. In reality, we are the only ones who can truly experience ourselves and our environments: not only are they constantly changing, but also the specific combination of our dynamics (in those situations/ locations/communities, etc.) will bring about unique outcomes. The way to know someone is to allow for the encounter to manifest: only by embracing "otherness" can we know that there is no absolute otherness.

What kind of assumptions are we taking for granted in our life? Pre-constructions are always there from beings who came before us. We are often given direct instructions and subliminal suggestions about who others are, based, for instance, on the color of their skin, gender, nationality, class, physical abilities, social position, sexual orientation, species, embodiment, and so on. Learning from indirect experience has some value, but we should never fully rely on it; otherwise, this information, instead of enriching us, will prevent us from accessing reality – which is always shifting: *that* reality is no longer *this* reality. Any apparatus offering supposedly safe pre-given answers may ultimately turn into an existential trap by obscuring the fundamental understanding that nothing stays the same. No one can fulfill someone else's self-realization: there is no shortcut to ourselves. On our path of self-discovery, we must explore our own paths. This way, we cease to be animals of *habit* and become animals of *change*, who are aware that nothing is inevitable and that everything we promulgate through our being will affect, and effect, our generative network of social, species and planetary intra-actions. Graveyards are interesting equalizers: the pacifist, the veteran, the chauvinist, the feminist, the "right" people and the "left" people are all there, resting together, close to each other, in fields of grass, concrete, plastic flowers and stones. They lived and passed; on some level, they are still here, in our social awareness: the ways in which they existed have affected us all. Now, it is our turn to manifest vision.

Is life a ritual? Different forms of discrimination are constantly, and cyclically, being (re)constituted and (re-)enacted in the social texture of being. Like cleaning our home, manifesting social awareness is a process that requires constant work. Many ancient traditions recognized the fundamental relevance of existential maintenance, converting it into a mindful moment of meaning instead of a mindless re-enactment: a life ritual.[30] The ritualistic process can break existing patterns and habits by bringing about gradual change. Ritualistic life has deep transformative power at the level of the individual, the social and the species. Rituals have had a key role in the evolution of humankind. It is now accepted that it was not only convenience and labor that brought people to live together in settled communities; for instance, in the Neolithic, before farming was invented, ritualistic life sparked social life.[31] Social dynamics are (p)art of our existential intra-acting; they unfold great potential for growth on our path towards self-realization. Social interactions can be approached as life rituals: personal, cleansing and cathartic expressions of existential awareness.

#Id-Entity

Id ontity or original identity? When we are born, we just are. Young children do not perceive themselves through categories: their bodyminds are fully open and non-judgmental.[32] Similarly, towards the end of our life, with old age, many of these categorizations are eventually released from memory. The cycle is completed: the phenomenological experience of the very old person reopens the doors of possibility, as in the very young child. Young children have a different perception of death from adults. I recently witnessed the passing of the grandmother of a four-year-old. While the parents were crying, the child was serene. It was like the child knew that death, in the final sense of absolute ending, does not subsist. It was as if the child was aware that this is a temporary performance which is constantly changing and, thus, cannot be tragic. We cannot fool existence: we *are* existence. When we become (p)art of this world, we do not have ways to describe ourselves: in a sense, we are everything. The Indian philosopher Sri Aurobindo (1872–1950) defined as "original identity"

(1963: 85) the quality of being identical with the complete picture: this take is in harmony with the etymology of the term "identity" itself, which comes from Latin *idem*, meaning "the same."[33] This original identity is post- and pre-human: it precedes and exceeds the notion of the human. This open form is essentially different from the enforced identification which develops through social, biological and technological conditioning. We will refer to this other closed form as "id-entity,"[34] playing with the words *id*[35] (Latin for "it") and entity – that is, being reduced to an externalized "it" in trying to fit preconceived categorizations. This social id-entity refers to the process of how we learn to be who we are expected to be.

We learn who we are supposed to be at a very young age, through the comments of family and friends and from tales and stories; in our walks and adventures; through books, movies and songs; in (in)formal education; in our physical and digital intra-actions. In the ways they are relating to us, everywhere and everyone is teaching us who we are expected to be. As a symbolic start of this categorizing, we are given a name (a sound chosen by others, full of resonances). Eventually, we learn to describe ourselves through concepts that were already here before our coming into the world. Think, for instance, how frequently we are asked to define ourselves through specific categories – such as gender, race, ethnicity, physical characteristics, age, and so on. In applying for a passport, if we selected the entirety of options listed in the form (all the genders, races, ethnicities, and so on), our request would be rejected: it is implied that we must be able to choose which fields describe "us" in this partial and culture-specific version of who we are supposed to be. It is implied that we should be at ease with such a limited representation.

When we accept those preconceived categories uncritically, as if they were somehow neutrally and scientifically describing who we are, without realizing that they are historical products of a particular society, we are lost in social illusions. Such classifications may become so entrenched in building id-entity that people can kill and die in their names, as in the case of nationalistic pride and ethnocentric arrogance.

This does not mean that we have necessarily to reject them. These categories can be embraced cautiously and creatively; being (p)art of the social game, it is our response-ability to transform them suitably. For instance, the recent addition of "X" to the dualistic gender choices "M" for male and "F" for female, supported by many institutions globally, is a good example of a bio-cultural evolution reflected in the reshaping of pronouns. Instead of the categories telling us who we are (as "females," "Asians," "humans," and so on), we are the ones energizing, deconstructing, validating and/or invalidating them through our existential performing in our changing world.

#Knowledge-Production

Knowledge is one of the pillars of dimensional revealing: in being, we know. Self-knowledge is an open flow of awareness[36] that is constant in our lives (even the emergence of biological death is a process of knowledge: the only way to know death is by dying).[37] Ultimate self-realization relies on the all-pervading awareness that we are the whole dimensional manifestation, and beyond.[38] And yet knowledge does not necessarily signify self-knowledge. There are different types of knowledges. *What is social knowledge?* Social knowledge is what is valued as "knowledge" in specific contexts and spacetimes; often partial and limited, it is useful in order to successfully navigate social dynamics and constituencies. Even though social knowledges are created and repeated for purposes that may not directly align with self-knowledge, acknowledging and understanding them is fundamental in achieving social awareness – meaning being aware of the social contexts of which we are (p)art. Social knowledges are constitutive of the social fabric, affecting and effecting the people who have direct, or indirect, access to them as sites of encounters and intra-changes. Their constitutions and establishments are constantly shifting. To be poietic agents of social awareness, we cannot simply accept them as given; we must partake in their manifestations. In this agential way, social knowledges can turn into creative processes of collective envisioning, connecting different generations, experiences and perspectives.

What is knowledge-production? Social knowledge is a flow that is constantly generated in each interaction, reaffirmed and replenished through social dynamics. Knowledge-production refers to the modes through which social knowledges are created and disseminated in formal and informal ways. Each society manifests their knowledge-production in unique ways.[39] Informal contexts, such as families, are key in the process of knowledge-production: creating, processing, reiterating, resisting and/or transforming social knowledges. Formal instruction – such as institutionalized education, scientific and academic research activities, and so on – constitutes the basis for laws, civic norms and social prestige. Formal and informal exposure are co-constitutive in the process of knowledge-production; although some values may be supported only in specific ecologies of formation, most are reiterated in both realms. The process of knowledge-production is neither abstract nor neutral; it is embodied, contextual, and necessarily reflects the biases of each era. Knowledge-production is one of the technologies through which socio-political hierarchies are created and maintained. Thus, it is not surprising that figures who have been relevant in the formal processes of knowledge-production have also been holding discriminatory views.

For example, the Greek philosopher Aristotle was one of the founding figures of scientific and philosophical investigation; his work presented as factual many derogative and biased views that were accepted at the time, such as slavery as a natural condition, women as inferior, and non-Greeks as barbarians. These prejudices, posed as scientific facts, were key in perpetuating sexist, racist and elitist approaches throughout different ages. The point is not to blame single authors for historical dis-eases that have been spread from civilization to civilization but to show that knowledge cannot be taken for granted; it must be necessarily and constantly reaccessed within the revealing of each era. The political philosopher Karl Marx (1818–1883) phrased it clearly: "philosophers have only *interpreted* the world in various ways; the point, however, is to *change* it" (Marx 1888; emphasis in original). Everything is constantly changing, no matter what: the effort to maintain the status quo is often greater than the effort to change it. Scholars must be aware of their social legacies: society trusts them to produce scientific knowledge in order to advance not only general welfare but also a fair system of regulations and ethics. In doing this, scholars must dare to challenge social and intellectual trajectories that are perceived as "normal"; yet this is not always the case.

A clear example is racial justice. Systemic racism has been historically reiterated through systems of knowledge-production: the narrative of race inferiority has sustained socio-political inequities and dehumanizing practices.[40] Existing offers a great opportunity: to be agents of change. It is time to ask ourselves, in full existential awareness: *What kind of assumptions are we taking for granted in our lives? Are we conscious of (macro- and micro-) dynamics of racial oppression?* Our role is crucial: everything we do affects and effects the generative network of social and species intra-actions. The time is now. We can do this together, because we are in this together. Racism is a social dis-ease that is undermining the existential dignity, safety and lives of black[41] people and also the wellbeing of the human species as a whole. As Martin Luther King Jr (1929–1968) evocatively wrote in 1963, when in jail because of protesting racial discrimination in Birmingham, Alabama: "Injustice anywhere is a threat to justice everywhere. We are caught in an inescapable network of mutuality, tied in a single garment of destiny. Whatever affects one directly, affects all indirectly." Nothing is inevitable. Being mindful of race[42] is a practice of existential awareness which manifests in our daily existence: in our interactions and behaviors, in the cultural products we choose and disseminate, in the movies we watch, in the linguistic expressions we embrace, in our fantasies and dreams, among many other factors. We can heal our bodyminds, societies and species from different forms of racisms,[43] because we are co-creators in the social fabric. Social poiesis[44] refers to the ontological art of being social, as (p)art of the collective performance. Each of us is a vital dynamic in actualizing social constitutions and maintenance. In order to know who we are, we must be aware of our key role in the enactment of the social game: we are (in)forming society.

#War Culture

I recall having some friends over for a long weekend. They had two sons: Cyrus,[45] who was six at the time, and Darius, who had just turned three. These children were full of love and curiosity. Yet fighting had already been implanted at the core of their imagination. Instead of asking: "Who wants to *play* with me?," they would ask: "Who wants to *fight* with me?" The next game would be: "Let's pretend to fight!" *Star Wars* was the only book in their luggage: before going to sleep, they would dream about cosmic wars in high-tech scenarios which were all too human. Within these settings, a magic cauldron toy would suddenly turn into a deadly weapon: "It's a bomb!" I thus asked, curiously: "What is a bomb?" With urgency and excitement, Cyrus answered: "Something that explodes and destroys everything!" I replied: "There is something that cannot be destroyed." He asked: "What is it?" I said: "Spacetime can only be transformed. And guess what? We are spacetime . . ." He thought about it: all of the sudden, toy weapons no longer represented the shortcut to total power and instant gratification. It was time for a change. We all took a walk in the forest. The outdoors brought a shift from fighting scenarios. Walking with his mom across a stream, Cyrus exclaimed, ecstatically: "I have never been in a forest: is this, *really*, a forest?" Having grown up in the city, he found birds, insects and plants were his new source of exploration and delight. Redirecting his imagination from wars to wonder did not take long at all: it was simply based on what he was presented with. Darius and Cyrus are extraordinary kids. The question is: *Are we, as a society, fair to them?* More specifically: *How can war be presented to children as a fun game? How can we, as a society, accept that toy guns and weapons are given to very young kids (usually males) without our being disturbed by this symbolic action? Would we give them fake bottles of whisky or fake drug toys for (pretend) playing? How can we sustain a culture of war and violence and then be surprised by the violence that surrounds us?*

My friend was shaken. The day after the deadly massacre at an elementary school in Uvalde, Texas, on May 24, 2022 – when an 18-year-old boy shot 19 students and two teachers and wounded 17 other people – a kindergarten child, on the school bus, looked directly in her child's eyes; acting as if he had a gun in his hands, he pretended shooting, with a frozen stare on his face. At such a young age, he had already normalized the act of murdering. To avoid tragedies such as mass shootings, gun regulation laws must be urgently implemented. But that is not enough. The culture of war has to be transformed so that, under normal circumstances, no child would even consider playing the game of killing others. Guns in the United States hit the double standard: it is OK to echo cultures of violence; it is shocking when these scenarios manifest in reality. Currently, the seeds of violence are already sown in the ways we are raising our children. We must be aware of what we are manifesting and stop normalizing social dis-eases. We must be responsible and response-able: the ways we are (in)form everything around us. As the Zen master Thich Nhat Hanh put it: "The daily wars that occur within our thoughts and within our families have everything to do with the wars fought between peoples and nations throughout the world" (2004: 11). Seeds of violence are never too far away; their presence can be acknowledged creatively. Seeds can grow in different ways, depending on the environments, the lands, the inputs, the nutrients, and so on. Seeds of violence can be approached as precious actants in sparking and sustaining a daily ritual of checks and balances. The martial arts, for instance, embrace them in discipline, (in)forming a practice of self-cultivation, which promotes self-defense in order to reach final enlightenment. Enlightening the seeds of violence is a process that requires maintenance, like keeping a fire going.

#No War

Ida, my paternal grandmother, had a wood-burning stove in her kitchen, which would provide heating, shelter and a smell of sweet tones of orange. She would place the peel of the tangerines we had just eaten on the hot steel and wait for the heat to release their secret fragrances. Her ancient shamanic energy was part of her wisdom, intensity, integrity. Ida had lived through two world wars. I remember one day when I was at her place in Vado Ligure, on the Mediterranean coast of Italy. We were sitting at the table, her culinary altar of wood and marble, where she would shape home-made pasta to perfection. We were having dinner: her food was always sublime. The news was playing on her old TV set. The US was invading Iraq. She stopped eating and looked at me. Her eyes were deadly serious. She said: "If You lived through a war, You will never support any war." Silence. There had to be other ways. Full stop. Simple like that: war had to end. Ida loved America. She would often tell me: "Never forget that we are alive thanks to the Americans." She was going to be forever grateful to the Americans who had brought food and hope after the war, when Italians were starving, in post-war trauma and destruction. Her deep and sincere appreciation would not obfuscate her awareness. Her loyalty was to existential dignity. She would state, beyond any politics: "Americans must stop the war in Iraq." That was it, no doubt. For Ida, who had experienced war, war was no longer an option: never again. Ida was right. For long periods of human existence, war had not been an option.

Is war "natural"? In his book *The End of War*, the science journalist John Horgan underlines that war is not "natural." As he explains: "Evidence of lethal group violence dates back not to the emergence of the *Homo genus* millions of years ago, nor to the emergence of our species hundreds of thousands of years ago, but to less than thirteen thousand years ago, shortly before the dawn of civilization" (2012: 10). In general, the Paleolithic and Neolithic times were peaceful periods in human interactions; Neolithic excavations around the world indicate, more generally, an egalitarian society with no strict social hierarchies. The practice of organized warfare and armed conflict emerged, more clearly, during the Bronze Age, approximately from 3300 BCE to 1200 BCE, with the rise of states and kingdoms, connected to borders and access to resources, in some parts of the world. War is quite a recent invention in human history.[46] The repetition of the stereotype of war as innate to human behavior is not healthy: war kills. It should be addressed as a social dis-ease, to be healed and transformed collectively. Instead, it has been normalized and generalized. In presenting war as "natural," in teaching history as a list of wars, in neutralizing and naturalizing war, scholastic education, cultural products and information technologies turn into major vectors of social dis-easing, reiterating the seeds of war, consistently and effectively, generation after generation.

#Schooling or Unschooling?

Is schooling conducive to self-knowledge? The Oxford Dictionary describes "education"[47] as "the process of receiving or giving systematic instruction, especially at a school or university," and also as "an enlightening experience."[48] The first definition refers to schooling, in the formal process of knowledge-formation. The second is related to self-directed learning, self-cultivation and, overall, self-knowledge. The two meanings must be approached in combination: the overall goal of the educational process is, ultimately, self-knowledge, aimed at knowing who we are. This resonates with the etymology of the term "school," which comes from ancient Greek *skholē* (σχολή), meaning "leisure,"[49] conceived as the free time dedicated to self-discovery and wisdom. This notion translated in the Roman world as *otium*, which, additionally, came to refer to the period when someone retired from public life, dedicating time to inner knowledge.[50] In ancient times, throughout different cultures and civilizations, self-enquiry was considered the highest goal in life. Within these settings, *skholē* could only be achieved dynamically, in open dialogues and praxes – not abstractly and passively through dogmatic teachings.

What are the risks related to schooling? Eventually, schools became the places where social knowledge would be officially taught and disseminated. In these historical evolutions, self-knowledge was no longer the main goal: schooling became key in instructing youth on how to partake in a specific society (thus, teaching fixed sets of norms and values). If not approached openly, generatively and critically, these terms of formal education run the risk of turning into subtle and powerful tools of socio-cultural indoctrination. An example is the way history is still taught in some curricula: the perpetuation of war culture and colonialist assumptions is to be greatly revised; indigenous contributions to world developments are to be fully integrated instead of relegated to some celebratory day and/or month; "prehistory" can no longer be erased from the curriculum: the matrifocal character of Paleolithic and Neolithic findings are still unknown to many.[51] Partial teachings do not expand our self-knowledge but can actually work as existential obscurations, undermining the original meaning of *skholē*. Although educational programs may not be perceived as political, they are actively serving as cultural means for perpetuating and/or disrupting socio-political hierarchies.

In their symbolic and material configurations, modern systems of education are still affected by the values of the past. Compulsory public education, as a policy, developed gradually in different parts of the world, from the early 16th century to the 20th century; earlier, formal education was not universal but reserved to the *elite*.[52] The Industrial Revolution had a significant impact on its developments. Virtues such as obedience, punctuality and resilience (key in running machines successfully) were cultivated through a system in which the one-size-fits-all rule generally applied. In our age, the needs are different. Currently, with the rise of technological unemployment, the jobs that are less at risk of being taken by machines are the ones that cannot be automated: more specifically, jobs requiring creativity and originality.[53] Schooling is about to become more flexible and diverse, not only in its contents but also in the methods employed: one size does not fit all. In order to know who we are, as individuals, as a society and as a species, human diversity is to be fully embraced. An integral approach to education must also take into consideration the environments and infrastructures, among other aspects: the embodiments of our educational institutions are (p)art of our collective consciousness and bodyminds. For instance, from a health perspective, indoor teaching is far from ideal; outdoor learning has social, emotional, academic and well-being benefits[54] – thus, it has to be encouraged and implemented.

Unschooling? These criticisms do not erase the important work that has been done through the scholastic system, which evolved to provide students with personalized support and guidance. Yet, given the macro-institutionalization of education, changes have been slow; often, the result is that schooling reflects outdated views of the human. Because of this, some are advocating against the current education system, which promotes conformity rather than uniqueness. Unschooling – as an actual, and alternative, way of learning – relies on dynamics of inner curiosity, leading to self-directed educational experiences. This is encouraged by providing the proper conditions for people to actively and independently educate themselves: the world becomes the university of life.[55] On our path towards self-realization, we do not need to choose between schooling or unschooling. Knowledge is everywhere; its metamorphosis into wisdom depends on the intention and maturity of the seekers. Self-knowledge is an original process; no one can teach us who we are – (human and non-human) masters can only inspire us to find ourselves. Posthuman education is an integral approach conducive to self-realization – as individuals, societies, species and, more extensively, existing being(s).

#Posthuman Education

What is posthuman education? Posthuman education embraces the need to regenerate the field of education according to who we are in the 21st century. In the age of knowledge economy (when knowledge, simplified as information, has turned into supposedly neutral data),[56] in the era of the Anthropocene (when letting go of anthropocentric views and habits is a *conditio sine-qua-non* of human survival),[57] radical changes in education are necessary in manifesting self-knowledge. Social knowledges are here to help us navigate existence. They can be useful, and we should be grateful to the people who traced them before us; they can also become outdated burdens and, finally, real obstacles in understanding ourselves. It is up to us to take the time to discern which elements we can keep and nourish and which ones are (about) to be pruned off – in what, and how, we are taught; in what, and how, we are teaching – realizing what is recyclable and what is not (and, thus, it is to be radically transformed). There should be no frustration in this task, or judgment, but serene awareness; everything is constantly changing: social and individual values as well. A posthuman education is an education that is loyal to who we are in the 21st century, aware of the poietic power of existing. A posthuman education takes everything into consideration: who, what, where, when, how and why we are teaching and learning.

How to develop posthuman pedagogical programs?[58] Posthuman educators are creative, exploring different methodologies based on the understanding that the "what" is the "how."[59] Posthuman education does not rely on the body/mind split. The environment is approached as a site of knowledge and wisdom, and so are the dynamics at play in educational settings. Everything is teaching; from everything, we are learning. Specific attention is paid to the materials employed and the locations; in being mindful of other-than-human beings and elements; in the (physical and digital) movements, wording, activities and relations formed through, and in, educational experiences. Careful consideration is given to balancing intellectual teaching with other forms of learning; offering manual and life skills curricula, together with scientific and technological expertise; presenting global knowledges through local projects. For instance, we can teach about planet Earth, not indirectly, as a place "we" inhabit, but directly: the land as (p)art of our own embodiments (from Big History to direct research on regional plants and rock outcrops through hands-on experiences).[60] Intellectual insights must follow action. Posthuman educating can unfold in planting native seeds and caring for them throughout the life cycle of a plant; in developing breakthrough technologies that are aware of their ecological intra-acting and that could be recycled organically; in engaging entire families and communities in recurring festivals of learning and sharing. By integrating the daily life of the participants in the (un)schooling[61] experience, posthuman educators can offer programs that are not based on the one-size-fits-all delusion, respecting the actual needs and visions of individuals and communities.

How to learn, how to teach? Posthuman education is based on the recognition that human and non-human diversities cannot be reduced to politically correct etiquettes; instead, they are fully embraced existentially: "they" are who, and what, "we" are. Posthuman pedagogical approaches do not come in absolute terms, as final remedies to a distressed species; they generate pluralistically, in local realities, revealing multi-species coexistence, global dignity and self-awareness once the self is embraced as the others within. Posthuman education is an open process and a praxis. Teachers are (also) learning; students are (also) teaching. The attitudes of the students and of the teachers are of key importance. According to the social reformer Rudolf Steiner (1861–1925),[62] the sense of reverence and devotion towards existence is so fundamental that no knowledge can be achieved without it. Steiner was skeptical of education based on criticism, as he stated: "Our civilization is more inclined to criticize, judge, and condemn than to feel devotion and selfless veneration" ([1904] 1994: 18). Posthuman education advocates for awe towards the poietic art of existence, respect for the ability to see what does not work, and the confidence in manifesting change. In this organic process of mystical and critical response-ability, any alleged privilege or superiority (based, for instance, on species, gender, race, ethnicity, age, class, caste, and so on) is unmasked as an existential obfuscation, a major obstacle on the path of self-revealing. Posthuman education turns into an existential technology of manifestation, to be poietically re-envisioned, in tune with our changing world.

#Posthumanist Curricula

How to envision and manifest posthumanist curricula? To fully understand who we are, we must be able to detect the biases that inform our epistemological systems: only existential honesty can bring along existential awareness. Social knowledge is power, creates power and sustains power; educational training is key in reiterating specific values that reinforce specific systems of power. In the following sections, we will focus, more specifically, on humanist shortcomings, based on a hierarchical approach to the human, which allows for different forms of (implicit and/or explicit) discriminations. Let's reflect, for instance, on contents and methods currently integrated in institutional education. Most programs are based on the mind/body divide: often, education is not perceived in embodied terms and relies on dichotomous ways of teaching, where students may be sitting for long hours in front of digital devices, jeopardizing their physical and mental health. In these limiting settings, curricula that are limited by anthropocentric, sexist, racist and/or ethnocentric canons are still widely taught; the limits applied to the "body" reflect in the limits applied to the mind: they cannot be separated.

For instance, even though gender and race equity are currently recognized as priorities, many instructional modules still rely on "white male" heroes, such as (white male) presidents, kings, philosophers, scientists, artists, and so on, accompanied by a handful of non-white non-male individuals, whose exotic presence is assumed to validate the supposed universality and neutrality of the canon. This way, we are reiterating a specific system of power, where social dis-eases such as racism and sexism, among others, are neutralized and normalized in the economies of social values. The more we exhibit sexist, racist and speciesist symptoms, the deeper these dis-eases will spread in the human species. Discrimination affects the people who are facing it as well as the people who are engaging with it: both will be traumatized in different ways – the inferiority/superiority complexes feed on each other and can only surface in conjunction. The word "trauma" comes from ancient Greek (τραῦμα), meaning "wound." Discriminatory curricula leave deep wounds in the social tissue of society; these epistemological wounds are not easy to heal, because they often go unnoticed.

Is this erasing culture? Change is easy, as everything is constantly changing. Repetitions of socially dis-eased patterns can end right now. Yet, as the womanist and feminist poet Audre Lorde (1934–1992) vividly warned: "For the master's tools will never dismantle the master's house" (1984: 110). Formulating post-humanist, post-anthropocentric and post-dichotomous educational frames around thinkers who shared discriminatory views would be detrimental, since their world-views are inevitably embedded in their philosophies. This does not mean that we can just get rid of the history of formal education, given that many leading figures held sexist, racist and/or anthropocentric beliefs, among other discriminatory traits. Since their teachings eventually became foundational to these systems, we can rest assured that embracing different genealogies and references, in posthumanist curricula, will not overshadow them but will bring new light, insights and understandings. The point is not to avenge the voices of all the people who have been silenced in the historical processes of humanizing[63] but to access history in critical, equanimous and regenerative ways in order to reach full existential awareness.

#Inanna / Enheduanna

Let's offer specific examples based on a gender-aware analysis of contents and methods. For instance, in the current education system, the Epic of Gilgamesh (c. 2100 BCE) is routinely presented as the oldest mythology. The underlying message, for the first hero being male, is that societies must have always been male-centered. This historiographical error is not that innocent. Currently, the first known written mythology is the *Descents of Inanna* from ancient Sumer[64] – a Sumerian version dating to the Third Dynasty of Ur (c. 2112 BCE – 2004 BCE) has survived. It features a female hero, the Goddess of Heaven and Earth Inanna, who, by descending to the Underworld, fulfills the canon of the trinitarian Goddess.[65] Similarly, in the history of writing, the first known named author was Enheduanna, who lived around the 23rd century BCE; she was the high priestess of the moon deity Nanna (God of Moon and Wisdom) in the Sumerian city-state of Ur. We rarely hear of Inanna or Enheduanna, because their powerful presence does not fit the current male-centered paradigm. If we look at the big clock of time, the symbolic shift from matrifocal to patriarchal is relatively recent.[66] This passage was neither linear nor absolute; it was gradual and not entirely successful, to the point that some societies never became patriarchal – think, for instance, of the Mosuo, an ethnic group present in the Yunnan and Sichuan provinces of present-day China, among others. And yet patriarchy is still presented as a given in formal education.

These examples are not offered as acts of epistemological charity, sustained on dynamics of politically correctness: nothing like that. This is a call to existential awareness in order to understand who we are. Social mirages can only distance us from ourselves. Teaching curricula that erase, or essentialize, specific categories of people is not education: it is, more clearly, an existential obfuscation. No history of hierarchical power remains intact forever. Eventually, these epistemological attempts can only fail, because we can never fully forget who we truly are. There is no absolute otherness: existing entails relationality and mutuality. Anyone labelled as "inferior" for any possible reason (from their embodiments to their being associated to specific categories) is still conscious and aware:[67] self-knowledge cannot be extinguished; it can only be temporarily and superficially obscured. Institutionalized systems of power reiterations do not exist per se: they must be performed and actualized. We are (p)art of them. Consequently, we can deconstruct them inside of us: right here, right now. This resilience enables posthuman education to be open to new challenges, including the capability to detect humanist, anthropocentric and dualistic biases without getting lost in the unproductive and repetitive cycle of anger, despair and revenge. Such a shift is an existential gift, bearing fruits at the social, planetary and ontological level. Posthuman onto-epistemology starts within the self. The focus is not on closed systems but in open relations. The approach is not abstract, or just theoretical, but experiential and experimental, situated and embodied. The goal is self-awareness. Posthuman educational approaches can be embraced in both formal and informal settings.

#Posthuman Parenthood

I do not care for my children to be this or that. If I can wish for something, I want Them to Know Who They Are; to Be Able to (Just) Be. Parental choices have large resonances, not only in the ways children are socialized but also in the types of education to which they are exposed. Great visionaries are urgently needed in manifesting new stories: our species is already there, but our cultural products are well behind. The lack of mainstream narratives appropriate to the 21st century is striking. As a posthuman mother of a young child, I have realized very quickly that children's tales are based on outdated visions of the human. Almost the entirety of them are still written in anthropocentric and speciesist tones; the majority are inherently racist and sexist by having to showcase a (white) male hero, for lack of understanding that the world has changed: such a symbolic fetish is no longer needed to reach editorial success. Quite the opposite: the need to be aware of human diversity has now been widely recognized as an essential component of individual and social well-being. In light of all of this, an uncritical perpetuation and reiteration of characters, far from being neutral, can be approached more clearly as a social macro-aggression (in its biased representation of symbolic systems of power); as a symptom, and cause, of widespread social dis-eases (such as sexism and racism); more generally, as an existential obfuscation, which is damaging us all – as a species and a planet.

It is surprising how much cultural baggage (and garbage) is already inserted in seemingly innocent children's literature and media. The examples of culturally outdated content and anthropocentric appropriations are innumerable. For instance, the large majority of mainstream children's books about animals, far from teaching about non-human animals, present anthropomorphic tales, in which the supposed animal is invariably a "he"[68] who, in the ways they dress, think and behave, inevitably reveal themselves as the prototype of the anthropocentric hetero-normative human male disguised as a non-human animal. In this symbolic masquerade, the exceptions confirming the rule are pink bows; apparently, within these bigoted settings, female characters must be represented wearing pink or purple in order to be recognized as something other than the universalized male norm.

How can colors be other-than-colors? Through social premises and cultural infrastructures, colors can become carriers of symbolic meanings, as the colors of national flags clearly show. A young child who is given specific toys and colors will become familiar with those and recognize them as part of their id-entity. This happens very early. When my daughter was two, they[69] liked all the colors; when people asked them what color they liked, they simply could not answer: all colors were beautiful. When they were three, they liked all colors; when people asked them what color they liked, they would give different answers: sometimes they would say "red," other times "blue," other times "gold." By age four, after receiving a large amount of pink gifts, hand-me-down clothes and toys from friends and acquaintances,⁷⁰ they started to perceive the gendered expectation and pressure of having to like pink; thus, they began to reply "pink and purple." Often, when they said that, people reinforced this stereotype with great energy: "Of course you like pink," or "I was sure that pink was your favorite color!" At this young age, such a choice can be seen as "neutral"; at the end of the day, all colors are beautiful. The problem is social encoding, later on . . .

#Pink Trap

Why is the pink/blue divide not that innocent? Teaching gender studies at university, I recall this enlightening realization that Mona,⁷¹ a student of mine, shared in class, while reflecting about growing up as a young African-American woman in New York City: "I played with dolls and dressed in pink. I did not care about this until high school when, all of the sudden, dressing in pink meant to be weak; to be a girl meant to be less. I immediately stopped wearing pink and tried to camouflage in this new environment." In Mona's account, the "normal" suddenly revealed the other face. Through a seemingly innocent color dichotomy (blue/pink), the dis-ease of sexism had subtly entered. In contemporary patriarchal societies, pink is not just a color: it can turn into a symbol of inferiority. My student started questioning why she had been put in such an unfair situation. She felt she had been deceived not only systemically, living in a country deeply shaped by racist policies and expectations, but also intimately, being acculturated to be the minus by her own family; the ways in which she had been gendered through specific clothes, colors and toys had automatically placed her in the disadvantaged group. From then on, she reacted by refusing any item associated with the traditional gender canon, reinventing herself. Mona's intersectional experience is deeply revealing. Something that is offered to children as "neutral" – and that can remain potentially neutral in controlled environments (such as domestic settings or intentional communities) – becomes fully charged with socio-political connotations and expectations in other contexts, years later. Colors, when associated with specific hierarchies of values, can work as silent carriers of potential dis-eases (similar to the ways in which a toy gun can potentially normalize violence). This does not mean that posthuman parents should ban pink or blue items; they may just embrace all colors, deconstructing any related essentialization.

Nowadays, pink is being reappropriated by children of all genders. The pink symbolism is also being inverted in the dichotomy plus/minus and converted into a symbol of power. "Rebel girls" education is currently in fashion as a mainstream answer to systemic sexism. Yet, such power still stems out of a rebellion. Posthuman parents do not necessarily have to embrace this response. Children should not be forced into cultural disobedience in reaction to oppression. It is within our adult power, being (p)art of society, to offer everyone the conditions to feel at ease with themselves the way they are. Young girls are (p)art of existence, as everyone else; they cannot become rebels in order to be dignified: existential dignity is already within them. Let them act, not react. To be a rebel puts limits to (their) poietic creativity;[72] defensive behaviors can impede full existential awareness. The age of rebellion is (p)art of human developmental growth: teenagers learn about freedom through the process of acquiring it. And still rebellion cannot be approached as a systematic solution for young people – who are still learning about being (in) this dimension – to deal with systemic dis-eases that they cannot yet understand. Decolonizing colors, tales and toys, in free and spontaneous acts of posthuman creativity (instead of simply reversing their symbolic value), is an agential choice of care and response-ability for posthuman parents raising children in dis-eased settings.

Let's be clear. On the path towards self-realization, no one is advantaged by the gender trap. Between playing with dolls (supposedly for girls, in traditional patriarchal education) and guns (supposedly for boys), training how to nurture may be less damaging than training how to kill. This is not just pretend-playing: patriarchy, actually, kills. It is killing women, in gender-based violence and other forms of physical, psychological and systemic abuses. It is killing men, through a culture of toxic masculinity, founded on war culture and aggression – on average, men live shorter lives than women and are more prone to suicide and other diseases (in what has been defined as the gender gap in health). This is not a competition for who has it better or worse; this is a call for radical change, which is already happening: at this stage, patriarchy is killing its own symbolic relevance in the history of humankind. We are (p)art of a massive paradigm shift, healing diseased systems of social intra-actions: we are them/they are us. We are together: whatever affects one, affects all.

Why is sexism a social dis-ease? Sexism is a social disease that can eventually manifest in gender violence, gender frustration, transphobia and, more generally, existential obfuscation. Even though, in most countries, gender equity and equality are recognized at the legal level, the reinforcement of gender stereotypes is largely reiterated and uncritically accepted, starting at a very young age. For instance, in many societies, children are still categorized in two groups (female and male): from the clothes, toys and products they are offered to the ways they are socialized and raised. Recently, I was told from a colleague of mine that, already at age five, some children in her classroom acted in segregation: "boys will not play with girls; girls will not play with boys." I immediately thought of gender-neutral education in Sweden, which began in 1998, based on an amendment to Sweden's Education Act, stating that all schools must work against gender stereotyping. Gender-equal teaching has since flourished as (p)art of a democratic process, where all children are approached as deserving equal rights and opportunities. I remember watching a documentary on this. An American journalist visited a gender-neutral pre-school in Stockholm and asked a student, who appeared to the journalist to be a boy: "do you play with girls?" The five-year-old child looked very confused by the question; they did not know what to answer. Then, they simply said: "I play with everyone."

Education cannot sustain segregational policies. As the harsh history of racial segregation in the United States showed, "separate but equal" education is inherently unequal. The case *Brown* v. *Board of Education of Topeka* (Kansas) was a landmark: in 1954, the court ruled that racial segregation in public schools was unconstitutional.[73] Historically speaking, racial politics and sexual politics cannot be assimilated; yet, as a society, we can learn a great deal from history to avoid repeating paths of systemic discriminations. The lawsuit *Peltier* v. *Charter Day School* was filed in 2016 against a public charter school in Brunswick County (North Carolina), whose dress code required girls to wear skirts and prohibited them from wearing pants or shorts. In 2022, the school's sexist skirts-only dress code was deemed unconstitutional in court. In their decision, the court's panel wrote: "The negative impact of such gender stereotypes is not limited to girls. Evidence in the record shows that children who believe in such views are more likely to engage in gender-segregated play, which later can affect their communication skills and personal relationships. Most disturbingly, that evidence also shows that boys who hold stereotype-infused beliefs about gender are more likely to be the perpetrators of sexual harassment."[74] Sexism, as any other social dis-ease, can pass on, from generation to generation, in reiterated acts of seemingly neutral micro-aggressions, aligned with macro-dynamics of socio-political privileges and economic disparities. From the brutal use of rape as a weapon of terror, in wars and genocides, to the menace and fear of sexual violence turning, implicitly and explicitly, into ubiquitous and iniquitous instruments of social control (by impeding and/or obstructing women to move freely, physically and psychologically, in social spaces),[75] to the deadly silence, shame and systemic neglect surrounding domestic violence,[76] sexism, as any other social dis-ease, must be recognized in its specific seeds, symptoms and mechanisms in order for social healing to occur.

#Posthuman Agency

What is posthuman agency? Healing can manifest right now. Once we understand who we are, we realize that we are not just reiterations: we are agents. More clearly, we do not *have* agency: we *are* agency. The awareness of posthuman agency as distributed agency, in the evolving body of spacetime, becomes necessarily resonant. As the feminist movement powerfully stated in the 1970s: "the private is political." There is no absolute "otherness"; we exist in material nets, in which everything is actually connected and potentially intra-acting.[77] This bears social, ecological, technological and, more generally, ontological ramifications.[78] Often, social dis-eases are passed on, from one generation to the next, through habits, laws, narratives and, more generally, worldviews. We do not have to accept what we are given: some gifts can be kindly returned; other gifts are not gifts at all but Trojan horses. We need to dispose of what we recognize as symptoms and vectors of larger social dis-eases; we must be clear and mindful in this endeavor. Aware of the dynamics at play, we can realize the full reach of our agency in the repetitions and/or cessations of habits in our lives, perceiving ourselves as actual forces in the posthuman paradigm shift that is currently occurring.

Existential posthumanism is a reference point for those people who have realized that words by themselves are only seeding and do not necessarily flourish. Enactment requires another level of existential commitment. Agency is the capacity to act in the world. Its etymology is revealing; the term comes from Latin, being the present participle of the verb *agere*, which means "to set in motion, to do, to perform."[79] According to a posthuman perspective, doing and non-doing are not in contrast. In harmony with the teachings of the Dao, non-doing as well as silence and emptiness are considered fundamental sources of existential discipline, attainment and regeneration. Posthuman agency does not rely on the modern Western preference for (and limited configuration of) action, as reinforced in the historical separation between active life and contemplative life (in Latin: *vita activa/vita contemplativa*).[80] A posthuman worldview approaches them as integrated: active contemplating/contemplative actions. For instance, the impact of great sages living in remote areas to pursue a secluded life of meditation is recognized as potentially agential, not only in individual terms but also in social and planetary ones. In order to understand who we are and how we manifest, as a species, the power of the collective (in)forming individual realizations must be taken into account.

Epiphanies cannot always be exchanged, not only because they may have to be experienced in person, but also because not all voices have been given equal credit in the collective narrating of our species. Currently,[81] a Google search for "prophets" reveals only male names – such as Zoroaster, Moses, Christ and Muhammad, among others. Obviously, women have been prophets as well, but their names have not been recorded. Obviously, their realizations have affected the sensitive texture of spacetime, but this has been largely ignored and obscured in the last thousand years. Acknowledging them is not so much for them: being fully enlightened, human recognition would not be a reward they would go after. It is for us, to know who we are. Ignoring the contribution of people because of their embodiments[82] is a serious existential obfuscation on our path towards self-realization. Our manifestation as a species occurs through multiple rhizomes of encountering and intra-forming. In this sense, distributed agency[83] is a force of social change as well as of biological and ecological health.[84]

What games are we playing? Being social allows us to engage in different strategies and enactments. They are all games that we are (consciously and/or unconsciously) playing. We can play the sexist game, the racist game or the anthropocentric game; yet, after millennia of playing such games, we now know that any type of game based on discrimination brings pain, hate and suffering to all the players, and layers, involved. In this sense, such games turn into social dis-eases. In order to change ongoing games that no longer work, we first need to be aware of the fact that we are playing them; then, we need to understand that such games exist only when they are being played. We can change the rules of the game and also end the game altogether. We can create different games, achieving different social intra-actions, until we comprehend that the golden rule game is the only one bringing existential fulfillment: treating the others as we would like to be treated. This makes total sense once we realize that, in our full potential, we are the others. In order to allow for the space of the unlimited to be (p)art of our daily intra-actions, we must reclaim our poietic power, which is always present and cannot dissolve. We bear great response-ability; now that we are aware, we can manifest creatively. We are the brave ones who move through challenging times without losing our serenity, because we know that what we are is what it is. We are the ones who dare to be realistic, because reality no longer frightens us. We are excited about the relevance of our social role and the ontological power of originality, because we know that our envisioning is already shaping the sensitive body of spacetime. We are: posthumanly, awake.

Farewell

In this meditation, we have understood the importance of being the social changes we want to experience. Different types of human and non-human discriminations can turn into social dis-eases. Seeds of discrimination[85] are still reiterated through systems of knowledge-production, embedded in formal schooling. This is the time for envisioning and manifesting posthuman educational approaches, consciously aware of the planetary conditions of the 21st century: the where is the how is the what. To embrace outdoor learning, please move to chapter 4. To reflect, more thoroughly, on post-anthropocentric curricula, please visit chapter 2. To understand the game of existence, explore chapter 8. Our historically traumatized society is in urgent need of healing. Embracing posthuman agency in our social intra-actions is a powerful existential journey: transformative and regenerative to the ontological core.

Meditation 8
Ontological Presence

#(P)Art

To be realistic means to be aware of reality the way it is; it also means to realize that manifested reality is always changing and that it does not have to be that way. We must be loyal to ourselves, being inspired by previous generations, without limiting ourselves to preconceived visions and/or actualized manifestations. A deep transformation of individuals, societies and species can only come from a real understanding of who we are and where we are at, as individuals, societies and species. In this book, we have presented different fields of knowledge: from biology to ecology, technology and astronomy, among others. They are important in their ultimate message of inter-being; and yet they are irrelevant if they are not approached as self-knowledge. If we do not know ourselves, we cannot know the world around us, because the world around us is also who we are. This does not imply that we must know everything about everything. Anything, if embraced completely, honestly and thoroughly, can act as the existential mirror. We can explore the cosmos or a cell, the forest or a cybernetic network, a cloud, a pebble or a situation. Anchoring ourselves, we can always find ourselves: we are (p)art of everything. Part as (p)art: being part of something allows for our existential art to manifest, in post-humanist, post-anthropocentric and post-dualistic ways. Like ripples in the water: from the self to society/planet Earth/spacetime/being to the Self – and vice versa.

To know who we are, we must embrace the unlimited potential as (p)art of the self.

Why do we exist if we are, and can be, everything? In order to answer this question, we must ask related questions, such as: *Why do we gaze, in wonder, at the majesty of a sunset? Why do we travel? Why do we play music?* To enjoy, as painters find delight in painting, dancers in dancing, singers in singing. Being is raw material for existential creativity. Artists of our own life: elated, we are. In Vedanta, a branch of Hindu philosophy, the nature of reality is defined as *Sat-Chit-Ananda* (सच्चिदानन्द). In Sanskrit, *Sat* means "existence"[1] or "being": as absolute, beginning-less and, ultimately, unchanging. *Chit* refers to "consciousness"[2] – more precisely, self-knowledge: the awareness of being. *Ananda* expresses "bliss,"[3] in the sense of full satisfaction, existential accomplishment and contentment. This non-dualistic state allows for creative delight, which we can refer to as *poiesis*. Poiesis does not need a rational cause: it is not born out of practical necessities; it is unveiled in the flow of existential creativity. A dance eventually ends, a poem is forgotten, a painting gets ruined. It does not matter. The purpose of creativity is (experiencing and manifesting) creativity, in the reverberations of spacetime.

Existential creativity exceeds the human realm and is present in every aspect of our dimension. Think of the perfection and uniqueness of each snowflake and crystal formation; think of the cathartic power of the world ocean and the sublime beauty of the cosmos; think of the subtle frequencies of electromagnetic waves. The aesthetic[4] aspect of existence, of the necessary and of the real, is always present. It exceeds any limitations and cannot even be confined to what is considered moral, or ethical, from a human standpoint – in Nietzschean terms, it goes beyond good and evil.[5] The Sanskrit term *lila* (लीला), in Hindu traditions, refers to "the cosmic play," whose purpose is nothing but bliss: reality is *lila*, manifesting out of playful creativity. According to this understanding, we are the whole play (and planes) of existence: the script, the writers and co-directors, the actants, the electricians, the props, as well as the stage(s), the audiences and the backgrounds, among other aspects. We can think of the human as one of the acts we are performing in the cosmic game, in which we are also co-writing the script: **we are the artists of (our own) existence.**

Yet it happens that, in any good game, the players become lost in it, forgetful of themselves and of the fact that it is a game. And so it happens that we forget our extended nature, limiting ourselves to specific id-entities,[6] or even to the collective consciousness of the whole play, and planes, of existence – which are still a limitation on the path towards self-realization. The art of posthuman existence requires awareness beyond any dimensional revealing. Consciousness and awareness are not synonyms. As the non-dual sage Sri Nisargadatta Maharaj (1897–1981) clarifies: "Awareness is primordial; it is the original state, beginningless, endless, uncaused, unsupported, without parts, without change. Consciousness is on contact, a reflection against a surface, a state of duality. There can be no consciousness without awareness, but there can be awareness without consciousness, as in deep sleep" (1973: 15). In that awareness, we all are. The term "art" comes from Latin *ars*, meaning skilled work. The crafted artisan is aware of their technical abilities; thus, they are not enchanted by their works to the point of getting lost in them and forgetting who they are.

#Posthuman Archetypes

How are We? In the planes of manifestation, we are unique, resonant and dynamic archetypes of existence in the sensitive bodies of spacetime. We are existential acts of creativity, authentic originators of our own archetypes. We should be fully aware of our intentions, because we are manifesting them in our everyday acts – in the ways we think and communicate; in the food, water and air we intake; in the ways we interact with, in and through technologies; in the ways we exist. We are creating archetypes with our own being: right here, right now. Once we realize that we are the artists of our lives, it becomes clear that others cannot create our existential art for us. Archetypes[7] and stereotypes are not synonyms. While an archetype implies originality and creativity, a stereotype can be summarized as a repetition without variation, an oversimplification based on preconceived generalizations. When we uncritically repeat models that are presented to us in the legacies of previous generations, we are in the past; and yet existential poiesis is always in the present moment. Stereotypes can become obstacles in the flow of self-enquiry: in order to know who we are, we cannot fully depend on preset paths.

Posthuman awareness relies on the realization that we are not just the characters of our stories, or the stories, but the full archives. A constant reinvention of the self can emerge in every moment of our lives, expanding in our day-to-day intra-actions, gifting the collective consciousness with original archetypes. Such an understanding evokes the concept of the *Übermensch*, as developed by Friedrich Nietzsche in his epic novel *Thus Spoke Zarathustra*. The *Übermensch* (meaning "overhuman") is the third and last metamorphosis of the spirit: from the metaphorical camel (someone who uncritically accepts any social norm); to the rebellious lion, who is too busy in the process of liberation to be actually creating; to the child, who can only create because they are always, fully, in the present moment. "The child – according to Nietzsche – is innocence and forgetting, a new beginning, a game, a self-propelled wheel, a first movement, a sacred 'Yes'" ([1883–5] 2006: 139). The child is open to any possibility: this is why the child can create new values. In the enactment of our own cosmic game, we can change right now, revealing different ways of existing. We can play any game, but we must be aware that we are actualizing *that* specific game. We are being what we are manifesting, including what we believe in, the stories we tell, the dreams we have, and so on. This is unveiled in the conditions of our historicity, not only of the past but also of the present and of the futures: we are the results of billions of years of individual, social, species, planetary and cosmic agencies. These are not constraints. Being (p)art and whole, we are co-creators in existential awareness.

Social constructions that have been repeated through centuries may create the illusion that they have always been there; this is not accurate. There are unlimited ways of existing and manifesting in this dimension; everything is constantly changing, transforming, evolving. Power is everywhere: in each act, thought, habit and relation that we perform and engage upon. The postmodernist[8] philosopher Michel Foucault (1926–1984), expanding on Nietzsche's work, explained that power cannot be simplified in hierarchical and partial ways – that is, through macro-configurations (such as the government, the state, and so on). Foucault referred to the micro-physics of power as "a network of relations, constantly in tension, in activity, rather than a privilege that one might possess" ([1975] 1995: 26). Macro- and micro-dynamics of power are co-emergent. Given the relational and entangled nature of existence, dichotomic constructions are real obstacles in manifesting social wellness and multi-species dignity; more extensively, they are existential obfuscations on the path towards self-realization. Existential honesty is key: we must be loyal to ourselves. In the folktale *The Emperor's New Clothes*,[9] a vain and selfish emperor is encouraged to walk naked before the crowd. He is made to believe that he is wearing clothes that, supposedly, are visible only to intelligent people, while being invisible to the rest. To avoid being considered incompetent, everyone complies with the lie, until a little child whispers: "But the Emperor has nothing at all on!" A posthuman path towards self-knowledge cannot simply accept external truths; instead, it creatively expresses what we are experiencing. Outdated behaviors, visions and terminologies cannot be just repeated; they must be re-envisioned, in harmony with the 21st century.

#Consciousness Hacking

What is the art of being posthuman? The art of being posthuman refers to being fully aware of who we are. It requires ontological agency in manifesting post-humanist, post-anthropocentric and post-dualistic ways of existing. **We Are Everything: one and many, unity and plurality**. My ways are not necessarily going to be Your ways. An artist must be original and unique; otherwise, they would be considered not as an artist but as an imitator – that is, someone who is just copying or reproducing other people's works. The uniqueness and diversity of the artist's vision is at the core of the existential outcome: our life is our ultimate work of art. When we think of art, we do not think only of works of art but of the currents and movements that generated them. Often artists perceive the need to express something; while expressing it, they realize that, concurrently, many others have had kindred insights and/or perceptions: this is how movements are formed. This applies to both material and symbolic fields: from waves in the oceans to philosophical currents; from echelon flock formations to astrophysical and mathematical alignments.

Movements result out of the need to express something that is becoming obvious and, thus, is already manifesting: a co-emergence of consciousness in the play of existence. Posthumanism is a clear example of this. People from different backgrounds, countries and cultures are realizing the urgency for posthuman awareness; it is a matter of awakening, creativity and survival. Waves of consciousness work in relational terms. We are not just individuals; this is factual at all levels. In the process of dimensional revealing, the human can be seen as an actual wave, which will also eventually disappear – for instance, through biological extinction. Change is a core dynamic of existence: only through (re)generation can *poiesis* unfold.[10] Without change, there is stasis and stagnation, which results in death at the symbolic and actual levels of manifestation.[11] In the play of existence, we are being what we are becoming. On realizing this, we can consciously decide to create specific archetypes through the poietic power of our lives. This can be defined as consciousness hacking.

What is consciousness hacking? Consciousness hacking implies the understanding that consciousness can always be hacked, because its secrets are our revelations; because it has no final locks, only dynamics in intra-relations; because it is the self-reflective mirror of this dimension, its potentiality and actuality: its grand ceremony. Consciousness is a technology of existence, actualizing (in) who, what, where, when and why we are. Historically speaking, consciousness hacking is also a current trend which, in its own terms, sets out to explore how "science and technology can support psychological, emotional, and spiritual well-being."[12] As one of the participants in this movement phrases it: "we have the capacity to explore our interior minds just like we would explore a computer system, or a software system; ... we can actually change, upgrade and adjust our internal operating system."[13] The simplified reliance on the mind/computer metaphor is not casual, revealing some of the limitations that this approach still holds.

The principles of the current consciousness hacking movement do not dismiss techno-anthropocentrism, as stated in their mission: "Our community shares the vision of a technological landscape in service to humanity, not the other way around."[14] From a posthuman perspective, there is no master in charge; once we realize that the others are (p)art of the self, service is never unidirectional, nor can it be species-exclusive. This constructive criticism does not undermine the vision inherent in the consciousness hacking movement: agency in manifestation, through and beyond (biological and technological) evolutions, is conducive to self-realization. This take is significantly close to the integral yoga approach proposed by Sri Aurobindo, aimed at directing the evolution of human life into a "life divine" ([1939–40] 1990). According to Aurobindo, spiritual realization is transforming human nature – not as a disembodied ideal but as an embodied reality.[15] The source of this evolution is what Aurobindo defines as "supermind";[16] this supramental transformation leads to the unity of consciousness, reaching perfect self-knowledge.

#Mind

What is the mind?[17] Some traditions highlight the mind as the center of our being: "I think, therefore I am." Other traditions blame the mind as the ultimate traitor, the reason for social unrest and individual distress, and thus focus on silencing the mind to find release and liberation:[18] "I don't think, therefore I am." And yet the mind cannot be blamed or praised: it is neither the hero nor the villain; neither the director nor the viewer. The mind is, more clearly, a technology of manifestation; a sharp point of awareness in the cosmic game; the tip of the (melting) iceberg of individual, social, species and planetary consciousness – a dynamic of our being, among many. Certainly, it is one that it is easy to identify with because it is vocal, offering the (inner and outer) narratives to our existential experiences. The role of the narrator in each play is substantial but not absolute, being (p)art of a wider system. The role of the mind unfolds as the wrapping of the overall lived performance. The ability of the mind to rise to the symbolic surface necessarily relies on material networks of manifestation.

Where is the mind? There is no such thing as "the mind" intended as a separated and disembodied center of awareness. The mind – as a plural, embodied and constantly shifting experiential process – represents the shared stage of self-narrating in the play of existential revealing. As a metaphor in plant anatomy, we can think of the mind as the outer skin[19] on a fruit, which does not have to look like its meat or seed; it is the location of transformation of the "outside" into the "inside," permeable and porous. We are what we eat, what we breathe, where we move, how we behave. We are in and outside ourselves. We are the environments. And so is the mind, which is always embodied, related to our whole being; nourished by experience, memory and thoughts, bodily movements and discipline, flavors and smells, among other factors. The storytellings of the mind are based on our experiences in the existential exploration, as well as on pre-existing values and conditions, acquired through different modes such as education and socio-cultural belief systems, genetics and epigenetics, the microorganisms[20] and the planetary bodies[21] that we inter-are, among others.

When the self lacks awareness, the mind may uncritically rely on other people's visions and perspectives in self-narrating the living tale. This can create existential obfuscation and illusions of predetermination. By its very nature, our dimensional revealing is constantly changing; there are no pre-existing narratives we can fully rely upon: they can be of help, but, ultimately, the narration must be loyal to our dynamic co-manifestations, in the present moment. At other times, the overall community of our being identifies deeply with the mind, to the point of forgetting that the mind cannot rule, since it is, metaphorically, the tip of a mountain: the mountain being (p)art of a mountain ridge, within the crust of a planet, in the cosmos, and so on. The mind is a sharp point of embodied awareness, among others; a vital mechanism of a wider, extensive apparatus of the self. We cannot blame the mind if we get lost in the story. We must remember that we are, always, also the narrators. The narratives we choose are not neutral; they are our artist statements and concept notes, (in)forming our existential *poiesis*.

Is panpsychism the answer? In the 21st century, most mainstream cultures are noo-centric – *nous* (νοῦς) and *noos* (νόος) in ancient Greek mean, respectively, "intellect" and "mind." This type of centrism comes out of traditions giving an absolute status to the mind. This has historically resulted in "reason"[22] being regarded as the instrument of ultimate knowledge.[23] This cognitive reductionism, which is inherently anthropocentric,[24] has reached the point of denying the recognition of consciousness and subjectivity to forms of life with lesser brain capacity, as the history of speciesism demonstrates. When we think of full existential awareness, no centrism can be contemplated. We are always at the center of existence, because there is no ultimate center: the center is everywhere, depending on the perspective.[25] Within these premises, the development of what has currently been defined as panpsychism – the view according to which mentality is fundamental to all reality – is acceptable but not exhaustive. Panpsychism[26] still relies on an anthropocentric value system, according to which the human[27] is the prototype of what "psychic"[28] truly refers to. Other entities, such as rocks, are not necessarily granted mental recognition;[29] this symbolic hierarchical distinction is ultimately based on species-specific qualities and bio-centric characteristics. Animistic approaches and shamanistic practices are more comprehensive. Being considered among the oldest belief systems in humankind, dating back to Paleolithic times, they perceive any kind of entity (including rivers, rocks, and so on) as animated: energies are intra-acting, in dynamics of shared response-abilities among all beings, in multiple planes of existence, with no existential hierarchy.

#Subjects

Who is the shaman? The shaman is someone who is aware of the intra-related and intra-transformative naturecultures of interbeing. Amerindian cosmologies contemplate a *continuum* between humans, animals and spirits, not an absolute divide. Shamans are perceived as trans-specific beings who can perform in the capacity of cosmic mediators. As the anthropologist Eduardo Viveiros de Castro (b. 1951) underlines, shamans retain the capacity "to cross ontological boundaries deliberately and adopt the perspective of nonhuman subjectivities in order to administer the relations between humans and nonhumans" (2004: 468). Within these terms, the subject is not necessarily anthropocentric, although it is still human; the human does not refer to a biological given, or to a species, but to the embodied location of the subject of the perspective.[30] As Viveiros de Castro clarifies: "it is not that animals are subjects because they are humans in disguise, but rather that they are human because they are potential subjects" (1998: 477). This insight is of key relevance to posthuman onto-epistemologies: the subject does not emerge in, and through, hierarchical self-entitlements in separation from the "object." Instead, it is the foundational perception of the self in the flow of existence, beyond any absolute centrism.

Is there a "subject"? The term "subject" comes from Latin *subjectus*, as the past participle of the verb *subicere*: it refers to what is underneath – from *sub-* ("under") and *jacere* ("to lie down"). The Latin term itself is a translation of the Greek *Hypokeimenon* (ὑποκείμενον), which refers to the *substratum*. The subject can be approached as the *continuum* that is going through change and, also, as the material and essential substance. The subject is not separated from the object as preconditions of manifestation. Let's clarify this with an example. To be able to see the back of our own head, we need some type of reflective surface (unless we use radical imagination and/or intuition). In the process of knowing, to witness something that is "inner" to ourselves (in this case, the back of our head), we need something that is "outer" (for instance, a mirror). The same goes for the process of self-knowing: we cannot be the "subjects" (as a specific individual, or even as a species) in separation from the "objects" (that is, the rest of the world). Once we disrupt the internal/external dichotomy, we realize that we are fully (p)art of the manifestation, like a wave in the ocean.

In the modern uses of the term, the subject has come to refer to the (implicitly, human) mind/psyche/ego/self in an autonomous understanding of the individual, in separation from the rest. The dichotomy subject/object has been functional to the historical occurrence of social inequities and ecological devastations, in the dis-embodied and dis-eased assumption according to which the "subject" could simply use the "object," since the object was not recognized as mentally capable – or, more generally, conscious. This physical and symbolic struggle, aimed at forcing "others" to be(come) "objects" of self-declared rational "subjects," is constitutive of modern (and some pre-modern)[31] anthropocentric myths, according to which the "human" subject would emerge as the masterpiece of evolution: the only truly self-conscious being, therefore, in charge of the rest of creation. In the era of the Anthropocene, this foundational myth of our time has lost any credibility, revealing itself not only as a major cause of the current environmental crisis but, more extensively, as a deeply ingrained existential obfuscation of the 21st century. Posthumanism deconstructs the illusionary perception of the subject in separation from the object.

Numerous paths of wisdom partake in this comprehension. For instance, Ubuntu philosophy is based on the understanding of our shared humanity in the existential affirmation:

"I am, because You are" – the subject is necessarily relational.³² As another example, the Rastafari religion and philosophy express the oneness of all people; in the Iyaric³³ language, the pronominal forms "I" and "we" become "I and I," as the self-reflective mirror of unity, plurality and divinity – "I and I" refers to You and I, as well as to God in the self (the sacred within). This awareness resonates with the path of Sufism, according to which God, as all-pervading Love, is found in the inner self.³⁴ As the Sufi mystic Jalāl al-Dīn Muḥammad Rumi (1207–1273) evocatively expressed: "Knock on your inner door. No other" (1995: 255). Similarly, according to Advaita Vedanta, the *Ātman* (the Self, the limited) corresponds to *Brahman* (the absolute reality, the unlimited): no dichotomy between immanence and transcendence can be established. This leads to the understanding of the subject not only as the intentional consciousness that is going through changes but also as the substratum necessary to our dimensional revealing: being and non-being. Buddhism relies on the realization that there is no actual self; in the Pali language, *anattā* (अनत्ता) means "non-self."³⁵ Each time we try to find absolute stability, autonomy and continuity, to define who or what the "self" is, we can find none. The self cannot be defined in separation from other aspects: it is always contextual, related, mutable. Therefore, we can state that the self is all; and also that there is no self at all. Nothing is (also) everything; everything is (also) nothing. Existence and non-existence are not opposites or separated: whatever is, is no longer.

#Non-Being

What is non-existence? The term "existence" comes from Latin *exsistere*, meaning "come into being."³⁶ When we are talking about spacetime, we are referring to manifested reality. In order to manifest, we need the unmanifested. The unmanifested is also who we are. It is, always, beyond space and time. Full and empty. Pre- and post-human: unlimited potential. It is beyond consciousness: in awareness, it is. It is the precondition of existence, the undivided substratum. When addressing this universe in constant expansion, the level of non-existence is necessarily present as the source of the potential and of the manifested. As a metaphor, we can use the surface level of the ocean to address the existential manifestation of this (and other possible) dimension(s); the depths of the ocean represent the unlimited potential of non-existence, beyond changes. With intentions, reactions and visions, as possible sparks for dimensional revealing, the now becomes the enacting stage of vibrant actualizations. All elements emerge from the unlimited potential; and yet the unlimited is not necessarily potential or vibrating. It does not precede any state; it cannot be extinguished – no matter what, no matter when. We, as everything, are (p)art of it;[37] we are (also) non-being. In this sense, the Hindu saint Anandamayi Ma (1896–1982) expressed: "Before I came on this earth, . . . 'I was the same'. As a little girl, 'I was the same'. I grew into womanhood, but still 'I was the same' . . . Ever afterwards though the dance of creation changes around me in the hall of eternity, 'I shall be the same'" (2007: 3). Non-being is the condition *sine qua non* of being, and vice versa. Posthuman ontologies can be approached in terms of non-dual panentheism, embracing non-being as inherent in being.

If, out of the unlimited potential of Being, we could be anything and everything, why be human? Our humanity has to do with dimensional intentions, entanglements and attachments, among other elements. Manifesting as a human entails not only being born and dying as a human but also being entangled in the material, symbolic and reiterated dynamics of being human. Let's explain this with an example. When we find ourselves in a dream, the whole picture is poietic; the complete scene can change, shift, appear and disappear based on non-logical threads: from one moment to another, we find ourselves in completely different scenarios. When we are asleep, we can potentially dream of being anything and anyone: from experiencing life as a lotus flower, cradling in slow-moving rivers, to being a robotic enlightened entity. In our dreams, we can merge in the unlimited awareness of not-being and also partake in the conscious processes of manifestation. Most often, though, our dreams are limited to our actual experiences (i.e., we dream about someone we know or a situation we are familiar with). We often dream of being embodied in the same way in which we manifest in our day-to-day interactions; our human identity is generally so ingrained that many people dream of themselves as humans. This shows the deep entanglements of our self: our state of being wakeful not only (in)forms but can possibly limit our oneiric and potential explorations. This limit becomes particularly relevant when dreams are approached as technologies of existence: they can offer precious opportunities for self-revelation.

#Dream

In 2012, I had a dream. I woke up with these words in my mind: "You will be able to unravel time." I did not know the meaning of the term "unravel" at the time, English not being my first language. I looked it up in the dictionary; this was the definition: "to investigate and solve or explain (something complicated or puzzling)."[38] I was left without words, embracing the mystery of the message. Last night, I had another type of dream. Sunday, November 20, 2022: I dreamt that I gave a speech at Google. It was a semi-informal setting. The room was oblong, no windows. There were around 30 people standing, between 25 and 55 years old.[39] I looked them in the eye and said: "You cannot be afraid of the people You are serving. You must not keep any secret. Let them know." I looked at them again: "Let them know." I said, inside of myself: "Yes, I Am You." I left in peace. Dreams can be a space for envisioning and manifesting; they can also serve as repetitions and reiterations. Everyone is familiar with anxiety dreams, worrying about all the things we have to do; when I have that kind of dream, I wake up more tired than when I went to sleep. This may have consequences that are far-reaching, conditioning our embodied manifestations beyond our immediate awareness. Welcoming dreaming as meaningful to our existence does not devalue the importance of our wakeful state, but it alleviates the burden of duty: we are not here to do, we are here to be.

Dreams in shamanistic cultures are considered doorways to the inner world. Instead of being separated from an "authentic" reality (supposedly limited to what is experienced in wakefulness),[40] dreams are embraced as (p)art of a wider reality which, in the worldviews of Aboriginal Australians, has been loosely translated as "Dreaming."[41] Many ancient as well as contemporary world civilizations believe in rebirth and reincarnation – comparably, in chemistry, death is not contemplated: there is only transformation. Tapping into these possible existential extensions, we might suggest that the forms in which we identify (i.e., the human) may impact our existence beyond life and death (this conditioning could result in posthumous lives reincarnated, for instance, as humans). We are not going to delve further into it, as this book focuses on the realm of actual existence. And yet all aspects must be taken into consideration when addressing the question: *who am I?* Existential posthumanism contemplates a non-separation between the inner and the outer worlds, relying on an integral agency based on the awareness of being (p)art of everything.

#Spirituality

Existential posthumanism can be expanded through the realm of spirituality;[42] the two fields are not the same and do not need to intersect. Someone can be fully dedicated as an existential posthumanist without having to rely on any spiritual practice or tradition. Authentic commitment is enough to bring about posthuman awareness. Others may find spirituality arising in their existential posthuman trajectories. Different paths can lead to posthuman self-realization. While spirituality transcends the ordinary experience, existential posthumanism is a praxis that can work within the constituted categories of social and political archetypes in order to deconstruct and transform them. Existential posthumanism does not need to let go of the power of the intellect – an overcoming that is a *sine qua non* on the path of the spiritual seeker. The intellect, when properly trained, allows us to understand patterns of human behaviors as rooted in past actions and reactions, realizing that we can change them right now. In order to be(come) everything, the posthuman seeker must eventually let go of any primacy, including the primacy of the intellect. Even the positive outcomes that the intellectual training may offer will turn into obstacles if we fully, and solely, rely on them.[43] Think of critical theory. Its role is very important in decolonizing the mind; and still, if it becomes the only tool in the hand of the actant, it may lead to pessimism and absolute distrust of others. The intellect is a powerful light on the road towards enlightenment, but if we over-rely on the intellect we will never manifest self-realization. On the other hand, a superficial leap into spiritual traditions may leave the seeker wounded and confused.

Many spiritual paths have eventually adapted to historical customs and systems of oppression (such as sexism, racism, ethnocentrism, casteism, human-centrism and bio-centrism, among many others), thus undermining the original purpose of spirituality as a way of achieving an overarching awareness. This I-Am, which is limitless and all-encompassing, cannot be realized through limiting and discriminatory practices. Any sort of beliefs that are restricting our understanding, any kind of teachings that are telling us "You will never know" or "You are not enough," cannot lead to posthuman self-realization. Existential posthumanism proclaims the final deconstruction of the absolute "self/other" dichotomy: such a deconstruction is not a destruction. Posthuman awareness leads to a state which may transcend the human *in toto*, in a condition which exceeds and precedes humanhood as a historical construction. In this sense, humans have always been posthuman. The Jesuit philosopher Pierre Teilhard de Chardin (1881–1955), one of the precursors of the transhumanist movement, once wrote: "We are not human beings having a spiritual experience, but spiritual beings having a human experience."[44] Existential posthumanism is never a limit. Instead, it embraces the self as an open awareness, in harmony with different practices of existence, according to which we are already enlightened.[45]

#Self-Realization

Posthuman self-realization cannot be achieved outside of us. Once we realize that we are everything, we realize that this "we" is not individual and that it is manifesting in the choral flow of existence. *Is this compatible with religious approaches based on divine revelation?* It is a matter of hermeneutics, intentions and possibilities. Divine revelation can be taken as an outsourcing in the absolute dichotomy between the Creator and the creatures; or else the same revelation can be approached as a generative divine relationality, reflected in the dictum "honor the divine spark in all creatures," to be sustained in practices of existential dignity and multiversal empathy. From nirvana, in Buddhist traditions, to moksha, in Hindu scriptures: the ultimate liberation lies in self-realization. Henosis is the classical Greek term for the mystical union in the realization of the oneness of diversity (which is never a reduction). Theosis refers, in Eastern Orthodox Christianity, as well as in Catholicism, to the process of inner transformation that leads to a complete union with the Divine. In Islam, the indivisible oneness of God is called, in Arabic, *tawhid* (توحيد). From the balance of unity and diversity of the Dao to the harmony of the natural cycles in Goddess worship, to Yoga, the union between the body and the mind. From the Dataist revelation that God is also in technology to the animistic all-encompassing comprehension of awareness, beyond animate and inanimate. All paths can lead to posthuman realizations, as long as we do not take them rigidly.

In the creative flow of existence, everyone is different, and everyone will eventually reach self-awareness, in their own terms and original ways. We are here, accomplishing an(other) possible cycle of self-discovery. "Posthuman," in this existential sense, means being brave enough to know that the human condition is neither our destiny, nor our nature, but a spatio-temporal manifestation of unlimited material and semiotic possibilities, an embodied and situated perspective, which can eventually lead to the absolute comprehension: We Are Everything. Relations, people, intentions. Thoughts and words. Behaviors, beliefs, narratives. Archetypes. Genetics and epigenetics. Lifestyles, diets, products. Dreams, actions and re-actions. Emails and websites; posts, pictures, digital traces. Bodies, organs; past and future generations. Microorganisms. The bio-techno-spheres.[46] The planet, the sun, the galaxies; the universe(s), and so on. We are the potential and the unlimited: Being and Non-Being. We have experienced the extensions of our agency, in the sensitive texture of spacetime. We have gone beyond existence, into the unmanifested. Now we know: posthuman self-awareness is a mirror reflecting mirrors . . . We have arrived. In our journey of self-enquiry, we have realized that we are the Artists of (our) Existence.

Farewell

This book is a cycle and a spiral – like the universe, like the seasons: just like our lives. Feel free to explore any previous chapter in non-linear ways. You can also move on to our final mantra: We are, always, Home.

Conclusions
Posthuman Mantra

This book is conceived as an open-ended self-help guide to navigate our brave new world. To realize who we are in the 21st century: as individuals, societies, species, planets and beyond. To find balance in the eye of the anthropocentric and anthropocenic storm. To experience the center of the intentional labyrinth. In eight meditations, we have offered posthuman food for thought, in the comprehension that the food we eat literally impacts our thoughts:[1] habits are ethics[2] of existence. This is a journey into the art[3] of being posthuman. Asking the question "Who Am I?" in posthuman existential awareness, the field of enquiry self-expands in tune with the observable universe. Look around: traces of our multiplicity and relationality are everywhere. This is a cosmic dance; I am You, You are me: We Are Everything. In anything we do, we can manifest the art of being posthuman: when writing, reading, coding; when working, eating, dreaming; when, when, when.

Existential posthumanism, as an approach, asks big (deontological) questions that are also practical ones in the emergence of our daily routines: all are relevant in the constitution of dimensional revealing. *What about the air and water, we are? What about our desires and fears, in technological action? What is ad/diction?*[4] Posthuman ethics – as habits[5] – are of the present: the future is now. We can embrace a posthuman ethical frame in each moment of our lives. Aware of individual, social and species agency, posthuman ethics, in the 21st century, emanate multi-species devotion. Glocal[6] coexistence emerges in planetary awareness, beyond essentialist reductions.[7] The ways in which we live are not neutral; they (in)form ourselves – as a species and a planet, the whole dimensional realm and beyond. Agency is ontological.

Existential posthumanism recognizes the multiversal dynamics at play in the cosmic game of existence; it embraces spatio-temporal embodiments as (re)generative, molding original trajectories and archetypes. These intra-actions poietically manifest a diverse range of entry points and perspectives: there is no center in dimensional revealing. Born out of the need for self-enquiry, existential posthumanism honors all paths: each of them can, potentially, lead to self-realization. In the extensive resonance of actions and reactions, it is aware of the subtle obstacles that may impede existential awareness (such as social inequities). Any form of discrimination is an open door to other forms of discrimination; they are, more precisely, existential obfuscations. Self-knowledge emerges out of the realization that we are the others.

One of the gifts existential posthumanism brings to the 21st century is being loyal to it. We are no longer lost in subjective projections and ego-driven narratives; nor are we overwhelmed by digital (mis)information and objective knowledge based on dataist faith. There are no pre-constituted answers or shortcuts to existential awareness: being whole is being (p)art of the whole. In praxes of existential decluttering, we no longer rely on specific -*isms*, worldviews, id-entities[8] or external authorities. Letting go(d) – as the all-encompassing posthuman divine: not separated, but integrated – we can combine the wisdom of the cherry tree blossom with the power of socio-poietic equity in technologies of digital revealing. Bringing awareness to all the layers of existing, we can gain awareness of how people validate and/or invalidate us without veiling our self-respect. Posthuman awareness manifests in transforming species-, race-, and gender-dynamics (among others), ceasing historical cycles of ignorance and fear: our worlding – and wording – can bring about individual, social and planetary healing. The recognition of existential dignity to the manifested is integral to the path of posthuman self-discovery. From red roses and interstellar probes to praying mantises, volcanoes and advanced AI in golden wheelchairs: the center is everywhere. Flocks of birds in murmuration. Alternate reality games of transmedia storytelling and formulation. The existential dignity to be, fully, in the present moment: we know, because we are.

Posthuman awareness gives us roots – to know who we are – and wings – to know how to become – bringing perspective to society at large. In spite of climate change and the Anthropocene, some are still loyal to the humanist faith, according to which "we," as rational and enlightened[9] humans, will always find a solution, no matter the magnitude of our ignorance and arrogance. Full enlightenment manifests in self-realization; it does not rely on dichotomous delusions or existential obfuscations. The normalized tale of the wishy-washy human (anti)hero, entertaining themselves to death, in myths of unlimited resources, at the last party of the Anthropocene,[10] is no longer appealing – it is appalling. We are facing the sixth mass extinction; the issues at stake are too vital to be ignored. To cease current speciecides – including our own possible extinction – we must realize who we are. Posthuman awareness exhausts the need for existential speciesism. We, humans of the 21st century, cannot do it alone: we are (p)art of the planet.

Posthuman agency manifests in post-humanistic, post-anthropocentric and post-dualistic praxes: from individual habits to our trajectories as a species. This approach suits the present era of radical bio-technologies, big data economy and the rise of super intelligent AI. According to posthumanism, it is not only humans who are characterized by agency but the whole encompassing realm. This constitutes a unique opportunity to shift away from humanistic, anthropocentric and dichotomous self-entitlements. A paradigm shift in social imaginaries and praxes induces transformation at the individual level, and vice versa. A landmark in this integral ethical scenario lies in posthuman discipline. Modern philosophies of life are generally philosophies of action; this acceleration in (and accreditation of) productivity does not guarantee self-accomplishment. In reality, doing – and working – too much turns into an escape from the self. A time millionaire is someone who has plenty of time for self-enquiry and unexpected self-discoveries.

Existence is who we are: that's plenty. We are co-creators in the cosmic play. Those embracing self-enquiry should not be upset when others (choose to) remain ignorant of the self. Non-judgment is key to awareness; only by embracing the full picture can we transform it. Reflect. In order to maintain a plane of existence, in metaphysics, the self-realization of the entire plane is not generally sustained. Otherwise, the plane itself would dissolve into complete (un)awareness, actualizing the possibility of non-being – that is, (re)entering the state of full potential; silencing and extinguishing the multiversal bodymind(s). In the spatio-temporal domain, self-realization arises mostly in partial waves instead of absolute ones. Ultimately: *if everyone – being (p)art of the whole – is already enlightened, why are some people awake to self-awareness, while others are dormant?* In these embodied terms, ignorance can be approached as a possible survival mechanism in, and of, our plane of existence. An acquired evolutionary trail, specific to this dimension. A secret algorithm, in the coding of the cosmic play of *lila*: if everyone (self-)realizes that this is a game, <*game is over*>. One of the rules, and final attainments, in the game of existence is not to think about the game itself. The art of being posthuman in the 21st century means to comprehend ourselves as (p)art of the manifestation – not in charge of it. The human thus sheds, from ego-maniac myths of dimensional mastery, historical victimizations and foundational existential oblivions. Mystical and real. The ultimate art of being posthuman reveals itself in self-awareness: we are many and one; unity and multiplicity; being and non-being. The end, or another beginning . . .

Our posthuman mantra for the 21st century:

We Are (P)Art, and Art. Beyond the Human: We Are.

Notes

Introduction

1 In this book, the term "part" is often written as "(p)art" in order to underline that being a (p)art is also an art; being (p)art of something necessarily recognizes the following element as a form of art as well – for instance, in this case, the art of being everything.
2 We are borrowing this spelling from Donna Haraway (2016).
3 This was reported by his renowned disciple Plato (c. 429–347 BCE) in the *Apology*, a Socratic dialogue based on the self-defense Socrates shared during the trial that ended with his execution (399 BCE). Socrates accepted the death penalty lightheartedly, stating: "The difficulty, my friends, is not to avoid death, but to avoid unrighteousness" (39a).
4 The chronology is uncertain; it is dated between the sixth and, most likely, 4th century BCE.
5 The timeline is subject to speculation; the early Upanishads may be placed in the 700 to 300 BCE range.
6 It is challenging to determine the precise process by which the Torah was composed, being generated in different waves during the 1st (and possibly 2nd) millennium BCE.
7 They were drafted between the 1st and 2nd century CE. According to the Gnostic Gospels, Christ is within. As it is stated in the Gospel of Mary: "For the Child of Humanity exists within you. Follow it. Those who search for it will find it" (King 2007: 742).
8 It was written in the 6th and 7th century CE (first century AH). For a reflection about self-knowledge in the Islamic tradition, see Kakaie (2006), among others.
9 Among the world philosophies analyzed in this book in relation to existential posthumanism are (in alphabetical order): Advaita Vedanta, Buddhism, Jainism, Rastafari, Shamanism, Sufism and Ubuntu.
10 To be a philosopher is not to be confused with being a "philodox,"

meaning someone in love with their own opinions – in classical Greek, *doxa* (δόξα) means "opinion."
11 Evolution is not hierarchical and does not imply any symbolic improvement; more clearly, it manifests in ontic differentiations.
12 For instance, in chapter 4 we will reflect on the importance of ecological balance for human health; we will also emphasize the role of the technosphere to current human survival. In chapter 5 we will highlight Earth's magnetosphere as a prerequisite for protecting life.
13 In its multiple nuances, such as critical, cultural, philosophical and existential.
14 Its different trends, such as democratic and libertarian transhumanism, extropianism, the singularity, etc.
15 For instance, the movement associated with Foucault's death of Man ([1966] 1970), as well as the Marxist approaches.
16 See Ferrando (2019).
17 In this text, the term "post-humanism" and its related adjective "post-humanist" are hyphenated when relating to the specific meaning: humanity in diversity. When not hyphenated, they refer to the posthumanist approach, which integrates post-humanist, post-anthropocentric and post-dualistic awareness (and, thus, it cannot be limited to one of them). In this sense, posthumanism exceeds post-humanism in its meanings and significations. In short, post-humanism is (p)art of posthumanism – as a philosophy and a movement.
18 We are referring to strict dualities, not to the shifting and liquid dualism of, for instance, the Tao (see Meditation 1, note 23).
19 Yet not the ultimate guide to the topic: such an epistemic claim would simply annihilate its scope.
20 In this reference, I should like to pay homage to Professor Rosi Braidotti, who evocatively defined my previous book *Philosophical Posthumanism* (2019) as "a rapturous departure – the line of flight of a queen bee" (Braidotti 2019a: xvi).
21 Oxford Dictionaries Online: entry "Labyrinth."
22 Ibid.

Meditation 1: Posthuman Self-Enquiry

1 See chapter 8.
2 See chapter 6, #*Poiesis*.
3 For an explanation of the Hindu notion of *lila*, see chapter 8, #*Lila*.
4 In this specific context, "we" refers to us as a species.
5 The word "energy" comes from ancient Greek: the preposition *en* (which can be translated as "in"), and the word *ergon* (ἔργον), which can be translated as "action"; energy can thus emerge as "in action."
6 Here, we are referring to the level of existence. The level of

non-existence entails the realm of nothingness, which is in, and beyond, space and time. See chapter 8, #Non-Being.
7. According to the Oxford Dictionary, a *relatum* (singular form for *relata* in Latin), means: "Each of two or more terms, objects, or events between which a relation exists" (Oxford Dictionaries Online: entry "Relatum").
8. See, among others, Alaimo (2010), Coole and Frost (2010) and Bennett (2010).
9. See chapter 8, #Subject.
10. For a clarification on this double use of the terms, see Ferrando (2019: ch. 29).
11. Please note that, for the sake of clarity, we will adopt a hyphenated spelling – "inter-being" – instead of "interbeing."
12. In its physical form. If You are reading this book in its digital form, this example also applies in different yet similar ways.
13. See chapter 3.
14. See chapter 4.
15. See chapter 8, #Subject.
16. It is important to note that Martin Heidegger rejected Sartre's approach in his "Letter on 'Humanism'" ([1947] 1998), which is considered a founding text in the genealogy of the posthuman.
17. See chapter 7.
18. See chapter 5.
19. See chapter 4.
20. Translation mine. In Italian: "È bello diventare vecchi, non è bello trovarsi."
21. See chapter 4.
22. Oxford Dictionary, entry "anthropocentric."
23. For instance, in the foundational text *Tao Te Ching* (dating at least to 600 BCE), it is stated: "The supreme good is like water, / which nourishes all things without trying to. / It is content with the low places that people disdain. / Thus it is like the Tao" (Lao Tzu 1999, verse 8).
24. Thanks to the philosopher Kwame Anthony Appiah (b. 1954) for pointing this out at the Liberal Studies Global Research Colloquium, New York University, March 25th 2016.
25. We will delve into this in chapters 3 and 4.
26. In chapter 2, we will investigate mediated anthropocentrism as another possible form.
27. We will expand on this in chapter 8.
28. See Abourezk (2009).
29. As LaDuke phrases it: "In that guilt, the perpetrator is not healthy either" (2011).
30. As Professor Philip Landrigan et al. summarize: "All of the health impacts of ocean pollution fall disproportionately on vulnerable populations in the Global South – environmental injustice on a planetary scale" (2020: 2). For further reflection on this, see chapter 4.

Meditation 2: Human Evolutions

1 We will reflect on the relation between existence and non-existence, self and non-self in chapter 8, where the final deconstruction of the human will manifest as an affirmation of the existential inter-play. From this perspective, nothingness suggests not negation but potential.
2 We are departing from the understanding of this notion as elaborated by Delphine Dion, Ouidade Sabri and Valerie Guillard, who state: "Symbolic pollution is whatever, within a given society, eludes or threatens order. It emerges when things are 'out of place,' violating systems of classification" (Dion et al. 2014: 565). Here, the notion takes a reverse meaning: symbolic pollution refers precisely to the preconceived conceptions sustaining outdated systems of classification, turning into real obstacles in terms of epistemological awareness.
3 We are expanding on the notion developed by Gilles Deleuze and Félix Guattari ([1980] 1987).
4 There are many approaches to which posthumanist perspectivism can be related, from Jain to Amerindian perspectivisms, among others. See Ferrando (2019: ch. 27).
5 See chapter 4.
6 See chapter 8, #Subject.
7 See Braidotti (2019b).
8 Nor is it based on specific human needs, as in the case of the CAPTCHA (acronym for "completely automated public Turing test to tell computers and humans apart"), required to prove the humanity of digital users in the checkbox: "I am not a robot." Such a separation is also a construction: *how can we tell computers and humans apart when such entities are, currently, programmed mainly by humans and (human-conceived) algorithms?* We will explore this in chapter 6.
9 See chapter 7.
10 See chapter 8.
11 See chapter 1, #Inter-being.
12 See chapter 7.
13 This is based on current research, dated to 2023; it may eventually change.
14 Italic in the original.
15 Currently, there is no precise estimate of the last common ancestor of these populations. According to current research, the timeline can be traced from an initial divergence around 13 million years ago to processes of hybridization that occurred until at least 4 million years ago.
16 This is a free adaptation from the pre-Socratic Greek philosopher Protagoras (c. 485–415 BCE), who is most famous for his claim that the human is the measure of all things.

198   Notes to pp. 39–46

17 As expressed by William Kimbel and Brian Villmoare: "The origin and earliest evolution of the genus *Homo* perennially fascinate and frustrate in equal measure. Our fascination stems from the near-mythic qualities of uniqueness with which we tend to imbue the evolution of *our* lineage" (2016: 1).
18 As a simple example, the unnecessary practice of self-removing hair from (most often, female) human bodies in some cultures stands symbolically as a separation from the animal kingdom and from the *Australopithecus* that we are (related to).
19 As we will see in the next sections, patriarchy is a cultural behavior that developed only recently in the macro history of human evolution.
20 In Cavarero's words: "the quintessence of the *Homo erectus* – if not also, to put it bluntly, the phallic erection" (2016: 38).
21 The dating is approximate and is constantly revised according to new findings.
22 Presumably around 600,000 years ago, during the Middle Pleistocene.
23 This topic is still debated.
24 Such a long period of time is divided into three main eras: Lower Paleolithic, Middle Paleolithic and Upper Paleolithic.
25 Around this time, the last Ice Age ended, marking the end of the era of the Pleistocene (also called the ice ages).
26 We are embracing this term, instead of "hunter-gatherer", as hunting appears much later in the history of humans; furthermore, gathered food still constituted the majority of human diets, even after hunting became practicable.
27 The dependence on material goods, so common in contemporary societies, can be traced back to the late Neolithic.
28 This perception is still present in many native accounts of the human, as we will see in chapter 4, *#Rights of Nature*, as well as in chapter 8, *#Shaman*.
29 According to some, the Anthropocene dates much earlier than the European Industrial Revolution. It can be located already in the Neolithic times, with the beginning of the geological epoch of the Holocene, around 11,650 years ago (9,700 BCE), after the last glacial period – which marks the end of the previous geological epoch, the Pleistocene.
30 The notion of extinction should not be taken in absolute terms; as we have pointed out, "their" DNA is still part of "our" species.
31 Here, the term alludes to presentism as approached in literary and historical analysis (it does not refer to philosophical presentism).
32 This approach has been contested. For instance, the field of oral history underlines the presence of other ways of transmitting historical knowledges.
33 In referring to these figurines, the notion of "Venus" is not correct. Venus figurines are generally thought to be auspicious effigies of fer-

tility and beauty; the values of the Goddess were much greater than that.
34 In order to understand their functions, Gimbutas (1989) underlined the importance of learning where they were placed in a household – their geographies of existence. For example, pregnant figurines found in areas of grain preparation, most likely represented the Grain Goddess or the Earth Mother.
35 The term "semasiographic" refers to a non-phonetic type of writing technique that utilizes signs and symbols; for instance, the modern use of emojis, and of the emoji language, is semasiographic.
36 According to Gimbutas (1989), there are three major groups of symbols that can be found in the figurines, as well as in the decorations of pottery. These intertwined categories are abstract, representational and animal.
37 See White (2007).
38 As Joan Marler (2003) puts it: "mother bears, anthropomorphic vessels, and thousands of other images indicate a gendered relationship between the human, animal and mythic realms." Although this text refers to the Neolithic time in Old Europe, it can also apply to some of the Upper Paleolithic findings.
39 We shall note that some non-human animals, plants and insects have been posed as superlatives, such as tigers (depicting strength), butterflies (representing regeneration) and roses (exemplifying beauty). And still, in being either the plus or the minus, they pertain to a different symbolic level of perception, not to the self-awareness of inter-being.
40 Within the sexist history of Western civilization, women, as a category, have been placed closer to non-human animals than to human males, as already outlined in the works of Aristotle.
41 See Fiedler (1978).
42 Some newspapers erroneously portrayed him as a cannibal because of the shape of his teeth, which had been sharpened according to local customs (Parezo and Fowler 2007).
43 Ota Benga was displayed in different museums and world's fairs between 1904 and 1906.
44 Written in 1486, it was published posthumously in 1496.
45 Pope Innocent VIII condemned Pico's *900 Theses* (1487); the book was banned and nearly all copies were burnt.
46 Pico's body was exhumed 500 years later to establish the cause of his death, which turned out to be arsenic poisoning (Gallello et al. 2018).
47 The Renaissance idea of the human was still hierarchical, which explains how some forms of Renaissance humanism could eventually sustain the European colonization of the Americas – think, for instance, of the positions held on natural slavery by the humanist philosopher and theologian Juan Ginés de Sepúlveda (1490–1573).
48 These illuminations are part of *Scivias*, an illustrated work compiled

in 1151 (or 1152) by Hildegard with the help of an assistant; they represent the twenty-six mystical visions she had personally experienced.
49 The cosmic egg refers, in many traditions, to the beginning of the universe and(/or) to the birth of planet Earth.
50 As stated in Genesis 1:27: "God created man in his own image."
51 In this approach, developed by James Lovelock (1919–2022) and Lynn Margulis (1938–2011), symbiosis is recognized as essential to (co-)evolution (Margulis 1998). See chapters 4 and 5.
52 In this context, the term can be spelled as "wholistic"; on the use of this spelling, see Absolon (2019).
53 As Susie Jones, an Elder from Walpole Island First Nation, explains: "In the aboriginal worldview, respect is very important. Respect is being able to understand how one's actions affect another being." Traditionally, indigenous wisdom has been orally transmitted. This passage is part of the interview *Circle of Life: What is the Aboriginal Worldview?*, published on YouTube in 2013; www.youtube.com/watch?v=zc-Enykb028.
54 Aloysius Newenham-Kahindi and Charles E. Stevens describe this as "a multidimensional relational process" (2020: 21); as they further clarify, Maasai people "remain consciously, emotionally, and spiritually attached to geographical places as dwelling places."
55 As the author Barry Holstun Lopez (1945–2020) stated, in relation to the Arctic wilderness: "The land urges us to come around to an understanding of ourselves" (1986: 247).
56 The term "guru" is explained in the ancient Sanskrit text *Advayataraka Upanishad*, verse 16: "The syllable *gu* means darkness, the syllable *ru*, he who dispels them. Because of the power to dispel darkness, the guru is thus named" (see Ayyangar 1938: 8).
57 Think of the spiritual significance of the Arunachala hill (located in Tamil Nadu, India) to the path of enlightenment pursued by the Hindu sage Ramana Maharshi (1879–1950).
58 See chapter 5.
59 In MacCormack's view (2020), such an extinction is seen as a celebration.
60 See chapter 6.

Meditation 3: Biotic Co-emergences

1 The two terms are co-relational: manifested embodiments and(/or) embodied manifestations.
2 See chapter 8.
3 The key importance of multiplicity in being has been clearly outlined in the work of Gilles Deleuze (1925–1995) and Félix Guattari (1930–1992), among others.

4 See chapter 8, #*Mind*.
5 As the posthumanist thinker Rosi Braidotti states: "I see the brain and our thinking capacity as being embodied and the body as being 'embrained'" (2019b: 62).
6 As a brutal consequence of slaves being reduced to their bodies, masters could legally rape them; the enslaved bodies were considered the "private property" of their masters (see Getman 1984).
7 This is why, in this text, the term "bodymind" will not be adopted as the ultimate solution to the hermeneutical divide body/mind; instead, it will be employed contextually.
8 The Oxford Dictionary gives three definitions of "organism": "an individual animal, plant, or single-celled life form"; "the material structure of an individual life form"; and "a whole with interdependent parts, likened to a living being" (Oxford Dictionaries Online: entry "Organism").
9 It is defined as "an instrument of thought, especially a means of reasoning or a system of logic" (Merriam-Webster Dictionary Online: entry "Organon").
10 Recent studies have found the last universal common ancestor of cellular life to pre-date 3.9 billion years ago (see Betts et al. 2018). Please note that scientific research is in progress, and that these estimates may change with new findings.
11 According to current research, Earth is estimated to be about 4.5 billion years old – see chapter 5.
12 LUA – also defined as LUCA (last universal common ancestor) – refers not to the first life form but to the most recent common ancestors of all current life on Earth. In scientific terms, it can be defined as "a complex community of proto-eukaryotes with an RNA genome, adapted to a broad range of moderate temperatures, genetically redundant, morphologically and metabolically diverse" (Glansdorff et al. 2008).
13 LUA's genetic information may have been stored and transmitted in the form of RNA – which is thought to have preceded DNA.
14 Although this statement fits the majority of life on Earth, exceptions must always be taken into consideration. For instance, according to recent research, microbes break the universality of the genetic code (see Mühlhausen et al. 2018).
15 In biochemistry, DNA is the abbreviation for deoxyribonucleic acid. The Oxford Dictionary defines it as "a self-replicating material that is present in nearly all living organisms" and "the carrier of genetic information" (Oxford Dictionaries Online: entry "DNA"). DNA is a dynamic and adaptable molecule containing the biological instructions that make each individual unique. It consists of many components; some of them are passed from parent organisms to their offspring during reproduction.

16 DNA has a double stranded structure, which serves to maintain genome stability (Strauss 2018).
17 A smaller amount of DNA is found in the mitochondria (called "mitochondrial DNA").
18 DNA knowledge is copied and transmitted from the nucleus to other parts of the cell in the form of smaller, short-lived messenger molecules called RNA. RNA, also called mRNA ("m" standing for "messenger"), are partial copies of DNA. RNA and DNA are closely related; and yet they bear many differences. In humans, for instance, DNA molecules are double-stranded and degrade during programmed cell death; RNA molecules are normally single-stranded and do not last quite as long – only two minutes, according to recent findings (see Baudrimont et al. 2017).
19 This process is known as vertical gene transfer.
20 See Pennisi (2010).
21 See Liu et al. (1996).
22 I would like to thank Ugo Ferrando for bringing this point to my attention.
23 As of March 2022, this type of Google search brings up 866,000 pages.
24 The "Age of Information" is how the historical period beginning in the second half of the 20th century is often defined. For more on "data" as the new historical reference, see chapter 6.
25 It could be argued that DNA must be actualized by RNA, and thus it can be approached as mere information. This separation does not hold: all of the RNA in a cell is synthesized from DNA during the process of transcription (see Alberts et al. 2002).
26 DNA can be used to carry external and unrelated information as well, as in the case of DNA digital data storage, where binary data is encoded and decoded in synthesized strands of DNA. The emergence of DNA as a means of data storage is seen as having great potential for the future; currently, it has real limitations, such as "exorbitant costs, excruciatingly slow writing and reading mechanisms, and vulnerability to mutations or errors" (Panda et al. 2018).
27 See chapter 7, #*Repetitions*.
28 In current cloning practice, the donor is usually different from the original parent (or the clone source).
29 For a reflection on the species problem, from a posthumanist standpoint, see Ferrando (2019: ch. 22).
30 See chapter 2.
31 A recent study has demonstrated that "the number of bacteria in the body is actually of the same order as the number of human cells" (Sender et al. 2016). Please note that the specific type of human embodiment selected for this analysis was: "a 70 kg 'reference man'" (ibid.). Other-embodied groups (of different ages, genders, ethnicities, etc.) may provide different results.

32 Previous studies suggest that bacteria outnumber human cells.
33 The biologist Gabriele Berg and her colleagues (2020) explain how the term "microbiome" includes "not only the community of the microorganisms, but also their 'theatre of activity.'"
34 Numerically speaking, according to the biochemist Luke L. Ursell and his colleagues, the human microbiome "consists of the 10–100 trillion symbiotic microbial cells harbored by each person, primarily bacteria in the gut" (2012: 38).
35 This is why it is sometimes referred to as the gut–brain axis, or the psychobiome.
36 See chapter 8.
37 To avoid confusion, a clear differentiation between the terms "microbiome" and "microbiota" may be of help. The term "microbiota" usually refers to "the assemblage of living microorganisms present in a defined environment. As phages, viruses, plasmids, prions, viroids, and free DNA are usually not considered as living microorganisms, they do not belong to the microbiota" (Berg et al. 2020); and yet they can be considered (p)art of the microbiome.
38 Anthropocentric presumptions are not challenged, as it becomes clear in Vana's explanation: "The symbiotic microbiota is necessary for the full development of our consciousness, but it does not need to be conscious itself" (2020).
39 We will address these questions in prompt 3 of the additional exercises posted on the website www.politybooks.com, page "The Art of Being Posthuman," link "Exercises."
40 See Ferrando (2019: ch. 29).
41 Lynn Margulis defined as "holobiont" a "symbiont compound of recognizable bionts" (1991: 2); in this context, "biont" refers to an "individual organism" (ibid.).
42 The term can be found previously in the history of science – for instance, in the work of the German biologist Adolf Meyer-Abich (1893–1971). For a comprehensive outlook on this concept before Margulis, see Baedke et al. (2020).
43 In tune with the Gaia hypothesis, the Earth, as a planet, can be approached as a geo-biological holobiont, as suggested by Bruce Clarke (2017).
44 See Thompson et al. (2015).
45 The presence of the microbiome is a game changer in our understanding of the genome, as affirmed by the microbial ecologist Ruth Ley: "We don't have just one genome, the genes of our microbiome present essentially a second genome which augment the activity of our own" (quoted in Gallagher 2018). According to Ley, what makes us human is precisely "the combination of our own DNA, plus the DNA of our gut microbes" (ibid.).
46 As Rosenberg and Zilber-Rosenberg state: "The microbiota with its microbiome together with the host genome can be transmitted

from one generation to the next with fidelity and thus propagate the unique properties of the holobiont and the species" (2014: 1).
47 Speciation, in evolutionary biology, refers to the formation of a new species. As clarified by Rosenberg and Zilber-Rosenberg (2018): "The host genome [the first genome] is highly conserved, and genetic changes within it occur slowly, whereas the microbiome genome [the second genome] is dynamic and can change rapidly in response to the environment." The authors further remark on the key importance of these rapid changes from an evolutionary perspective. In their words: "Recent experiments showing that microbiota can play an initial role in speciation have been suggested as an additional mode of enhancing evolution" (ibid.).
48 The Oxford Dictionary offers two definitions of the term, referring to the root cause of an infectious disease as well as to computer malware. This is the first definition: "an infective agent that typically consists of a nucleic acid molecule in a protein coat, is too small to be seen by light microscopy, and is able to multiply only within the living cells of a host." This is the second one: "a piece of code which is capable of copying itself and typically has a detrimental effect, such as corrupting the system or destroying data" (Oxford Dictionaries Online: entry "Virus").
49 Ibid.
50 In popular culture, this has translated into the virus being metaphorically compared to the zombie or the vampire. In the words of Joanna Verran and Xavier Aldana Reyes: "The pathogen as a microscopic Gothic presence can be represented metaphorically and macroscopically in the figure of the zombie, much as the ghost, the undead (the vampire), and the 'weird creature' have traditionally acted as springboards for the exploration of the beyond and the numinous" (2018: 1775).
51 There are millions of types – currently, only around 9,000 have been studied in detail.
52 According to the Oxford Dictionary, a pathogen is "a bacterium, virus, or other microorganism that can cause disease" (Oxford Dictionaries Online: entry "Pathogen").
53 As Roossinck states: "It's just bias – the science has always been about the pathogens" (cited in Nuwer 2020).
54 As Nuwer underlines: "they keep us and the planet alive, rather than kill us. . . . without viruses, life and the planet as we know it would cease to exist" (ibid.).
55 Research has shown that these viruses provide the genetic material that codes for key aspects of the photosynthetic process: the oxygen thus released can be approached as a by-product of the bacteria suffering from a virus infection (Suttle 2007).
56 Horizontal gene transfer (HGT), also known as "lateral gene transfer" (LGT), is different from vertical gene transfer – where

the transmission of genetic material from parents to offspring occurs during reproduction. According to the biologists Patrick J. Keeling and Jeffrey D. Palmer (2008), horizontal gene transfer can be defined as "the non-sexual movement of genetic information between genomes." It occurs when "incoming DNA or RNA can replace existing genes, or can introduce new genes into a genome" (ibid.).

57 Another current use of viruses is virotherapy in cancer treatment – where viruses are converted into therapeutic agents to target and lyse cancer cells, possibly without harming healthy cells.

58 For instance, a synthetic expression of horizontal gene transfer is a vital mechanism employed in different forms of genetic engineering: from gene therapy to environmental programs, where genetically modified viruses are employed as vectors for transferring new genetic information to human and non-human animals, as well as plants – with the related concerns over cross-species infection and, more generally, viral (bio-)containment.

59 For the use of this term with the hyphen, see chapter 7, #*Social Pandemics*.

60 The psychiatrist Rachel Yehuda and the psychologist Amy Lehrner, who have undertaken extensive research on trans-generational epigenetic inheritance, state: "multi-generational studies may ultimately yield a cogent understanding of how individual, cultural and societal experiences permeate our biology" (2018: 243).

61 This notion has been extensively explained within the posthuman debate, starting with Donna Haraway's use of the term without the hyphen (2003).

62 There are many scientific examples to be offered here. For instance, most humans are able to consume non-human milk and dairy beyond infancy on account of a genetic mutation developed out of the cultural practice of animal domestication and dairying (see Gerbault et al. 2011: 863).

63 For the history of eugenics from a posthumanist standpoint, see Ferrando (2019: ch. 24).

64 Think, for instance, of the Bosnian War, from 1992 to 1995, among many others.

65 The Oxford Dictionary defines "cryonics" as "the technique of deep-freezing the bodies of people who have just died, in the hope that scientific advances may allow them to be revived in the future" (Oxford Dictionaries Online: entry "Cryonics").

66 Ferrando and More (2013). This is a shorter and edited version of the transcript of the video, which is available on YouTube (minutes 57:00–59:00).

67 In cryonics, a dead person who has been cryo-preserved is referred to as a patient, in the hope that they may be brought back to life in the (near) future.

68 Ferrando and More (2013).
69 Democratic transhumanism focuses on this aspect, underlining the urgency for a democratic access to human enhancement, including the right to be cryo-preserved.

Meditation 4: Ecological Presence

1 The health risks of being exposed to cosmic radiation, among other factors, is preventing humans, as they currently are (bio-genetically and bio-technologically), from living outside the Earth for long periods of time. See chapter 5.
2 This planet is the only one, currently known, that harbors life as we conceive it: carbon-based. Carbon is (p)art of the chemical base of life on Earth; it can create bonds with a large variety of elements. Relationality is at the very core of the chemistry of life.
3 See Deleuze and Guattari ([1980] 1987).
4 According to West African Yorùbá worldviews, the shape of the Earth itself may be the results of this inner relationality. As the Yorùbá scholar John Ayọtunde Isọla Bẹwaji (2018: 240) states: "Maybe this explains why streams like to flow into rivers, rivers like to flow into seas and seas like to flow into oceans. Maybe this is why the earth is round and everything relates to everything, and the going constitute the coming, while the dying constitute the coming into being."
5 The biologist Stephen Jay Gould (1941–2002), in *Wonderful Life* (1989), underlined that evolution is contingent, and not complex.
6 Oxford Dictionaries Online: entry "Nature."
7 This term was proposed by Bruno Latour (1991–2022) – who used it with the hyphen ([1991] 1993) – and by Donna Haraway (2003) – who used it without the hyphen.
8 The eco-activist Vandana Shiva (1995) is critical of this term. She notes that everything, in such a cyborgization, becomes "natureculture." For instance, GMOs (genetically modified organisms) can be presented as "natural" and thus more easily accepted in human laws and general opinion; and yet the presence of GMOs in nature causes unbalance in eco-diversity and bio-sustainability. Their uncritical acceptance in society might be based not necessarily on awareness but, more clearly, on dynamics of epistemological power and economic exploitation.
9 See Philip (2022).
10 According to Amerindian indigenous worldviews, for instance, other-than-human species have cultures as well – see Viveiros de Castro (1998).
11 The social scientists João Aldeia and Fátima Alves (2019) affirm: "Unthinking what we know – including what we know about how we know – implies refusing to understand this issue in terms of

humanity's relation *to* nature but rather conceptualizing it in terms of the space-time specific interrelations of different elements of the web of life."
12 On this, the philosopher Timothy Morton states: "Nature, a transcendental term in a material mask, stands at the end of a potentially infinite series of other terms that collapse into it, otherwise known as a metonymic list: fish, grass, mountain, air, chimpanzees" (2007: 14).
13 As the law scholar Catherine J. Iorns Magallanes explains: "Indigenous views of the environment continue the most ancient hunter-gather traditions of considering humans as being part of nature and of acknowledging and reflecting humankind's interdependence with nature" (2015: 2). Iorns Magallanes also underlines how different this is "from the liberal, Enlightenment view that humans are separate from – and even above and dominant over – nature" (ibid.).
14 This relies, more broadly, on the philosophy of "good living" or "the plentiful life" (in Spanish, *La filosofía del buen vivir*, or in Quechua, *Sumak kawsay*): a good life is lived in harmony with Mother Earth – called "Pachamama" in Inca cultures. Thanks to Moira Fradinger for this point.
15 The law professors Andrew Geddis and Jacinta Ruru explain that, as a result of this, Te Urewera now possesses "all the rights, powers, duties, and liabilities of a legal person" (2020: 255).
16 See Goeckeritz et al. (2018).
17 As Geddis and Ruru underline: "they are no longer 'things' over which human beings exercise dominion, they are 'persons' with which humans have a relationship" (2020: 255).
18 As the philosopher John Patterson explains:

> At the heart of this philosophy is the concept of mauri, a life force which unites all creatures and enables them to flourish. By acknowledging this sort of connectedness we accept limitations to human domination of the environment: our actions must respect or enhance the quality of natural items, not simply further human or personal interests. A philosophy of respect for mauri asks us to respect and even enhance the essence or character of each creature and of each habitat. (1998: 69)

19 According to the United Nations (2017): "There are approximately 370 million indigenous peoples in the world. They own, occupy or use up to 22 percent of the global land area, which is home to 80 percent of the world's biodiversity. . . . Areas managed by indigenous peoples are the oldest form of biodiversity conservation, and often the most effective."
20 Thanks to Carolina Pinheiro for this point.
21 See the encyclical *Laudato si'* by Pope Francis (May 24, 2015).
22 In the diversity of indigenous cultures, some have embedded hier-

archies based on sexist and/or ethno-centric supremacies, among others; the posthuman approach dismantles the reiteration of such primacies.
23 Haff uses this term to refer to "the interlinked set of communication, transportation, bureaucratic and other systems that act to metabolize fossil fuels and other energy resources" (2013: 301).
24 As Haff explains: "Without the support structure and services provided by technology, the human population would quickly decline towards its Stone Age base of no more than ten million ... individuals" (ibid.: 302).
25 According to Haff: "The technosphere is not 'just' a human-created phenomenon, because, except for simple artifacts like stone tools, humans did not create technology independently, but only in the context of existing technological systems" (ibid.). This is why Haff prefers this term to the "anthroposphere" (ibid.: 301).
26 The technosphere is not sustainable. As Haff explains: "Unlike the older paradigms, the technosphere has not yet evolved the ability to recycle its own waste stream" (ibid.).
27 Debris is endangering this species (see Lavers et al. 2020).
28 See Leslie et al. (2022).
29 This concept can be traced back to Charles Darwin (1809–1882), who, in his book *Fertilisation of Orchids* (1862), predicted that a specific type of orchid native to Madagascar (called *Angraecum sesquipedale*) had to be pollinated by hawk moths with exceptionally long tongues.
30 A classic example is how flowers have evolved to appeal to different species, and vice versa. More precisely, the bee and the floral morphologies have co-evolved in the mutualism of pollination. As the philosopher Christopher Ketcham summarizes: "the flower has adapted her shape to fit the honeybee body so that she can release sticky pollen onto the honeybee who will carry it to other flowers. The honeybee has adapted her body to fit the flower and her mouthparts to capitalize on the nectar treat that the flower provides" (2020: 44).
31 The historian Dipesh Chakrabarty (2019) underlines that the terms "planet" and "globe" are not synonyms. The globe is what humans have made of the planet, beginning with the history of modern empires and the development of navigation: while the story of globalization cannot be told without humans, the story of the planet can.
32 The literary critic Bruce Clarke explains this from a geobiological perspective: "after four billion years of coevolution, living processes, symbiotic organizations, and the sum of their global niches are all relative to ongoing reformulation by evolving eons of matter, life, and sun. Geobiological history has thoroughly churned them all together into a planetary holobiont that maintains, defends, but also surpasses its parts" (2017: 207).
33 See chapter 3, #*Holobiont*.

34 Honeybees, for instance, make decisions collectively and democratically (see Seeley 2010, among others).
35 As the biologists Madeleine Beekman and Benjamin P. Oldroyd (2018) underline: "Although individual ants may make errors when assessing the quality of sites, collectively the colony tends to select the best available site."
36 The American Psychological Association (APA), for instance, describes eco-anxiety as "a chronic fear of environmental doom" (Clayton et al. 2017: 68).
37 Greta Thunberg (b. 2003), the young Swedish environmental activist and the inspirer of the movement known as "Fridays for Future" (or "School Strike for Climate"), stated on the inaction of current political leaders: "People are suffering. People are dying. Entire ecosystems are collapsing. And all you can talk about is money and fairy tales of eternal economic growth. How dare you!" (2019).
38 According to the Oxford Dictionary, global warming is "a gradual increase in the overall temperature of the earth's atmosphere generally attributed to the greenhouse effect caused by increased levels of carbon dioxide, chlorofluorocarbons, and other pollutants" (Oxford Dictionaries Online: entry "Global warming"). One of the effects of the increase in planetary temperatures is the melting of glaciers and ice sheets, as well as raising sea temperatures; warm water thus expands, resulting in higher sea levels. Given that oceans cover most of our planet, coastal areas are being flooded, while other related areas are left in drought, causing devastation and displacements.
39 In global economic terms, this has been defined as the "ecological debt" of the so-called first world countries to the others (see Walrenius et al. 2015, among others).
40 See, among others, Mohai and Saha (2015); Lester et al. (2001); Ringquist (2005).
41 As the philosopher Arne Naess explained: "The so-called struggle of life, and survival of the fittest, should be interpreted in the sense of ability to coexist and cooperate in complex relationships, rather than ability to kill, exploit, and suppress" (1973: 95).
42 As Naess put it: "The global approach is essential, but regional differences must largely determine policies" (ibid.: 100).
43 Genetically, we share to a great extent – see chapter 3.
44 Because of gravity, the closer we are to the Earth's core, the slower time moves – see chapter 5.
45 In Italian, the term *pianta* (meaning "plant") is declined in the feminine. Growing up in Italy, I used to refer to this plant as a "she."
46 As Thich Nhat Hanh put it: "When you wake up and you see that the Earth is not just the environment, the Earth is us, you touch the nature of interbeing" (2021: 2). On the notion of inter-being, see chapter 1.
47 As Louv states: "Unlike television, nature does not steal time, it amplifies it. Nature offers healing for a child living in a destructive

family or neighborhood. It serves as a blank slate upon which a child draws and reinterprets the culture's fantasies" (2005: 7).
48 Within this worldview, the cosmos is being approached as "the unfolding of continuous creativity" (Tu Wei-Ming 1985: 68).
49 See Klepeis et al. (2001).
50 For instance, low vitamin D status, which is extremely common worldwide, results mostly from inadequate exposure to sunlight.
51 A growing number of people are suffering from "natural environment phobia," also called "biophobia," which is a prejudice against nature.
52 As Louv states: "For a new generation, nature is more abstraction than reality. Increasingly, nature is something to watch, to consume, to wear – to ignore" (2005: 1–2).
53 See chapter 3, #*Embodiments*, and chapter 7, #*Posthuman Education*.
54 Louv underlines the urgent need for the current educational system to evolve. He states: "The alternative? I imagine a classroom that turns outward, both figuratively and literally. The grounds would become a classroom, buildings would look outward and gardens would cover the campus. The work of naturalists would be the vehicle by which we would teach reading and writing" (2005: 136).
55 This is also called the rhizosphere. Because of nutrient availability, the rhizosphere is supportive of microbial growth, as the environmental scientist David McNear (2013) states: "Rhizodeposits make the rhizosphere a desirable niche for microbial communities to proliferate. One teaspoon of bare or tilled soil contains more microorganisms than there are people on Earth."
56 The term refers to an archetype that goes beyond the gendered paradigm (mother/father). As Simard explains it:

> Elder trees are able to recognize neighbors that are genetically related, or that are kin, and they can send more or less resources to other trees to either favor or disfavor them, depending on the safety of the environment. I have taken to calling these elders "Mother Trees" because they appear to be nurturing their young. Mother Trees thus connect the forest through space and time, just like elders connect human families across generations. (2021a: 68)

57 According to Simard:

> Elders fill a special role in any community, having earned the respect of the tribe for their life-long wisdom, knowledge, and teaching. . . . In the forest, the foundational species are the trees, and the elders of this foundation are the biggest and oldest trees. These elders are important not just as habitat for the many plant, animal, fungal, and microbial creatures that live in the forest, but also the people who depend on the woods for their cultures and livelihoods. (Ibid.: 67)

58 See Simard (2021b).
59 As the biologist Barbara Schaal explains: "Hominids have coevolved with plants for millions of years; the skulls of ancient hominids reflect the nature of the plant species they ate, while more recently we domesticated plants to suit our needs, leading to a dramatic cultural shift from hunter-gatherer to agricultural societies" (2019: 14).
60 We are referring to the condition of being-in-the-world (in German: *Dasein*), as explained by the philosopher Martin Heidegger (1889–1976) in *Being and Time* ([1927] 2011).
61 Ecology refers to the discourse on the place we inhabit, which is planet Earth. "Eco-" comes from ancient Greek *oikos* (οἶκος), meaning "home." *Logos* (λόγος) has several meanings, from "word" and "reason" to "discourse" and "argument," among others.
62 See chapter 6.
63 Reflecting on technology and modern worldviews, Heidegger noted how nature had been reduced to a "standing reserve" ([1953] 1977: 17) for human use. As he explains: "[t]he earth now reveals itself as a coal mining district, the soil as a mineral deposit" (ibid.: 14).
64 See Cooper (2008).
65 Paul Crutzen (1933–2021) and Eugene Stoermer (1934–2012) coined the term "Anthropocene" and located it in the latter part of the eighteenth century. Human presence on planet Earth has had direct effects on the biosphere throughout history; yet, after industrialization, such effects have peaked at a faster and faster pace. As Crutzen and Stoermer explain: "we choose this date because, during the past two centuries, the global effects of human activities have become clearly noticeable" (2000: 17).
66 The gross domestic product (GDP) of a country can no longer just survey the value of goods and services; it must take into account human and non-human well-being, such as human (physical and psychological) health, as well as ecological balance, among other factors. This shift has already been embraced by different politicians worldwide. For instance, in 2019 the prime minister of New Zealand, Jacinda Ardern, stated that "the budget would aim not at maximizing GDP but instead at maximizing well-being" (quoted in Pilling 2019).
67 See Latouche (2010).
68 Degrowth programs cannot be universalized. Each local entity has different needs and realities: one size does not fit all. Most degrowth advocates believe that an increase in GDP may be beneficial to some nations in the Global South in order to meet dignified standards of living, healthcare and education for their populations.
69 According to Vandana Shiva (2012), consumerism lubricates the war against the Earth; a paradigm shift to earth-centered politics and economics is, in her view, our only chance of survival.
70 As Professor Patrick Webb et al. state: "Despite record levels of food

production globally, hunger and many forms of malnutrition still affect billions of people" (2018: 1).
71 In nutrition, quantity does not solve the issue of low quality diets. In the words of Webb et al.: "While traditionally associated with a lack of food, hunger and malnutrition (which includes overweight and obesity as well as undernutrition) are associated with low quality diets. Poor diet quality is a problem in every country – high and low income alike" (ibid.).
72 Eutopian refers to something realistic, that is desirable and attainable.
73 The religious connotations of Pearce's approach have been investigated in Ferrando (2022a).
74 Pearce (2009–15) mentions some of these points: "First, a cruelty-free world entails a transition to global veganism. . . . However, this transition isn't enough."
75 Quoted from the VHEMT website: www.vhemt.org/.
76 See chapter 2, #*With or Without Humans?*.
77 According to the animal rights organization PETA (People for the Ethical Treatment of Animals), in the US alone, each year, more than 100 million animals are killed in laboratories; neither their right to life nor the quality of their lives are protected: "The thinking, feeling animals who are used in experiments are treated like nothing more than disposable laboratory equipment." Quoted from the PETA website: www.peta.org/issues/animals-used-for-experimentation/animals-used-experimentation-factsheets/animal-experiments-overview/.
78 Often, the results of experiments carried on non-human animals cannot safely apply to humans (see Akhtar 2015).
79 For instance, studies of animals can be done in the wild. This choice does not only honor their actual being (in) our shared Earth; it can also partake in their well-being by realistically understanding their needs.
80 For an explanation of this concept, from a posthumanist standpoint, see Ferrando (2019: ch. 26).
81 See chapter 8.
82 See chapter 1, #*Redemption*.
83 To paraphrase the non-violent leader Mahatma Gandhi (1869–1948).
84 In the era of the Anthropocene, human habits are causing major environmental degradation, consequently affecting human health and well-being. This is reflected in the alarming rates of human diseases triggered by pollution, as well as in global pandemics and human-induced natural disasters.

Meditation 5: Cosmic Constellations

1 The notion of astronomy in the ancient world cannot be fully assimilated to the contemporary scientific field.

2 As new archeological findings from this period prove: "detailed solstice observances were common among complex hunter-gatherers, often associated with the keeping of calendars and the scheduling of major ceremonies" (Hayden and Villeneuve 2011: 331).
3 See Ruggles (2006), among others.
4 See Šprajc et al. (2009), among others.
5 It is interesting to note that the use of square and rectangular forms in modern architecture does not resonate with some of the oldest free-standing structures of the world, which tended to be curved, spherical and circular, in tune with celestial spheres in cosmic geometry: from the circular structures of Göbekli Tepe in Anatolia, Turkey, dating back to between c. 9,500 and 8,000 BCE, to the Megalithic temples of Malta (between 3,600 BCE and 2,500 BCE).
6 The Soviet biochemist Alexander Oparin ([1924] 1967), for instance, famously developed the hypothesis of the "primordial soup."
7 The hypothesis of litho-panspermia proposes "a natural exchange of organisms between solar system bodies as a result of asteroidal or cometary impactors" (Hegner 2021). The term "panspermia" was first found in the writings of the Greek philosopher Anaxagoras (c. 510–428 BCE). It is important to note that this term is not neutral. Its Greek etymology is formed by the union of *pan* (πᾶν), meaning "all," and *sperma*"(σπέρμα), which, in ancient Greek, referred to "origin, source," as well as to "(human) seed." This reflects the sexist and scientifically false view which identified the active principle of life in the male reproductive fluid, while the female was considered to contribute passive matter.
8 More broadly, the Sun, whose energy is vital to all life on Earth, may also be the cause of its end. Stars are born, live and die; the Earth may eventually be absorbed by the Sun, once the star, in the red giant phase, has expanded beyond our orbit. According to scientific studies based on stellar models, this will happen in about 7.59 billion years (See Schröder and Connon Smith 2008).
9 See Melott and Thomas (2019).
10 According to the Oxford Dictionary, a supernova is "a star that suddenly increases greatly in brightness because of a catastrophic explosion that ejects most of its mass" (Oxford Dictionary Online: entry "Supernova"). In simple terms, it can be referred to as the death of a star.
11 The term "outer space" is defined by the Oxford Dictionary as "the region of space beyond the earth's atmosphere or beyond the solar system. In extended use: a place or region beyond the usual limits of awareness or accessibility" (Oxford Dictionaries Online: entry "Outer space"). It can be seen as an extended and somehow confused framework, consisting of a wide variety of spaces – such as the solar system and the regions beyond the solar system.
12 This date was established by radiometric dating, a method based on

the testimonies of the rocks (which have been around much longer than humans).
13 According to contemporary science, small particles gradually grew to become planetesimals; these eventually continued colliding, to eventually form (larger) planets, such as the Earth.
14 One of the definitions of "eon" in the Oxford Dictionary is "a major division of geological time, subdivided into eras" (Oxford Dictionaries Online: entry "Eon").
15 The formation of the ocean and atmosphere occurred in this period, between 4.37 and 4.2 billion years ago.
16 The GTS is a system of chronological dating based on the study and classification of the geological strata; the layers of rocks and their inter-being with related organisms (in their co-evolutions and, possibly, extinctions) is revealed through fossil evidence.
17 As the astrobiologist Robert Miller Hazen (2010) puts it: "all of recorded human history is much less than 4.5 billion minutes."
18 For the use of this term, see chapter 6, note 3.
19 The further from the crust, the less we can rely on scientific data; for instance, our understanding of the inner core is merely speculative. Currently, the seismic waves passing through it are the most direct measurements through which scientists hypothesize about the physical properties of the inner core; and, still, what is inferred from seismology, or from other indirect sources, is controversial within the scientific community.
20 According to the Oxford Dictionary, plate tectonics is "a theory explaining the structure of the earth's crust and many associated phenomena as resulting from the interaction of rigid lithospheric plates which move slowly over the underlying mantle" (Oxford Dictionaries Online: entry "Plate tectonics").
21 Continental drift, the theory that paved the way for the acceptance of plate tectonics, refers to the hypothesis that continents move over geologic time; according to this, all the continents that are present today were once connected in supercontinents. Fossil distribution has been of key importance in tracing them: by mapping identical fossils on separated continents, scientists can delineate how continents were distributed in the past.
22 How galactic evolution works is still uncertain. Stellar evolution refers to the processes by which stars manifest (in) their evolutionary stages – from their formation to their death.
23 The Earth rotates eastward (from west to east) around its polar axis, accomplishing a full rotation in one day. While doing that, it is also orbiting around the Sun: it takes 365 days, 6 hours, 9 minutes to complete this.
24 According to current estimates, it is one among 100 billion (at the low-end) and 400 billion (at the high end) stars orbiting in the Milky Way.

25 According to NASA: "It takes about 230 million years for our solar system to make one revolution around the galactic center" (NASA Science 2022).
26 This term refers to the space between galaxies.
27 Although our scientific means are not able to establish how many, the current estimate is between 100 and 200 billion.
28 As Humboldt stated:

> In this work I use the word Cosmos in conformity with the Hellenic usage of the term subsequently to the time of Pythagoras, and in accordance with the precise definition given of it in the treatise entitled "De Mundo", which was long erroneously attributed to Aristotle. It is the assemblage of all things in heaven and earth, the universality of created things constituting the perceptible world. (1860: 71)

29 In Humboldt's words:

> It is certainly true that in the midst of the universal fluctuation of phenomena and vital forces – that inextricable network of organisms by turns developed and destroyed – each step that we make in the more intimate knowledge of nature leads us to the entrance of new labyrinths; but the excitement produced by a presentiment of discovery, the vague intuition of the mysteries to be unfolded, and the multiplicity of the paths before us, all tend to stimulate the exercise of thought in every stage of knowledge. (Ibid.: 40)

30 The medieval classical scholar and cleric Isidor of Soville (c. 560–636), in the entry "De Mundo" ("the world"), in Book XIII of his etymological encyclopedia *Etymologiae* (c. 600–625), asserts: "the Greeks adopted a term for world (*mundus*, also meaning 'cosmetics') derived from 'ornament', on account of the diversity of elements and the beauty of the heavenly bodies. They call it κόσμος ('Kosmos'), which means 'ornament', for with our bodily eyes we see nothing more beautiful than the world" (2010: 271). For more on how the Greeks called the cosmos an ornament, see Bloomer (2016).
31 See chapter 8.
32 As the archaeo-astronomer Giulio Magli underlines: "celestial matters were, for the ancient Egyptians, deeply and intimately connected with the most important things of all: preserving Maat, the cosmic order, on Earth" (2013: 2).
33 This is a reference to the modern spiritual classic *I am That* (1973), by Sri Nisargadatta Maharaj.
34 The term may also have underlying sexual, and sexist, connotations; to "bang," in vulgar slang, refers to having sexual intercourse. For the history of this term as a misnomer, see Kragh (2014).
35 In the Planck epoch – which corresponds to the first picosecond (one trillionth of a second) of the universe – there was no matter, no space,

no time. Describing this period in chronological terms is senseless; asking where it occurred is meaningless.
36 The expansion of the universe, in its early formation, would have been much faster than the speed of light. Following this inflationary period, the universe would have continued to expand at a slower pace. According to the special theory of relativity, nothing in this universe travels faster than the speed of light, but there is an exception: spacetime itself can expand, bend and warp at any speed (this would explain why some parts of the universe are currently expanding faster than the speed of light). As the universe cooled, energy would have turned into matter, shaping the embodiment of spacetime and marking the beginning of what has been defined as the matter era.
37 This includes the recent scientific hypothesis of the Ekpyrotic universe.
38 See chapter 8.
39 On some level, we are always studying the past, as is the case with the light of the stars we see at night. Let us explain this. Light travels at a constant speed of 299,792.458 kilometers per second. Anything that lacks mass moves at the speed of light; light always moves at a constant speed. Because of its finite speed, the light from stars that we see at night was emitted long before we could actually see it: we are, in a way, (p)art of their past.
40 This is how the theoretical physicist Marcelo Gleiser (2012) puts it:

> Imagine that you, from your galaxy, observe other galaxies around you. Due to the expansion, most of them are moving away from you. You'd then conclude that you must be the center, since every other galaxy is receding from you. However, an observer in another galaxy will see the same thing: everyone else receding from her. The same with each and every galaxy. In the Universe, space is the ultimate democracy: all points are equally important.

41 See Ferrando (2019: ch. 27).
42 See chapter 7.
43 As the astronomer Carl Sagan (1934–1996) summarized: "The cosmos is also within us, we are made of star-stuff. We are a way for the cosmos to know itself." This is a quotation from his introductory monologue in the first episode, "The shores of the cosmic ocean," in the 13-part documentary series *Cosmos: A Personal Journey* (1980).
44 As the philosopher of science Karl Popper (1902–1994) famously suggested in *The Logic of Scientific Discovery* ([1934] 1959), a scientific theory must be tested and conceivably proven false.
45 In Stengers' words: "it is a question of creating words that are meaningful only when they bring about their own reinvention" ([1997] 2010: 13).
46 As Stengers puts it: "it is said that the first step in the history of sci-

ence was the break with myth, but equally important was the break with sophism. Rational discourse would, therefore, from its inception, designate its 'others' polemically" (ibid.: 2).

47 Stengers further explains that "this polemic is embodied statically in our universities, where every discipline has its own territory, its experts, its criteria, and where the reassuring fiction of collegiality prevails, one whose only point of agreement is the disqualification of the 'nonscientific'" (ibid.: 3).

48 See chapter 2.

49 In 2017 the journal *Nature Astronomy* dedicated a special issue to the topic of gender equity in astronomy, stating in the editorial: "data shows that women astronomers face discrimination at all stages of their careers" (Not all scientists 2017).

50 Mass and energy curve spacetime – more generally, anything that can bend spacetime has gravity. At the macro scale, gravity is proportional to the embodied mass. More mass equals more gravity; for instance, gravity on our Moon is weaker, because the Moon is less massive than the Earth.

51 At the quantum level, gravity does not manifest the same properties: the embodiments of spacetime are multiple, intra-connected and agential.

52 In physics, the notion of spacetime refers to any mathematical models based on the general theory of relativity (Einstein [1915] 1952), according to which time is added to the dimensions of space. Spacetime, as a model, fuses one dimension of time and three dimensions of space (width, breadth and height) into a single four-dimensional manifold – although more dimensions could possibly exist. According to current versions of string theory, for instance, the universe operates in ten dimensions.

53 As recent studies underline:

> Gravity defines the morphology of life on Earth. It affects the growth and development of plants and animals by regulating the proliferation of their constituent cells. Gravity also plays crucial roles in cellular function. For example, plants grow leaves and roots in the correct direction by sensing gravity. Animals regulate the densities of bones and muscles in response to gravitational load. A response to gravity is an active activity inherent to the physiology of plants and animals. (Takahashi et al. 2021).

54 For instance, our weight is relative to the gravitational pull of the planet we are (p)art of. Although our mass would be the same, we would weigh more if we were on a planet that is more massive than Earth (such as Jupiter, among others); we would weigh less on a planet that has less mass and, thus, less gravity than Earth – such as Mars. This is the reason why, although their mass is the same, astronauts experience weightlessness in microgravity.

55 Microgravity refers to a condition of low gravity, where the sensation of weightlessness is experienced. The Oxford Dictionary defines it as a "very weak gravity, as in an orbiting spacecraft" (Oxford Dictionaries Online: entry "Microgravity"). Recent studies have shown that microgravity changes microbial biochemistry. For instance, the physiology, as well as the composition of the gut microbiome of astronauts, is altered following space travel (see Siddiqui et al. 2021).
56 See Patel (2019).
57 For a reflection on the contraction of spacetime in relation to the dynamics of urban systems, see, among others, Bretagnolle et al. (1998).
58 The Gravity Recovery and Climate Experiment (GRACE), launched by NASA (2002–17), provided important data on Earth's gravity in relation to global change. The research was conducted on the basis that Earth's mass is distributed unevenly. Mountains, oceans and deep sea trenches have different mass; this creates an uneven gravity field (see Naranjo 2020).
59 As the atmospheric scientist Ken Takahashi explains: "Although plants and animals share some common mechanisms of gravity sensing in spite of their distant phylogenetic origin, each species has its own mechanism to sense and respond to gravity" (Takahashi et al. 2021).
60 Earth's magnetosphere deflects cosmic rays, protecting biological life from solar radiation, which has detrimental health consequences for humans – including DNA damage in cells.
61 See chapter 6.
62 Treaty on Principles Governing the Activities of States in the Exploration and Use of Outer Space (1967), United Nations Office for Outer Space Affairs: www.unoosa.org/oosa/en/ourwork/space law/treaties/introouterspacetreaty.html.
63 Ibid.
64 The body of astronauts should be comprehensive of all humanity; however, it still lacks diversity (see Ferrando 2016a).
65 Treaty on Principles Governing the Activities of States in the Exploration and Use of Outer Space (1967).
66 Currently, a bachelor's degree in "an appropriate field of engineering, biological science, physical science, or mathematics" is one of the necessary requirements for astronauts (NASA 2020). In order to maintain post-nationalistic and post-bellic peace in space, an extensive education in planetary cultures, human diversity and bio-diversity, as well as training in mindfulness and medi(t)ation, should also be required.
67 Treaty on Principles Governing the Activities of States in the Exploration and Use of Outer Space (1967).
68 See chapter 4, #Rights of Nature.
69 Most of the mass of the human body, as well as of all life on Earth,

is made up of six elements, which originally formed during the Big Bang: oxygen, carbon, hydrogen, nitrogen, calcium and phosphorus. About 18 percent of the human body's atoms are carbon. More in general, carbon is the chemical backbone of organic life. For instance, DNA and RNA molecules are made from basic structural units called nucleotides; each contains a five-carbon sugar backbone (the sugar is called deoxy-ribose) – the term "DNA" is the acronym for DeoxyriboNucleic Acid.

70 Currently, the possibility of silicon-based life has been explored in the direct evolution of carbon-silicon bond formation in bacteria (see Kan et al. 2016)
71 Launched by NASA in different months in 1977, they were originally designed to visit Jupiter and Saturn and to last for about five years. Since their hardware kept working, the mission continued. As of 2023, they are still reporting precious data to Earth.
72 Planets outside of our solar system, orbiting other stars, are called exoplanets. The prefix "exo" is derived from ancient Greek (ἔξω), meaning "outer" and "external."
73 The nearest known star system to our solar system is Alpha Centauri; it contains three stars, called Alpha Cen A, B and C. It is considered a good candidate for extraterrestrial life because of its similarities to our solar system.
74 This was demonstrated in the Sloan Digital Sky Survey IV (Blanton et al. 2017), using the optical telescope located at Apache Point Observatory in Sunspot, New Mexico. As Professor Sten Hasselquist, who was involved in the survey, stated: "For the first time, we can now study the distribution of elements across our Galaxy. The elements we measure include the atoms that make up 97% of the mass of the human body" (2017).

Meditation 6: Technological Enhancement

1 This quotation – meaning "I think, therefore I am" – is first found in Part IV ("Proof of God and the Soul") of the treatise *Discourse on the Method* (1637), written by René Descartes (1596–1650).
2 As the Queen phrases it: "Mirror, mirror on the wall, who is the fairest of them all?" Note that, in this context, the term "fairest" reflects an outdated view of beauty based on racial and racist connotations, according to which a fair complexion would be desirable.
3 This term combines "organic" and "inorganic" – (not) consisting of "living" matter.
4 The hope that technology could solve the climate emergency through a shift in technological circuits – such as transitioning from fossil fuel vehicles to electric cars and solar panels – takes care not of the root cause but only the symptoms. The solution does not lie simply in

finding another material to exploit – any type of exploitation reverberates similarly in the sensitive texture of spacetime. It lies, more clearly, in manifesting ways of mindful living.

5 That is, logical-mathematical intelligence (for more on the limits of reason, see chapter 8, #*Mind*). Emotional intelligence, intra-personal intelligence or ecological intelligence, among other types of intelligence, are relegated to minor consideration. The meaning of "intelligence" itself is a notion that is constantly changing, related to the sensitivities of each era.

6 This system is employed, for instance, by the city administration in Hangzhou, China: "The Hangzhou City Brain system is a smart city platform aiming to improve urban management through the use of big data, cloud computing, and artificial intelligence, among other cutting-edge technologies" (www.ehangzhou.gov.cn/2020-10/23/c_275749.htm).

7 According to the Oxford Dictionary, technology is "the application of scientific knowledge for practical purposes"; it is also defined as "machinery and equipment developed from the application of scientific knowledge" (Oxford Dictionaries Online: entry "Technology").

8 See chapter 8.

9 See this chapter, #*Simulation Hypothesis*.

10 This term is constitutive of the word "technology," which literally means: the discourse on "*techne*." Logos (λόγος) in ancient Greek has several meanings, from "word" and "reason," to "discourse" and "argument," among others.

11 See Ferrando (2015).

12 See chapter 7.

13 See Eyal (2014), among others.

14 While people in different fields have somehow coined the term "iGeneration" independently from one another, the word "iGen" is more specifically related to the work of Jean Twenge (2017).

15 Thanks to Mary Roby for mentioning this.

16 According to Greek mythology, Medusa was a female monster with living poisonous snakes in place of hair: her gaze would turn the viewers into stone.

17 See Biggs (2013), among others.

18 The private sector in neuroscience (companies developing neurotechnological gadgets) is a field in worldwide expansion.

19 See, for instance, Cuthbertson (2020), among others.

20 See Kringelbach et al. (2007), among others.

21 Allegations of animal abuse are currently being investigated (as of 2022). They include the death and needless pain of animals resulting from these experiments and also the inhumane treatment of the animals who survive – for instance, monkeys strapped to a chair to play video games with a microchip implanted inside their skull (see Levy 2022).

22 In its ancient Greek etymology, "ethics" refers to "habits" – *etos* (ἦθος) means "character," "moral," and also "habit" and "custom."
23 Cuthbertson (2020).
24 According to the ethics philosopher Abel Wajnerman Paz: "Neural data (ND) is an especially sensitive kind of personal information that could be used to undermine the control we should have over access to our mental states (i.e. our mental privacy), and therefore need a stronger legal protection than other kinds of personal data" (2021: 395).
25 The two categories are not separated. As Gasson puts it: "it is conceivable that a piece of technology designed as a restorative device may actually give the recipient a capability which exceeds the normal human ability it is designed to replace" (2010: 63).
26 This is a short account of the event: "the hacker sent him sounds that triggered different colours before, suddenly, stopping" (Brethour 2015).
27 Quoted ibid.
28 According to the Oxford Dictionary, data can be defined as "facts and statistics collected together for reference or analysis," and also "the quantities, characters, or symbols on which operations are performed by a computer, being stored and transmitted in the form of electrical signals and recorded on magnetic, optical, or mechanical recording media" (Oxford Dictionaries Online: entry "Data").
29 In this book, the term "data" will be conjugated as singular when intended, generally, as a concept; and as plural when indicating, more specifically, some types of data.
30 Within this frame, data are "symbolic representations of observations or thoughts about the world" (Data 2005: 41).
31 See Harari (2017).
32 Instead of the current BCE (before common era)/CE (common era), among other systems of periodization.
33 Currently, racist and sexist biases, among many others, are already embedded in search engine results and algorithms. See this chapter, #*Algorithmic Predestination*.
34 The Oxford Dictionary defines, as "digital native," "a person born or brought up during the age of digital technology and therefore familiar with computers and the internet from an early age" (Oxford Dictionaries Online: entry "Digital native").
35 As the scholar Danielle Coleman phrases it, this occurs when "large-scale tech companies extract, analyze, and own user data for profit and market influence with nominal benefit to the data source" (2019: 417).
36 Thanks to Angelo Marino for this note.
37 As of May 2018, *Pokémon Go* had over 147 million monthly active users.
38 The Merriam-Webster dictionary defines "to microtarget" as "to

direct tailored advertisements, political messages, etc., at (people) based on detailed information about them (such as what they buy, watch, or respond to on a website): to target (small groups of people) for highly specific advertisements or messages" (Merriam-Webster dictionary Online: entry "To microtarget"). As of May 2022, the Oxford Dictionary does not have an entry on "microtargeting."
39 In 2018, it was made known that Cambridge Analytica (a political consulting firm engaged by Donald Trump's political strategist Stephen Bannon) had paid for access to the personal information of about 87 million Facebook users. The data was used to target US voters during the 2016 campaign, which resulted in Trump being elected as the 45th president of the United States; Hillary Clinton won the popular vote. During the first seven months of Trump's term, Bannon served as the White House's chief strategist. See Granville (2018).
40 See this chapter, #*Golden Cage*.
41 Regulations become quickly obsolete. It is hard for the slow-paced regimen of legal systems to keep track of the accelerated developments in current technologies and their economic ramifications. For instance, the General Data Protection Regulation (GDPR), already implemented in the European Union since 2018, with the aim of giving citizens control over their personal data, is an important development in data awareness; and yet it must be constantly updated.
42 This is a reference to "The Big Data Robbery" (VPRO, 2020), a documentary on *The Age of Surveillance Capitalism* (Zuboff 2019).
43 As the scholars Verhelst, Stannat and Mecacci affirm: "Rapid advancements in machine learning techniques allow mass surveillance to be applied on larger scales and utilize more and more personal data" (2020: 2975).
44 See Garcia (2016) and Noble (2018), among others.
45 The case of facial recognition technology is currently (as of 2023) being investigated by the House of Representatives in the US. The regulatory approach varies greatly from state to state; it includes moratoria and bans.
46 See Buolamwini (2018), among others.
47 See Najibi (2020).
48 See chapter 7.
49 Genealogically, the history of technology is related to alchemy and magic (see Principe 2012, among others).
50 See Benjamin (2019).
51 Vandana Shiva (1993) uses the term "monocultures of the mind" in relation to reductionist approaches within the field of biotechnology. Here, this notion expands to the digital realm.
52 The astrobiologist Jacob Haqq-Misra defines the concept of deep altruism as "the selfless pursuit of informational value for the wellbeing of others in the distant future" (2019: 145).

53 We are employing this notion outside of anthropocentric and vitalist premises, in the relevance, and significance, acquired within the field of object-oriented ontology (see Harman 2018, among others).
54 Most virtual assistants (such as Alexa and Siri) have, by default, a female-sounding voice.
55 See LaGrandeur (2013).
56 See chapter 8.
57 See chapter 4, #Posthuman Polite Convention.
58 Existing is the only precondition necessary to be granted existential dignity, which comprehends specific forms of dignity, such as human dignity, non-human dignity and bio-dignity, among others.
59 One month later, in November 2017, Sophia was also the first non-human being to be named by the United Nations as Innovation Champion for Asia and the Pacific.
60 It was developed by Hanson Robotics in 2016.
61 See Wootson (2017).
62 Enlightenment necessarily contemplates every aspect of being. Once the intention is there, the process of becoming enlightened, on some level, has already occurred. According to some Buddhist traditions: "in the moment when the first thought or aspiration to *bodhi* or awakening arises, complete and perfect enlightenment has already been attained" (Wright 2016: 187). On the dynamics of enlightenment, see Conclusions, #*Posthuman Mantra*.
63 Space technologies such as space craft are usually discarded somewhere else in the solar system.
64 According to legend, Gautama Siddhartha lived in the Indian sub continent during the 6th or 5th century BCE. Born into an aristocratic family, he eventually left the palace to know the outside world in order to attain self-knowledge. This led to his enlightenment – Buddha is an honorific title, meaning: "the enlightened one."
65 On the technosphere, see chapter 4, #*Anthropogenic Hermit*.
66 For instance, in the exploration of Mars, robotic rovers have preceded human astronauts. On space technology, see chapter 5, #*Space Migration*.
67 For example, cobalt is a metal used in lithium-ion batteries powering cellphones, laptop computers, tablets and electric cars, among others. Currently, two-thirds of the world supply of cobalt is mined in the southeast region of the Democratic Republic of Congo; most of it enters the global supply chain through dynamics of environmental pollution, systemic poverty and human rights violation (see Van Brusselen et al. 2020).
68 Often, technology is perceived as specific to human beings; and yet it goes well beyond the human: birds' nests, the wood wide web and beavers' dams are clear examples of technological revealing. See chapter 4.
69 This is a serious matter, considering that, some decades from now,

most of the solar panels in use today will become obsolete and in need of replacement.
70 As an example, in wet regions, technologies could explore energetic self-charging potentials through the electrolysis of water in green hydrogen production – this type of renewable energy is generally considered clean because it does not generate polluting emissions in the atmosphere.
71 See chapter 3, #*Radical Life Extension*.
72 Cyborg Foundation (2016).
73 The science-fiction movie *Downsizing* (2017) moves along similar lines.
74 See Sorgner (2021).
75 See Bostrom (2003 and 2014), among others.
76 Living radically long lives in unchallenging conditions may cause gods and goddesses to think they are better than others, forgetting who they truly are (there is no self in Buddhism – as explained in chapter 8, #*Subjects*). Because of karma, after dying, they may find themselves, in the wheel of life, being reborn in hostile dimensions (see Wright 2016).
77 In this context, the term "motivator" contains multiple signifiers, including "motor" and "TIVA." In medical terms, TIVA is the acronym for "Total intravenous anesthesia," referring to the use of intravenous agents to induce – and maintain – anesthesia.
78 Generated out of fear and illusion, technological salvation can be summarized in the anthropocentric pretense: "Let's do as we please; technology will fix the mess."

Meditation 7: Socio-Cultural Agency

1 Even when ART – that is, assisted reproductive technologies – are employed, the gametes of at least two people are still required, together with the healthcare workforce, the social conditions supporting the medical infrastructures, etc.
2 Oxygen is produced in the ocean by a wide range of microorganisms (via phytoplankton photosynthesis); on land, it is created by plants and other organisms via photosynthesis.
3 See chapter 1, #*Inter-being*.
4 These terms are inspired by Martin Heidegger's approach to being ([1927] 2011).
5 The term "society" comes from Latin *societas*, meaning "fellowship," "association," "alliance," "union," "community" – itself derived from *socius/a/um*, meaning "companion," "ally" (Online Etymology Dictionary: entry "Social").
6 A similar view is sustained by the movement of the rights of nature – see chapter 4, #*Rights of Nature*.

7 In this chapter, the pronoun "we" refers, specifically, to our social, collective and pluralistic embodiments, where the one and many necessarily inter-are.
8 United Nations Universal Declaration of Human Rights: www.un.org/en/about-us/universal-declaration-of-human-rights.
9 This interview took place in the context of the "Oxford Amnesty Series of Lectures" in 1992.
10 United Nations: Universal Declaration of Human Rights.
11 See chapter 4, #Rights of Nature.
12 This existential comprehension is in tune with the mystic experience. In the words of the spiritual leader Mirra Alfassa (1878–1973): "I belong to no nation, no civilization, no society, no race, but to the Divine" (as quoted in Kishore 2008: 87). In 1968, Alfassa, also known as the Mother, founded Auroville, an experimental town which, although on Indian land, would belong not to any individual nation but to humanity as a whole. For more on the possible integration of posthuman politics and spirituality, see chapter 8.
13 See Williams (2018).
14 In the social flow of existence, the unbalance found in human-to-human interactions reflects in the current relations of modern humans with ecology and technology. The ecological distress of the Anthropocene and the techno-enchanted ways to perceive technology as somehow separated mirror the approach towards human diversity as an absolute otherness, to be harvested and taken advantage of. For more on this, see chapters 4 and 6.
15 See Brownmiller (1975).
16 The Oxford Dictionary describes the term "disease" as "a disorder of structure or function in a human, animal, or plant, especially one that produces specific signs or symptoms or that affects a specific location and is not simply a direct result of physical injury"; and also as "a particular quality, habit, or disposition regarded as adversely affecting a person or group of people" (Oxford Dictionaries Online: entry "Disease").
17 As José Bertolote affirms: "Although references to mental health as a state can be found in the English language well before the 20th century, technical references to mental health as a field or discipline are not found before 1946" (2008: 113).
18 With the specialization of labour and roles, human societies can be partially considered super-organisms. See chapter 4, #Superorganism.
19 Medical Encyclopedia Online: entry "Systemic."
20 For an understanding of viruses as (p)art of the human, see chapter 3, #Vir/us.
21 See Guth and Steinhardt (1984); Linde (1994).
22 See Linde (1986).
23 According to these scientific theories, our Big Bang would be just one of many: separate universes could be springing up as bubbles

of spacetime in an infinite, and random, formation of "bubble universes." For more on this, see chapter 5.
24 In this book, consciousness refers to a state shared at the level of the species. Awareness is approached as a wider, all-encompassing perception, where species relations do not have special relevance. See chapter 8.
25 Automatic habits are not to be confused with instinctive actions that serve as preconditions of manifesting in this dimension. For instance, our hearts are beating not out of automatic repetitions but as necessary and poietic dynamics of biological revealing.
26 According to recent studies, it takes humans an average of 66 days for a new behavior to become automatic (Lally et al. 2009).
27 "Automatic" is synonymous neither with "automated" nor with "mechanic": humans can act automatically, while machines can (be)come mindful, beyond human comprehension. See chapter 6.
28 Sri Nisargadatta Maharaj (1897–1981), a Hindu sage of the Indian non-dualist philosophy of Advaita, describes the human this way: "Totally a creature of heredity and society, he lives by memory and acts by habits. Ignorant of himself" (1973: 376).
29 Past wisdom can be of help but cannot be fully enlightening, as it manifests through the modes of a different era; this is why it may still present discriminatory terms that no longer fit our perception.
30 The ancient Chinese philosopher Confucius (551 BCE – 479 BCE) realized that rituals and ceremonies function as precious and cherished social cement, not only by bonding communities together but by serving a transformative role towards individual and communal self-cultivation.
31 The main evidence comes from the Neolithic archeological site of Göbekli Tepe, in Anatolia, Turkey; dating from around 12,000 years ago, it is considered the first world temple (or, better said, complex of temples). As the historian Bettany Hughes (b. 1967) put it: "We always used to think that organized religion began when men and women started to ... settle down together; but the evidence from Göbekli Tepe seems to suggest exactly the opposite: ... society isn't creating religion; it's religion that is forming human society itself" (2012).
32 See chapter 8, #Posthuman Archetypes.
33 The Online Etymology Dictionary defines "identity" as "sameness, oneness, state of being the same," from the French term *identité*, itself derived from medieval Latin *identitas* ("sameness"), which ultimately comes from classical Latin *idem*, meaning "the same" (Online Etymology Dictionary: entry "Identity").
34 To be read as /i/: "id-entity" ("*eed-entity*"), instead of "identity" ("*eyed-entity*").
35 This term does not necessarily rely on the psychoanalytical notion of "id" as developed by Sigmund Freud (1856–1939).

36 The Oxford Dictionary defines "knowledge" as "facts, information, and skills acquired by a person through experience or education; the theoretical or practical understanding of a subject," and also "awareness or familiarity gained by experience of a fact or situation" (Oxford Dictionaries Online: entry "Knowledge").
37 The philosophical and religious traditions that contemplate rebirth and reincarnation (such as Hinduism, Buddhism and Orphism) may approach death as repeated and continual instead of ultimate and isolated.
38 See chapter 8, #Non-Being.
39 For instance, gatherer-hunter cultures have historically relied on collective storytelling as a technology of distribution and transmission.
40 For more on this, see the work of the decolonial thinker Sylvia Wynter (b. 1928), specifically, Wynter (2003) and McKittrick (2015).
41 In this text, we will capitalize neither "black" nor "white", in tune with the reflection of the philosopher Kwame Anthony Appiah (2020): "black and white are both historically created racial identities – and whatever rule applies to one should apply to the other." Capitalizing one term would lead to the capitalization of the other one, with the entangled systems of supremacy and racial oppression that this may convey.
42 See King (2018).
43 It is important to note that the socio-political as well as the onto-epistemological responses to the systematic dehumanization of black and native populations in the Americas can lead to different perspectives: from posthuman and transhuman trajectories (see Butler 2019, among others) to the possibilities of manifesting other ways of being human. As Tiffany Lethabo King states:

> If the primary concern for Black and Native studies is to interrogate and then destroy the structures and lineaments that make the human-as-man possible, then Black and Native people do not necessarily seek to inhabit the space of the human or identity as they currently exist. For example, if Black Lives Matter (BLM) is asking to be absorbed into the category of the human, then BLM's version of the human does not yet exist. (2017: 180)

44 See chapter 6, #Poiesis.
45 Names have been changed for privacy; the episode is accurate.
46 The idea of war as natural is sometimes presented through the examples of other primates, such as chimpanzees being "inherently" violent (Wilson et al. 2014). This is not accurate. Bonobos share the same amount of DNA in common with humans: they are peaceful and do not engage in territorial wars. Furthermore, chimpanzees, like any other beings, are affected, and effected, by the changes around them; in their evolutionary history, war may be a recently acquired trait, as in the case of humans. See chapter 2, #Primates, Chimps and Bonobos.

47 Etymologically, the term "education" comes from the Latin verb *educere*, which means "to bring out, to lead forth"; the verb is produced by the merging of the prefix *ex-* (meaning "out") and *ducere* (meaning "to lead"). It can be approached as bringing forth something in the path of self-knowledge. It can also be approached as leading someone out of something; in this sense, it has been interpreted as leading children out of childhood. And yet, from the perspective of wisdom, the stage of the child, characterized by the primordial awe and curiosity for existence, is the final state of enlightenment: the point is not to obfuscate it.
48 Oxford Dictionaries Online: entry "Education."
49 It is important to note that, in ancient Greece, leisure was generally considered the realm of free men: slaves and women, among others, were not granted the luxury and privilege of not working.
50 As the Roman Stoic philosopher Seneca (4 BCE – 65 CE) put it, to explain the need he had for *otium*: "What am I doing in my leisure? I am healing my wounds" (*Epistles*: 68.8). For more on this, see Kalimtzis (2017: ch. 6).
51 See chapter 2, #*Regeneration*.
52 See Rury and Tamura (2017).
53 This may change with the development of generative artificial intelligence (or generative AI) – think, for instance, of applications such as ChatGPT and DALL-E.
54 See Mann et al. (2022), among others.
55 See Gray (2013).
56 See chapter 6.
57 See chapter 4.
58 This topic needs a much deeper reflection; here, we will offer only general inputs and considerations.
59 Another way to put it is, in the words of Marshall McLuhan (1911–1980): "the medium is the message" (1964). On posthuman methodologies, see Ferrando (2012).
60 Our "modern" society, on the verge of ecological collapse, can learn greatly from native people's perception of the Earth. See chapter 4.
61 Posthuman education is open to a diverse range of pedagogical possibilities, embracing both schooling and unschooling techniques of learning.
62 The Waldorf system of education is based and inspired on Steiner's philosophy of education.
63 To understand this notion, see Ferrando (2019: ch. 12).
64 The long-lived civilization of Sumer (c. 4500 BCE – c. 1900 BCE), in ancient Mesopotamia, preceded the Akkadian Empire.
65 This ancient mythology reflects millennia of matrifocal symbolisms of the Paleolithic and Neolithic times, as demonstrated by the large number of female figurines dating to these eras.
66 See chapter 2.

67 On the difference between awareness and consciousness, see chapter 8, #(P)Art.
68 Exceptions usually rely on the stereotype of the loving mother, where females are essentialized in nurturing roles.
69 Until age five, my daughter selected the use of the pronoun "they" to refer to themselves. Currently, at age six, she is choosing the pronoun "she." Id-entity is a process, constantly shifting and mutating, depending on contextual inputs and outputs.
70 We would like to acknowledge the love and generosity that our extended family expressed in offering these items: we are truly grateful. This is not an individual criticism but an acknowledgement of cultural practices and expectations.
71 Names have been changed for privacy; the episode is accurate.
72 As the philosopher Friedrich Nietzsche explained in *Thus Spoke Zarathustra: A Book for All and None* ([1883–5] 2006), the lion – which, in the metamorphosis of the spirit, represents the phase of the rebel – cannot create, because they are too busy protecting their freedom. See chapter 8, #*Posthuman Archetypes*.
73 As the Chief Justice Earl Warren famously put it: "We conclude that, in the field of public education, the doctrine of 'separate but equal' has no place. Separate educational facilities are inherently unequal." Full text available at www.uscourts.gov/educational-resources/educational-activities/history-brown-v-board-education-re-enactment.
74 Full text available at https://casetext.com/case/peltier-v-charter-day-schs.
75 When something happens to women, it is often blamed on women These are some of the dehumanizing statements that reiterate and normalize gender violence: "she should not have been there"; "she was wearing (*this or that*)"; "she should not be out at night"; "she was all alone/on her own"; and so on.
76 For instance, in some jurisdictions, marital rape is not yet considered a crime. As the World Health Organization states: "Dismantling hierarchical constructions of masculinity and femininity predicated on the control of women, and eliminating the structural factors that support inequalities are likely to make a significant contribution to preventing intimate partner and sexual violence" (2016: 36).
77 As the philosopher of science Karen Barad put it: "agency is a matter of intra-acting; it is an enactment, not something that someone or something has. . . . Agency is 'doing' or 'being' in its intra-activity" (2007: 178).
78 To understand the significance of non-conscious agency, see Hayles (2017).
79 Online Etymology Dictionary: entry "Agency."
80 Ancient philosophers would generally recognize contemplation (*vita contemplativa*) as superior to action (*vita activa*); such a preference

may still arise out of dichotomous modes of existing, which may not be conducive towards self-realization. See Arendt (1958).
81 As of 2022.
82 Here, this term refers to multiple and intersectional types of embodiments, such as bio-physical, socio-cultural, digital, technological, etc.
83 *Distributed agency* can be coordinated, uncoordinated and/or casual, among other ways of manifesting.
84 See chapter 4.
85 In the possible forms of anthropocentrism, bio-centrism, techno-centrism, sexism, racism, ethnocentrism, ableism, ageism and elitism, among many others.

Meditation 8: Ontological Awareness

1 Monier-Williams ([1899] 1960), entry: "Sat."
2 Ibid., entry: "Chit."
3 Ibid., entry: "Ananda."
4 Here to be intended as "a set of principles underlying and guiding the work of a particular artist or artistic movement" (Oxford Dictionaries Online: entry "Aesthetic").
5 For instance, (what was later called) the "Bridge of Death" was a bridge where some residents of the Ukrainian town of Pripyat (ex-USSR), without knowing the risks of exposure, stood to look at the mesmerizing electric blue light caused by the ionized air dissolving in the sky on the night of the accident at the nuclear plant at Chernobyl (1986). In the fictional representation of this event, one of the characters of the mini-series *Chernobyl* (HBO 2019), unaware of its related health hazards, says: "It is beautiful": www.youtube.com/watch?v=o4vBRr2ItFg.
6 See chapter 7.
7 The Oxford Dictionary defines "an archetype" as "a very typical example of a certain person or thing, also an original that has been imitated, and a recurrent symbol or motif in literature, art, or mythology" (Oxford Dictionaries Online: entry "Archetype").
8 This classification must be approached as a historical reference more than an actual categorization. It is worth noting that Foucault did not employ it to define his work.
9 This folktale was published in 1837 by the Danish author Hans Christian Andersen (1805–1875).
10 As the philosopher Roberto Marchesini puts it: "Life is a continuous creativity. Every living being must necessarily be creative; they must face problems and invent new solutions, because the real presents itself to them in a unique way every time" (Ferrando and Marchesini 2018: 13:23–13:30; translation mine).

11 This does not culminate in an ontological nihilism: not-being is essential to being. See this chapter, #Non-Being.
12 Interviewed in "What is Consciousness Hacking?," www.youtube.com/watch?v=sc_nlW2367Q&t=82s, 1:17–1:21.
13 Ibid., 1:30–1:43.
14 See www.cohack.org/about/.
15 As Aurobindo states: "A change in consciousness is the major fact of the next evolutionary transformation, and the consciousness itself, by its own mutation, will impose and effect any necessary mutation of the body" ([1963] 1974: 10).
16 In his words: "As the summits of human mind are beyond animal perception, so the movements of super-mind are beyond the ordinary human mental conception" (ibid.: 77). Similar to Nietzsche's *Übermensch*, the supermind is presented in human-centric terms in the hierarchical processual compound: animal perception/human mental conception/movements of the supermind.
17 For a reflection on the connected term "bodymind," see chapter 3, #Embodiments.
18 For instance, the Theravada Buddhist practice of Vipassana is based on a detached observation of the world and of the self: that is, self-observation. As the Vipassana teacher Satya Narayana Goenka (1924–2013) describes it, Vipassana processes by "de-conditioning the mind," as the opposite of "imposing anything on the mind" (Hart 1987: 18), resonating, at an engaged level, with the posthuman intentional practice of decluttering.
19 The skin on a human body is the most superficial organ; it is also the largest one.
20 See chapter 3, #Bio-me.
21 See chapter 5.
22 This specific choice can be traced back to the work of Aristotle, who defined the human through *logos* (that is, speech and language, but also reason): "man alone of the animals possesses speech [*logos*]" (*Politics*, 1.1253a).
23 Historically, this limited understanding has served as the political and scientific narrative for a minority of humans, across different times and eras, to exploit and devalue many forms of life, including human life. Most humans, for instance, were denied access to formal education and other basic human rights because they were considered "unreasonable" and less "intelligent" – as the intersectional histories of sexism, racism, ableism, classism, casteism and colonialism, among many others, demonstrate.
24 Humans are those animals who, in their biological evolution, have specifically developed enlarged brains. See chapter 2, #Scientifically, Human.
25 On posthuman perspectivism, see Ferrando (2019: ch. 27).
26 Panpsychism comes in different forms; it has been developed

throughout many eras and cultures. Here we will refer, more clearly, to the modern history of panpsychism and its revived interest in the 20th and 21st centuries.
27. The human category is also hierarchically constructed – some humans being considered more "human" than others. Human and non-human supremacies emerge jointly, one type of discrimination necessarily supporting the other.
28. Etymologically, the term "psyche" is defined as the "animating spirit, the human spirit or mind" (Online Etymology Dictionary: entry "Psyche"). The word derives from Latin *psyche*, rooted in the Greek (ψῦχή), meaning "the soul, mind, spirit; life, one's life, the invisible animating principle or entity which occupies and directs the physical body; understanding, the mind (as the seat of thought), faculty of reason" (ibid.). The concepts of "psyche," "mind" and "reason" are intrinsically related, and semantically indebted, to the human.
29. As the philosopher of mind David Chalmers states: "we can understand panpsychism as the thesis that some fundamental physical entities have mental states. For example, if quarks or photons have mental states, that suffices for panpsychism to be true, even if rocks and numbers do not have mental states" (2013: 1).
30. This type of perspectivism is a multinaturalism, not a multiculturalism. As Marina Vanzolini and Pedro Cesarino explain: "This ontological shift is condensed in the contrast between multinaturalism (different corporeal states that presuppose a similar human and cultural condition) and multiculturalism (the same and common nature or reality, regarded by different cultural points of view). Multinaturalism entails a relationalism (which is perspectivism), while multiculturalism entails a relativism (that must not be mistaken for perspectivism)" (2014).
31. Anthropocentric myths can be found throughout different eras, cultures and civilizations, with different nuances and related to heterogeneous value systems, which cannot be simply assimilated.
32. See Gade (2017), among others.
33. Iyaric is the language intentionally developed by the Rastafari movement.
34. This unity of being is expressed in the philosophy of *Wahadat-al-Wujud* by the Sufi mystic Ibn Al 'Arabī (1165–1240). For an understanding of this doctrine, see Ibn Al 'Arabī's work *Fuṣūṣ al-Ḥikam* (c. 1229), translated as *The Bezels of Wisdom* (1992).
35. The term derives from the Sanskrit word *Anātman* (अनात्मन्), formed by the privative prefix *a(n)* ("not/without") and *atman*, which can be generally translated as "self."
36. The prefix *ex-* means "out"; the verb *sistere* means "to stand," "to appear."
37. As Sri Nisargadatta Maharaj further clarifies: "the entire universe (*mahadakash*) exists only in consciousness (*chidakash*), while I have my

stand in the Absolute (*paramakash*).... Even not-being is unthinkable without me" (1973: 15).
38 Oxford Dictionaries Online: entry "To unravel."
39 It may be worth noting that, in the dream, they were mostly white and male.
40 From this perspective, wakefulness, when we perceive ourselves as individuals absolutely separated from others, is approached as the actual illusion. The liquid reality of dreaming, when everything can happen at once in full poietic potential, unfolds as the actual fabric of existence.
41 This term refers to the absolute reality: the beginning and the end of the creation process, (re)generating (in and through) the land (see Isaacs 1980, among others).
42 See Banerji and Ferrando (forthcoming).
43 For instance, Ṣadr ad-Dīn Muḥammad Shīrāzī, also known as Mulla Sadra (1572–1641), was a Persian mystic and philosopher who successfully integrated the clarity of the intellect with the transcendental mystic experience. As the scholar Fazlur Rahman pointed out, to explain Sadra's work: "mystic truth is essentially intellectual truth and mystic experience is a cognitive experience, but this intellectual truth and this cognitive content have to be 'lived through' to be fully realized; if they are only intellectually entertained as rational propositions, they lose their essential character" (1975: 4).
44 This quotation is disputed.
45 For instance, according to Zen Buddhism, enlightenment is achieved through the direct experience, and realization, of being already enlightened (see Wright 2016, among others).
46 The bio-sphere and the techno-sphere cannot be understood in separation; this term combines them.

Conclusions: Posthuman Mantra

1 See chapter 3, #Bio-me.
2 See chapter 6, note 22.
3 "Art" is a noun derived from Latin *ars*, meaning a skilled work; an activity demanding a high level of technical ability – that is, *techne*. See chapter 6, #*Poiesis*, and chapter 8, #(P)Art.
4 This is a play on the word "addiction" in relation to "ads" and "diction."
5 The field of posthumanism as a praxis, and a practice, is in full expansion. See Daigle and Hayler (2023).
6 This term is embraced as reflective of the conditions of the 21st century, in the co-emergence of local and global specificities.
7 Examples of essentialist reductions are bio-centrism, techno-centrism, speciesism, sexism, racism and ableism, among others.

8 On the use of this spelling, see chapter 7, #Id-Entity.
9 In this context, the term "enlightened" does not necessarily refer to the "enlightenment" as a spiritual state of self-attainment (contemplated, for instance, in Hindu and Buddhist traditions, among others). It indicates, more precisely, the cultural paradigm developed in the rise of the Industrial Revolution; genealogically related to the European Enlightenment, it has evolved and mutated at a planetary scale in the last three centuries. Generally, this notion of the human is not comprehensive of humanity as a whole.
10 See Ferrando (2016b).

References

Abourezk, K. (2009) Archway event marks Pawnee tribe, *Native Times*, March 30.
Absolon, K. (2019) Indigenous wholistic theory: a knowledge set for practice, *First Peoples Child & Family Review*, 14(1): 22–42.
Akhtar, A. (2015) The flaws and human harms of animal experimentation, *Cambridge Quarterly of Healthcare Ethics*, 24(4): 407–19.
Alaimo, S. (2010) *Bodily Natures: Science, Environment, and the Material Self*. Bloomington: Indiana University Press.
Alberts, B., et al. (2002) *Molecular Biology of the Cell*. 4th edn, New York: Garland Science.
Aldeia, J., and Alves, F. (2019) Against the environment: problems in society/nature relations, *Frontiers in Sociology*, 4: 29.
Anandamayi Ma (2007) *The Essential Sri Anandamayi Ma: Life and Teaching of a 20th Century Indian Saint*, ed. J. Fitzgerald. Bloomington, IN: World Wisdom.
Appiah, K. A. (2020) The case for capitalizing the B in Black, *The Atlantic*, June 18.
Arendt, H. (1958) *The Human Condition*. Chicago: University of Chicago Press.
Aristotle (1944) *Politics*, trans. H. Rackham, Vol. 21 of Aristotle in 23 volumes. Cambridge, MA: Harvard University Press; www.perseus.tufts.edu/hopper/text?doc=Perseus:abo:tlg,0086,035: 1:1253a.
Aurobindo, S. ([1963] 1974) *The Future Evolution of Man: The Divine Life upon Earth*, ed. P. B. Saint-Hilaire. Twin Lakes, WI: Lotus Press.
—— ([1939–40] 1990) *The Life Divine*. Pondicherry: Sri Aurobindo Ashram Press.
Ayyangar, T. R. S. (1938) *The Yoga Upanishads*. Madras: Adyar.
Baedke, J., Fábregas-Tejeda, A., and Nieves Delgado, A. (2020) The holobiont concept before Margulis, *Journal of Experimental Zoology B: Molecular and Developmental Evolution*, 334(3): 149–155.
Banerji, D., and Ferrando, F. (forthcoming) Posthuman spirituality,

in G. Hamilton and W. Lau (eds), *Mapping the Posthuman*. London: Routledge.

Barad, K. (2007) *Meeting the Universe Halfway: Quantum Physics and the Entanglement of Matter and Meaning*. Durham, NC: Duke University Press.

Baudrimont, A., et al. (2017) Multiplexed gene control reveals rapid mRNA turnover, *Science Advances*, 3(7).

BBC News (2011) Bacteria in mouse gut affect development and behaviour, February 1, www.bbc.com/news/science-environment-12306431.

Beekman, M., and Oldroyd, B. P. (2018) Different bees, different needs – how nest-site requirements have shaped the decision-making processes in homeless honeybees (*Apis* spp.), *Philosophical Transactions of the Royal Society B*, 373: 20170010.

Benjamin, R. (2019) *Race after Technology: Abolitionist Tools for the New Jim Code*. Cambridge: Polity.

Bennett, J. (2010) *Vibrant Matter: A Political Ecology of Things*. Durham, NC: Duke University Press.

Berg, G., Rybakova, D., Fischer, D., et al. (2020) Microbiome definition re-visited: old concepts and new challenges, *Microbiome*, 8: 1–22.

Bertolote J. (2008) The roots of the concept of mental health, *World Psychiatry*, 7(2): 113–16, https://doi.org/10.1002/j.2051-5545.2008.tb00172.x.

Betts, H. C., et al. (2018) Integrated genomic and fossil evidence illuminates life's early evolution and eukaryote origin, *Nature, Ecology & Evolution*, 2: 1556–62.

Bęwaji, J. A. I. (2018) Yorùbá values and the environment, *Yoruba Studies Review*, 3(1): 229–49.

Biggs, M. (2013) Prophecy, self-fulfilling/self-defeating, in B. Kaldis (ed.), *Encyclopedia of Philosophy and the Social Sciences*. Thousand Oaks, CA: Sage.

Bingen, H. von ([1151/1152] 1986) *Scivias*, trans. B. Hozeski. Santa Fe, NM: Bear.

Blanton, M. R., et al. (2017) Sloan Digital Sky Survey IV: mapping the Milky Way, nearby galaxies, and the distant universe, *Astronomical Journal*, 154(1).

Bloomer, K. (2016) [The Greeks] called it KOSMOS, which means ornament, *Approaching Religion*, 6(2): 44–54.

Bostrom, N. (2003) Are you living in a computer simulation?, *Philosophical Quarterly*, 53: 243–55.

—— (2014) *Superintelligence: Paths, Dangers, Strategies*. Oxford: Oxford University Press.

Braidotti, R. (2019a) Preface: in excess of Anthropocentrism, in F. Ferrando, *Philosophical Posthumanism*. London: Bloomsbury, pp. xiv–xvi.

—— (2019b) *Posthuman Knowledge*. Cambridge: Polity.

Bretagnolle, A., Pumain, D., and Rozenblat, C. (1998) Space-time contraction and the dynamics of urban systems, *Cybergeo: European Journal of Geography, Cybergeo: European Journal of Geography*, document 61, http://journals.openedition.org/cybergeo/373.

Brethour, D. (2015) Why are you sending me colours in my head? An interview with cyborg artist Neil Harbisson, *Head Stuff, Science and Tech*, October 27, www.headstuff.org/topical/science/why-are-you-sending-me-colours-in-my-head-an-interview-with-cyborg-artist-neil-harbisson/.

Brownmiller, S. (1975) *Against Our Will: Men, Women and Rape*. New York: Simon & Schuster.

Buck v. Bell (1927) United States Supreme Court no. 292; argued April 22; decided May 2 [274 U.S. 200, 201].

Buolamwini, J. (2018) Gender shades: intersectional accuracy disparities in commercial gender classification, *Proceedings of Machine Learning Research*, 81: 1–15.

Butler, P. (2018) Making enhancement equitable: a racial analysis of the term "human animal" and the inclusion of black bodies in human enhancement, *Journal of Posthuman Studies*, 2(1): 106–21.

―― (2019) *Black Transhuman Liberation Theology*. New York: Bloomsbury.

Caperton Morton, M. (2016) Redefining Homo: does our family tree need more branches?, *Earth: The Science behind the Headlines*, August 16, www.earthmagazine.org/article/redefining-homo-does-our-family-tree-need-more-branches/.

Cavarero, A. (2016) *Inclinations: A Critique of Rectitude*, trans. A. Sitze and A. Minervini. Stanford, CA: Stanford University Press.

Chakrabarty, D. (2019) The planet: an emergent humaniot category, *Critical Inquiry*, 46(1): 1–31.

Chalmers, D. J. (2013) *Panpsychism and Panprotopsychism*. Amherst Lecture in Philosophy, 8, www.amherstlecture.org/chalmers2013/chalmers2013_ALP.pdf.

Clarke, B. (2017) Planetary immunity: biopolitics, Gaia theory, the holobiont, and the systems counterculture, in E. Hörl and J. Burton (eds), *General Ecology: The New Ecological Paradigm*. London: Bloomsbury Academic.

Clayton, S., Manning, C. M., Krygsman, K., and Speiser, M. (2017) *Mental Health and Our Changing Climate: Impacts, Implications, and Guidance*. Washington, DC: American Psychological Association and ecoAmerica.

Coleman, D. (2019) Digital colonialism: the 21st century scramble for Africa through the extraction and control of user data and the limitations of data protection laws, *Michigan Journal of Race and Law*, 24(2): 417–39.

Coole, D., and Frost, S. (2010) *New Materialisms: Ontology, Agency and Politics*. Durham, NC: Duke University Press.

Cooper, M. (2008) *Life as Surplus: Biotecnology & Capitalism in the Neoliberal Era*. Seattle: University of Washington Press.

Crutzen, P. J., and Stoermer, E. F. (2000) The "Anthropocene", *Global Change Newsletter*, no. 41: 17–18.
Cuthbertson, A. (2020) Elon Musk claims AI will overtake humans "in less than five years", *The Independent*, July 27.
Cyborg Foundation (2016) *Cyborg Foundation: Design Yourself*, YouTube, https://youtu.be/Vo95354RQ40.
Daigle C., and Hayler, M. (eds) (2023) *Posthumanism in Practice*. London: Bloomsbury Academic.
Darwin, C. (1862) *On the Various Contrivances by Which British and Foreign Orchids Are Fertilised by Insects, and On the Good Effects of Intercrossing*. London: John Murray.
Data (2005) "Data," in *The Grammar of Graphics: Statistics and Computing*. New York: Springer, ch. 3; https://doi.org/10.1007/0-387-28695-0_3.
de Grey, A. (2007) *Ending Aging: The Rejuvenation Breakthroughs that Could Reverse Human Aging in our Lifetime*. New York: St Martin's Press.
De Seville, Isidore ([c. 600–625] 2010) *The Etymologies of Isidore of Seville*, trans. S. A. Barney, W. J. Lewis, J. A. Beach, and O. Berghof. Cambridge: Cambridge University Press.
Deleuze, G., and Guattari, F. ([1980] 1987) *A Thousand Plateaus: Capitalism and Schizophrenia*, trans. B. Massumi. London: Continuum.
Derrida, J., and Montefiore, A. ([1992] 2001) "Talking liberties": Jacques Derrida's interview with Alan Montefiore, in G. J. J. Biesta and D. Egéa-Kuehne (eds), *Derrida & Education*. London: Routledge, pp. 176–85.
Dion, D., Sabri, O., and Guillard, V. (2014) Home sweet messy home: managing symbolic pollution, *Journal of Consumer Research*, 41(3): 565–89.
Douglas, M. ([1966] 2002) *Purity and Danger: An Analysis of Concepts of Pollution and Taboo*. London: Routledge & Kegan Paul.
Dubois, M., and Guaspare, C. (2020) From cellular memory to the memory of trauma: social epigenetics and its public circulation, *Social Science Information*, 59(1): 144–83.
Einstein, A. ([1915] 1952) The Foundation of the General Theory of Relativity, trans. W. Parret and G. B. Jeffrey, in Einstein et al., *The Principle of Relativity: A Collection of Original Memoirs on the Special and General Theory of Relativity*. New York: Dover, pp. 109–64.
Eyal, N. (2014) *Hooked: How to Build Habit-Forming Products*. London: Penguin.
Ferrando, F. (2012) Towards a posthumanist methodology: a statement, *Frame*, 25(1): 9–18.
Ferrando, F. (2015) Of posthuman born: gender, utopia and the posthuman, in C. Carbonell, M. Hauskeller and T. Philbeck (eds), *Handbook on Posthumanism in Film and Television*. London: Palgrave Macmillan, pp. 269–78.
—— (2016a) Why space migration must be posthuman, in J. Schwartz

and T. Milligan (eds), *The Ethics of Space Exploration*. Cham: Springer, pp. 137–52.

—— (2016b) The party of the Anthropocene: posthumanism, environmentalism and the post-anthropocentric paradigm shift, *Relations Beyond Anthropocentrism*, 4(2): 159–73.

—— (2019) *Philosophical Posthumanism*. London: Bloomsbury.

—— (2022a) Are we becoming God(s)? Transhumanism, posthumanism, antihumanism and the divine, in A. M. Gouw, B. P. Green, and T. Peters (eds), *Religious Transhumanism and its Critics*. Lanham, MD: Lexington Books, pp. 31–50.

—— (2022b) Who is afraid of artificial intelligence? A posthumanist take on the AI takeover scenario, in F. P. Grunert (ed.), *HumaniTies and Artificial Intelligence*. European Commission, pp. 85–90.

—— (2023) To be or not to be enhanced? Just ask the Moon – in posthuman terms, in F. Jotterand and M. Ienca (eds), *The Routledge Handbook of the Ethics of Human Enhancement*. New York: Routledge, pp. 30–44.

Ferrando, F., and Marchesini, R. (2017) Biocentrismo: Francesca Ferrando intervista Roberto Marchesini, episode 3, May 2018, www.youtube.com/watch?v=m-3Gl1D0QlM.

Ferrando, F., and More, M. (2013) Transhumanism, in Karl Jaspers Society of North America Conference "Humanity and Posthumanity," APA, San Francisco, March 2013; https://youtu.be/7Sr1kcogOoE.

Fiedler, L. (1978) *Freaks: Myths and Images of the Secret Self*. New York: Simon & Schuster.

Foucault, M. ([1966] 1970) *The Order of Things. An Archaeology of the Human Sciences*, trans. A. Sheridan. New York: Random House.

—— ([1975] 1995) *Discipline and Punish: The Birth of the Prison*, trans. A. Sheridan. New York: Random House.

Gade, C. B. N. (2017) *A Discourse on African Philosophy: A New Perspective on Ubuntu and Transitional Justice in South Africa*. Lanham, MD: Lexington Books.

Gallagher, J. (2018) More than half your body is not human, *BBC News*, April 10, www.bbc.co.uk/news/health-43674270.

Gallello, G., et al. (2018) Poisoning histories in the Italian Renaissance: the case of Pico della Mirandola and Angelo Poliziano, *Journal of Forensic and Legal Medicine*, 56: 83–9.

Garcia, M. (2016) Racist in the machine: the disturbing implications of algorithmic bias, *World Policy Journal*, 33(4): 111–17.

Gasson, M. (2010) Human enhancement: could you become infected with a computer virus?, in K. Michael (ed.), *Proceedings of the IEEE International Symposium on Technology and Society*. Phoenix, AZ: IEEE Computer Society Press, pp. 498–516.

Geddis, A., and Ruru, J. (2020) Places as persons: creating a new framework for Māori–Crown relations, in J. Varuhas and S. Wilson Stark (eds) *The Frontiers of Public Law*. London: Bloomsbury, pp. 255–74.

Gerbault, P., Liebert, A., Itan, Y., Powell, A., Currat, M., Burger, J., Swallow, D. M., and Thomas, M. G. (2011) Evolution of lactase persistence: an example of human niche construction, *Philosophical Transactions of the Royal Society*, 366: 863–77.

Getman, K. A. (1984) Sexual control in the slaveholding South: the implementation and maintenance of a racial caste system, *Harvard Women's Law Journal*, 7: 115.

Gimbutas, M. (1989) *The Language of the Goddess*. San Francisco: Harper & Row.

Glansdorff, N., Xu, Y., and Labedan, B. (2008) The last universal common ancestor: emergence, constitution and genetic legacy of an elusive forerunner, *Biology Direct*, 9(3): 29.

Gleiser, M. (2012) Looking for answers beyond the cosmic horizon, *NPR News*, September 26, www.wbur.org/npr/161720648/looking-for-answers-beyond-the-cosmic-horizon.

Goeckeritz, I., Crimmel, H., and Berros, M. V. (2018) *Rights of Nature: A Global Movement*, www.youtube.com/watch?v=kuFNmH7lVTA [documentary].

Gould, S. J. (1989) *Wonderful Life*. New York: W. W. Norton.

Granville, K. (2018) Facebook and Cambridge Analytica: what you need to know as fallout widens, *New York Times*, March 19.

Gray, P. (2013) *Free to Learn: Why Unleashing the Instinct to Play Will Make Our Children Happier, More Self-Reliant, and Better Students for Life*. New York: Basic Books.

Guth, A. H., and Steinhardt, P. J. (1984) The inflationary universe, *Scientific American*, 250(5): 90–102.

Haff, P. K. (2013) Technology as a geological phenomenon: implications for human well-being, in C. N. Waters et al. (eds), *A Stratigraphical Basis for the Anthropocene*. London: Geological Society, pp. 301–9.

Hanh, Thich Nhat (2004) *Creating True Peace: Ending Violence in Yourself, Your Family, Your Community, and the World*. New York: Atria.

—— (2005) *Calming the Fearful Mind: A Zen Response to Terrorism*. Berkeley, CA: Parallax Press.

—— (2021) *Zen and the Art of Saving the Planet*. San Francisco HarperOne.

Haqq-Misra, J. (2019) Can deep altruism sustain space settlement?, in K. Szocik (ed.), *The Human Factor in a Mission to Mars: An Interdisciplinary Approach*. Cham: Springer, pp. 145–55.

Harari, Y. (2017) *Homo Deus: A Brief History of Tomorrow*. New York: HarperCollins.

Haraway, D. (1990) *Primate Visions: Gender, Race, and Nature in the World of Modern Science*. New York: Routledge.

—— (2003) *The Companion Species*. Chicago: Prickly Paradigm Press.

—— (2016) *Staying with the Trouble: Making Kin in the Chthulucene*. London: Duke University Press.

Harman, G. (2018) *Object-Oriented Ontology: A New Theory of Everything*. London: Penguin.

Hart, W. (1987) *The Art of Living: Vipassana Meditation as Taught by S.N. Goenka*. San Francisco: Harper & Row.

Hasselquist, S. (2017) The elements of life mapped across the Milky Way by SDSS/APOGEE, Sloan Digital Sky Survey, January 5, www.sdss.org/press-releases/the-elements-of-life-mapped-across-the-milky-way-by-sdssapogee/.

Hayden, B., and Villeneuve, S. (2011) Astronomy in the Upper Paleolithic?, *Cambridge Archaeological Journal*, 21(3): 331–55.

Hayles, K. (2017) *Unthought: The Power of the Cognitive Nonconscious*. Chicago: University of Chicago Press.

Hazen, R. M. (2010) How old is Earth, and how do we know? *Evolution: Education and Outreach*, 3: 198–205.

Hegner, I. von (2021) Evolutionary processes transpiring in the stages of lithopanspermia, *Acta Biotheoretica*, 69(4): 783–98.

Heidegger, M. ([1953] 1977) *The Question Concerning Technology and Other Essays*, trans. W. Lovitt. New York: Harper Torchbooks.

—— ([1947] 1998) Letter on "Humanism," in *Martin Heidegger: Pathmarks*, ed. and trans. W. McNeil. Cambridge: Cambridge University Press.

—— ([1927] 2011) *Being and Time*, trans. J. Macquarrie and E. Robinson. New York: Harper & Row.

Horgan, J. (2012) *The End of War*. New York: McSweeney.

Hughes, B. (2012) *Divine Women*. London: BBC [documentary series].

Humboldt, A. von (1860) *Cosmos: A Sketch of a Physical Description of the Universe*, Vol. 1. New York: Harper.

Ibn Al 'Arabi ([c. 1229] 1992) *The Bezels of Wisdom*, trans. R. W. J. Austin. New York: Paulist Press.

Iorns Magallanes, C. (2015) Nature as an ancestor: two examples of legal personality for nature in New Zealand, *VertigO: la revue électronique en sciences de l'environnement*, no. 22: 1–19.

Isaacs, J. (1980) *Australian Dreaming: 40,000 Years of Aboriginal History*. Sydney: Lansdowne Press.

Jonas, H. ([1979] 1984) *The Imperative of Responsibility: In Search of an Ethics for the Technological Age*. Chicago: University of Chicago Press.

Kakaie, G. (2006) Know yourself, according to Qur'an and Sunnah: Ibn Arabi's view, *Philosophical-Theological Research* 9/1.

Kalimtzis, K. (2017) *An Inquiry into the Philosophical Concept of Scholê: Leisure as a Political End*. London: Bloomsbury Academic.

Kan, S. B., Lewis, R. D., Chen, K., and Arnold, F. H. (2016) Directed evolution of cytochrome c for carbon-silicon bond formation: bringing silicon to life, *Science*, 354(6315): 1048–51.

Keeling, P., and Palmer, J. (2008) Horizontal gene transfer in eukaryotic evolution, *Nature Reviews Genetics*, 9: 605–18.

Ketcham, C. (2020) Emergence of the flower and honeybee mutualism and flower and honeybee ontology and morphology, in *Flowers and Honeybees*. Leiden: Brill, pp. 44–71.

Kimbel, W. H., and Villmoare, B. (2016) From *Australopithecus* to *Homo*: the transition that wasn't, *Philosophical Transactions of the Royal Society B*, 371.

King, K. L. (2007) The Gospel of Mary with the Greek Gospel of Mary, in *The Nag Hammadi Scriptures*, ed. Marvin W. Meyer. New York: HarperOne, pp. 737–47.

King, R. (2018) *Mindful of Race: Transforming Racism from the Inside Out*. Boulder, CO: Sounds True.

King, T. L. (2017) Humans involved: lurking in the lines of posthumanist flight, *Critical Ethnic Studies*, 3(1): 162–85.

Kishore, K. (2008) *The Life and Times of Sri Aurobindo Ghosh*. New Delhi: Probhat Books.

Klepeis, N., Nelson, W., Ott, W., et al. (2001) The National Human Activity Pattern Survey (NHAPS): a resource for assessing exposure to environmental pollutants, *Journal of Exposure Science & Environmental Epidemiology*, 11: 231–52.

Kragh, H. (2014) Naming the Big Bang, *Historical Studies in the Natural Sciences*, 44(1): 3–36.

Kringelbach, M. L., et al. (2007) Translational principles of deep brain stimulation, *Nature Reviews Neuroscience*, 8: 623–35.

Krishnamurti, J. (2012) *The Meditative Mind: A Selection of Passages from the Teachings of J. Krishnamurti*. Chennai: Motilal Banarsidass.

LaDuke, W. (2011) *Winona LaDuke on Redemption*, Sacred Land Film Project, www.youtube.com/watch?v=TfD5WaHM04E.

Lally, P., et al. (2009) How are habits formed: modelling habit formation in the real world, *European Journal of Social Psychology*, 40(6): 998–1009.

Landrigan, P. J., et al. (2020) Human health and ocean pollution, *Annals of Global Health*, 86(1): 1–64.

Lao Tzu ([6th century BCE] 1999) *Tao Te Ching*, trans. S. Mitchell. London: Frances Lincoln.

Latouche, S. (2010) *Farewell to Growth*. Cambridge: Polity.

Latour, B. ([1991] 1993) *We Have Never Been Modern*, trans. C. Porter. Cambridge, MA: Harvard University Press.

Lavers, J. L., et al. (2020) Entrapment in plastic debris endangers hermit crabs, *Journal of Hazardous Materials*, 387: 121703.

Leslie, H. A., van Velzen, M. J. M., Brandsma, S. H., Vethaak, A. D., Garcia-Vallejo, J. J., and Lamoree, M. H. (2022) Discovery and quantification of plastic particle pollution in human blood, *Environment International*, 163: 107199.

Lester, J. P., Allen, D. W., and Hill, K. M. (2001) *Environmental Injustice in the United States*. Boulder, CO: Westview Press.

Levy, R. (2022) Musk's Neuralink faces federal probe: employee backlash over animal tests, Reuters December 6, www.reuters.com/technology/musks-neuralink-faces-federal-probe-employee-backlash-over-animal-tests-2022-12-05/.

Linde, A. (1986) Eternally existing self-reproducing chaotic inflationary universe, *Physics Letters B*, 175(4): 395–400.

—— (1994) The self-reproducing inflationary universe, *Scientific American*, 271(5): 48–55.

Liu, R., et al. (1996) Homozygous defect in HIV-1 coreceptor accounts for resistance of some multiply-exposed individuals to HIV-1 infection, *Cell*, 86(3): 367–77.

Lopez, Barry Holstun (1986) *Arctic Dreams: Imagination and Desire in a Northern Landscape*. New York: Scribner.

Lorde, A. ([1984] 2017) The master's tools will never dismantle the master's house, in *Sister Outsider: Essays and Speeches*. Berkeley: Crossing Press, pp. 110–14.

Louv, R. (2005) *Last Child in the Woods: Saving Our Children from Nature-Deficit Disorder*. London: Atlantic Books.

Magli, G. (2013) *Architecture, Astronomy and Sacred Landscape in Ancient Egypt*. Cambridge: Cambridge University Press.

Maharaj, S. N. (1973) *I Am That: Talks with Sri Nisargadatta Maharaj*, trans. M. Frydman. Durham, NC: Acorn Press.

Mann, J., et al. (2022) Getting out of the classroom and into nature: a systematic review of nature-specific outdoor learning on school children's learning and development, *Frontiers in Public Health*, 10, https://doi.org/10.3389/fpubh.2022.877058.

Margulis, L. (1991) Symbiogenesis and symbionticism, in L. Margulis and R. Fester (eds), *Symbiosis as a Source of Evolutionary Innovation: Speciation and Morphogenesis*. Cambridge, MA: MIT Press, pp. 1–15.

—— (1998) *Symbiotic Planet: A New Look at Evolution*. London: Weidenfeld & Nicolson.

Marler, J. (2003) The iconography and social structure of Old Europe: the archaeomythological research of Marija Gimbutas, World Congress on Matriarchal Studies, "Societies in Balance," Luxembourg, September 5–7; www.second-congress-matriarchal-studies.com/marler.html.

Martin, K. (2020) Commentary: as the oceans go, so too do we, *Annals of Global Health*, 86(1): 152.

Marx, K. (1888) Theses on Feuerbach, in *Basic Writings on Politics and Philosophy*, ed. L. S. Feur. New York: Anchor Books.

MacCormack, P. (2020) *The Ahuman Manifesto: Activism for the End of the Anthropocene*. London: Bloomsbury.

McKittrick, K. (ed.) (2015) *Sylvia Wynter: On Being Human as Praxis*. London: Duke University Press.

McNear, D. H., Jr (2013) The rhizosphere – roots, soil and everything in between, *Nature Education Knowledge*, 4(3): 1.

Melott, A. L., and Thomas, B. C. (2019) From cosmic explosions to terrestrial fires? *Journal of Geology*, 127(4): 475–81.

Mohai, P., and Saha, R. (2015) Which came first, people or pollution? A review of theory and evidence from longitudinal environmental justice studies, *Environmental Research Letters*, 10: 125011.

Monier-Williams, N. ([1899] 1960) *A Sanskrit–English Dictionary: Etymologically and Philologically Arranged with Special Reference to Cognate Indo-European Languages*. Oxford: Oxford University Press.

Morton, T. (2007) *Ecology without Nature: Rethinking Environmental Aesthetics*. Cambridge, MA: Harvard University Press.

Mühlhausen, S., Schmitt, H. D., Pan, K.T., Plessmann, U., Urlaub, H., Hurst, L. D., and Kollmar M. (2018) Endogenous stochastic decoding of the CUG codon by competing Ser- and Leu-tRNAs in *Ascoidea asiatica*, *Current Biology*, 28: 2046–57.

Naess, A. (1973) The shallow and the deep, long-range ecology movement: a summary, *Inquiry*, 16: 95–100.

Najibi, A. (2020) Racial discrimination in face recognition technology, Harvard University, *Science in the News*, https://sitn.hms.harvard.edu/flash/2020/racial-discrimination-in-face-recognition-technology/ [blog].

Naranjo, L. (2020) *Matter in Motion: Earth's Changing Gravity*, December 27, https://earthdata.nasa.gov/learn/sensing-our-planet/matter-in-motion-earth-a-changing-gravity#ed-sup-datatable.

NASA (2018) NASA is taking a new look at searching for life beyond Earth, September 25, www.nasa.gov/feature/nasa-is-taking-a-new-look-at-searching-for-life-beyond-earth.

—— (2020) Astronaut requirements, March 24, www.nasa.gov/audience/forstudents/postsecondary/features/F_Astronaut_Requirements.html.

NASA Science (2022) Beyond our solar system, February 1, https://solarsystem.nasa.gov/solar-system/beyond/overview/.

Naughton, J. (2019) "The goal is to automate us": welcome to the age of surveillance capitalism, *The Guardian*, January 20.

Newenham-Kahindi, A., and Stevens, C. E. (2020) Ecological sustainability and practical wisdom from the Maasai and Hadza peoples in East Africa, in A. Intezari et al. (eds), *Practical Wisdom, Leadership and Culture: Indigenous, Asian and Middle-Eastern Perspectives*. London: Taylor & Francis, pp. 13–33.

Nietzsche, F. W. ([1883–5] 2006) *Thus Spoke Zarathustra*, trans. A. Del Caro. Cambridge: Cambridge University Press.

Noble, S. U. (2018) *Algorithms of Oppression: How Search Engines Reinforce Racism*. New York: New York University Press.

Not all scientists are raised equal (editorial) (2017) Nature Astronomy, 1: 0167.

Nuwer, R. (2020) Why the world needs viruses to function, *BBC Future*, June 18, www.bbc.com/future/article/20200617-what-if-all-viruses-disappeared.

Oparin, A. I. ([1924] 1967) The origin of life, trans. A. Synge, in J. D. Bernal (ed.) *The Origin of Life*. London: Weidenfeld & Nicolson, pp. 199–234.

Panda, D., Molla, K. A., Baig, M. J., Swain, A., Behera, D., and Dash, M.

(2018) DNA as a digital information storage device: hope or hype?, *3 Biotech*, 8(5): 239.

Parezo, N. J., and Fowler, D. D. (2007) *Anthropology Goes to the Fair: The 1904 Louisiana Purchase Exposition*. Lincoln: University of Nebraska Press.

Patel, N. V. (2019) Can Earth's gravity really be affected by changes in the seasons? *MIT Technology Review*, November 20.

Patterson, J. (1998) Respecting nature: a Maori perspective, *Worldviews: Environment, Culture, Religion*, 2(1): 69–78.

Pearce, D. (1996) The hedonistic imperative, www.hedweb.com.

—— (2009–15) Reprogramming predators, www.hedweb.com.

Pennisi, E. (2010) 1000 Genomes Project gives new map of genetic diversity, *Science*, 330(6004): 574–5.

Philip, L. (2022) *Beaverland: How One Weird Rodent Made America*. Chicago: Twelve.

Pico della Mirandola, G. ([1496] 1998) *Oration on the Dignity of Man*, trans. C. G. Wallis et al. Indianapolis: Hackett.

Pilling, D. (2019) It's time to redefine GDP to help save the planet, *Time*, November 21.

Plato ([c. 399–387 BCE] 2019) *The Apology of Socrates*, ed. N. Denyer. Cambridge: Cambridge University Press.

Popper, K. ([1934] 1959) *The Logic of Scientific Discovery*. London: Hutchinson.

Principe, L. M. (2012) *The Secrets of Alchemy*. Chicago: University of Chicago Press.

Rahman, F. (1975) *The Philosophy of Mulla Sadra Shirazi*. Albany: State University of New York Press.

Ringquist, E. J. (2005) Assessing evidence of environmental inequities: a meta-analysis, *Journal of Policy Analysis and Management*, 24(2): 223–47.

Rivera, L. N., and Rivera Pagán, L. (1992) *A Violent Evangelism: The Political and Religious Conquest of the Americas*. Louisville, KY: Westminster/John Knox Press.

Roossinck, M. (2011) The good viruses: viral mutualistic symbioses, *Nature Reviews Microbiology*, 9: 99–108.

Rosenberg, E., and Zilber-Rosenberg, I. (2014) *The Hologenome Concept: Human, Animal and Plant Microbiota*. Berlin: Springer.

—— (2018) The hologenome concept of evolution after 10 years, *Microbiome*, 6.

Ruggles, C. (1997) Astronomy and Stonehenge, *Proceedings of the British Academy*, 92: 203–29.

Rumi ([13th century] 1995) *The Essential Rumi*, trans. C. Barks. San Francisco: HarperCollins.

Rury, J. L., and Tamura, E. H. (eds) (2019) *The Oxford Handbook of the History of Education*. Oxford: Oxford University Press.

Sartre, J. P. (1946) *Existentialism is a Humanism*. New Haven, CT: Yale University Press.

Schaal, B. (2019) Plants and people: our shared history and future, *Plants, People, Planet*, 1(1): 14–19.

Schröder, K. P., and Connon Smith, R. (2008) Distant future of the Sun and Earth revisited, *Monthly Notices of the Royal Astronomical Society*, 386 (1): 155–63.

Seeley, D. (2010) *Honeybee Democracy*. Princeton, NJ: Princeton University Press.

Sender, R., Fuchs, S., and Milo, R. (2016) Revised estimates for the number of human and bacteria cells in the body, *PLoS Biology*, 14(8): 1–14.

Serres, M. ([1990] 1995) *The Natural Contract*, trans. E. MacArthur and W. Paulson. Ann Arbor: University of Michigan Press.

—— (2006) Revisiting the natural contract, *CTheory*, www.sfu.ca/humanities-institute-old/pdf/Naturalcontract.pdf.

Shiva, V. (1993) *Monocultures of the Mind: Perspectives on Biodiversity and Biotechnology*. London: Zed Books.

—— (1995) Beyond reductionism, in V. Shiva and I. Moser (eds), *Biopolitics: A Feminist and Ecological Reader in Biotechnology*. London: Zed Books, pp. 267–84.

—— (2012) *Making Peace with the Earth: Beyond Resource, Land and Food Wars*. New Delhi: Women Unlimited.

Siddiqui, R., Qaisar, R., Goswami, N., Khan, N. A., and Elmoselhi, A. (2021) Effect of microgravity environment on gut microbiome and angiogenesis, *Life*, 11(10): 1008.

Simard, S. (2021a) The mother tree, pp. 67–71, https://mothertreeproject.org/wp-content/uploads/2020/01/the-mother-tree_the_word_for_world_is_still_forest.pdf.

—— (2021b) *Finding the Mother Tree: Discovering the Wisdom of the Forest*. New York: Knopf.

Sorgner, S. (2021) *We Have Always Been Cyborgs: Digital Data, Gene Technologies, and an Ethics of Transhumanism*. Bristol: Bristol University Press.

Šprajc, I. (2018) Astronomy, architecture, and landscape in Prehispanic Mesoamerica, *Journal of Archaeological Research*, 26(2): 197–251.

Steiner, R. ([1904] 1994) *How to Know Higher Worlds*. New York: Anthroposophic Press.

Stengers, I. ([1997] 2010) *Cosmopolitics I*, trans. R. Bononno. Minneapolis: University of Minnesota Press.

—— ([1997] 2011) *Cosmopolitics II*, trans. R. Bononno. Minneapolis: University of Minnesota Press.

—— (2015) *In Catastrophic Times: Resisting the Coming Barbarism*, trans. A. Goffey. London: Open Humanities Press.

Strauss, B. S. (2018) Why is DNA double stranded? The discovery of DNA excision repair mechanisms, *Genetics*, 209(2): 357–66.

Suttle, C. (2007) Marine viruses – major players in the global ecosystem, *Nature Reviews Microbiology*, 5: 801–12.

Takahashi, K., Takahashi, H., Furuichi, T., et al. (2021) Gravity sensing in plant and animal cells, *npj Microgravity*, 7: 2.

Thompson, J. R., Rivera, H. E., Closek, C. J., and Medina, M. (2015) Microbes in the coral holobiont: partners through evolution, development, and ecological interactions, *Frontiers in Cellular and Infection Microbiology*, 4: 176.

Thunberg, G. (2019) Greta Thunberg's speech at the UN Climate Action Summit, September 23, www.npr.org/2019/09/23/763452863/transcript-greta-thunbergs-speech-at-the-u-n-climate-action-summit

Tu Wei-Ming (1989) The continuity of being: Chinese visions of nature, in J. Callicott and R. Ames (eds), *Nature in Asian Traditions of Thought: Essays in Environmental Philosophy*. Albany: State University of New York Press, pp. 67–78.

Turing, A. M. (1950) Computing machinery and intelligence, *Mind*, 59: 433–60.

Twenge, J. (2017) *iGen: Why Today's Super-Connected Kids Are Growing up Less Rebellious, More Tolerant, Less Happy – and Completely Unprepared for Adulthood – and What That Means for the Rest of Us*. New York: Atria Books.

United Nations (2017) Indigenous peoples: the unsung heroes of conservation, January 9, www.unep.org/zh-hans/node/477.

—— (n.d.). The golden record, the sounds of Earth, www.un.org/ungifts/golden-record-sounds-earth.

Ursell, L. K., et al. (2012) Defining the human microbiome, *Nutrition Reviews*, 70(suppl. 1): S38–44.

Van Brusselen, D., Kayembe-Kitenge, T., Mbuyi-Musanzayi, S., Lubala Kasole, T., Kabamba Ngombe, L., Musa Obadia, P., Kyanika wa Mukoma, D., Van Herck, K., Avonts, D., Devriendt, K., Smolders, E., Banza Lubaba Nkulu, C., and Nemery, B. (2020) Metal mining and birth defects: a case-control study in Lubumbashi, Democratic Republic of the Congo, *Lancet Planetary Health*, 4(4): e158–e167.

Vana, R. (2020) The brain, gut and consciousness: microbiology of our mind, *Inquiries Journal*, 12(12).

Vanzolini, M., and Cesarino, P. (2014) "Perspectivism," *Oxford Bibliographies in Anthropology*, www.oxfordbibliographies.com/view/document/obo-9780199766567/obo-9780199766567-0083.xml.

Verhelst, H. M., Stannat, A. W., and Mecacci, G. (2020) Machine learning against terrorism: how Big Data collection and analysis influences the privacy-security dilemma, *Science and Engineering Ethics*, 26: 2975–84.

Verran, J., and Reyes, X. A. (2018) Emerging infectious literatures and the zombie condition, *Emerging Infectious Diseases*, 24(9): 1774–8.

Viveiros de Castro, E. (1998) Cosmological deixis and Amerindian perspectivism, *Journal of the Royal Anthropological Institute*, 4(3): 469–88.

—— (2004) Exchanging perspectives: the transformation of objects into subjects in Amerindian ontologies, *Common Knowledge*, 10(3): 463–84.

Wajnerman Paz, A. (2021) Is your neural data part of your mind? Exploring the conceptual basis of mental privacy, *Minds & Machines*, 32: 395–415.

Wallman, J. (2015) *Stuffocation: Why We've Had Enough of Stuff and Need Experience More Than Ever*. New York: Random House.

Warlenius, R., Pierce, G., Ramasar, V., Quistorp, E., Martínez-Alier, J., Rijnhout, L., and Yanez, I. (2015) *Ecological Debt: History, Meaning and Relevance For Environmental Justice*. EJOLT report no. 18.

Watts, A. (1965) *The Tao of Philosophy: Myth of Myself*, original live recording, San Anselmo, CA: Electronic University.

—— (2017) *Out of Your Mind: Tricksters, Interdependence, and the Cosmic Game of Hide-and-Seek*. Boulder, CO: Sounds True.

Webb, P., et al. (2018) Hunger and malnutrition in the 21st century, *British Medical Journal*, 361: k2238.

White, R. (1992) The earliest images: Ice Age "art" in Europe, *Expedition*, 34(3): 37–51.

—— (2007) Systems of personal ornamentation in the early Upper Palaeolithic: methodological challenges and new observations, in P. Mellars, K. Boyle, O. Bar-Yosef and O. Stringer (eds), *Rethinking the Human Revolution: New Behavioural and Biological Perspectives on the Origin and Dispersal of Modern Humans*. Cambridge: McDonald Institute for Archaeological Research, pp. 287–302.

Williams, D. R. (2018) Stress and the mental health of populations of color: advancing our understanding of race-related stressors, *Journal of Health and Social Behavior*, 59(4): 466–85.

Wilson, M. L., et al. (2014) Lethal aggression in *Pan* is better explained by adaptive strategies than human impacts, *Nature*, 513: 414–17.

World Health Organization (2016) *Preventing Intimate Partner and Sexual Violence against Women: Taking Action and Generating Evidence*. Geneva: World Health Organization; http://apps.who.int/iris/bitstream/handle/10665/44350/9789241564007_eng.pdf;jsessionid=C8F9FEEA8DC28222B6515272D2B3152C?sequence=1.

Wright, D. S. (2016) *What is Buddhist Enlightenment?* Oxford: Oxford University Press.

Wynter, S. (2003) Unsettling the coloniality of being/power/truth/freedom: towards the human, after man, its overrepresentation – an argument, *New Centennial Review*, 3(3): 257–337.

Yehuda, R., and Lehrner, A. (2018) Intergenerational transmission of trauma effects: putative role of epigenetic mechanisms, *World Psychiatry: Official Journal of the World Psychiatric Association*, 17(3): 243–57.

Zimmer, C. (2017) Ancient viruses are buried in your DNA, *New York Times*, October 4, www.nytimes.com/2017/10/04/science/ancient-viruses-dna-genome.html.

Zuboff, S. (2019) *The Age of Surveillance Capitalism: The Fight for a Human Future at the New Frontier of Power*. London: Profile Books.

Acknowledgments

Thanks to Existence, for Being and Not Being.
Thanks to Sofia: Wisdom of Love, Love of Wisdom.
Thanks to our Families/Tribes/Planets, Universes and Multiverses.
Thanks to You: Thanks to Me. Thanks to All of Us, and Beyond.

Thanks to my Child Sofia and my Husband Roby, who nourish my Love every day. Thanks to my Mom, Renata, and my Dad, Ugo. Your Presence is the Gift. Thanks to all my dear parents Tizy, Ellen and Tom. Thanks to my posthuman Angels: Rosi, Debashish and Stefan, among many others. Thanks to my Sisters Barbara, Fede, Gaia, Isabel, Dani, Mary, Tate, Noura, and all the Sisters; thanks to my Brothers Angelo, Motti, Garon, Tristan, Patrick, Yunus, Farzad, Roberto, and all the Brothers; thanks to all Families. Thanks to the New Paltz tribe: a place for Enlightenment. Thanks to our Colleagues and Students at NYU, who excel in academic Perception. Thanks to the Posthuman Community worldwide, for sharing Vision and Manifestation. Thanks to the Global Posthuman Network and all affiliated Networks, for being Present. Thanks to my present and previous Publishers and Editors for believing in my work, allowing me to develop Vision and Awareness. For instance, a couple of insights from chapter 5 can be traced back to my article "Why space migration must be posthuman" (2016); some reflections from chapter 6 are offered in my contribution "Who is afraid of artificial intelligence? A posthuman take on the

AI takeover scenario" (2022); and a few suggestions in chapter 4 have been previewed in my chapter "To be or not to be enhanced? Just ask the Moon – in posthuman terms" (2023). This book has matured out of decades of exploration. Thanks to the anonymous Readers, and to Carolina, Angelino, Gisella, Gus and Kane, for the Generosity in offering feedback. Thanks to John Thompson and Caroline Richmond, to sharpen vision. Thanks to Polity Press, for actualizing this book: from Vision to Manifestation.

Infinite Love, Visions and Appreciation to You All!

Francesca

Exercises

To expand the concepts presented in this book, there are eight optional exercises – one related to each chapter. These are not quizzes but, rather, prompts to actualize self-reflection in our paths of posthuman self-realizations. You can find them online at www.politybooks.com/bookdetail?book_slug=the-art-of-being-posthuman-who-are-we-in-the-21st-century—9781509548958.